ACCESS My eLab

My eLab | Efficient teaching, effective learning

My eLab is the interactive environment that gives you access to self-graded exercises related to your coursebook. Thanks to your personal dashboard, you can easily view your progress, as well as any upcoming assignments. Be sure to register for **My eLab** to ensure your success!

TO REGISTER

1. Go to **http://mybookshelf.pearsonerpi.com**
2. Click on "NOT REGISTERED YET?" and follow the instructions. When asked for your access code, please type the code provided underneath the blue sticker.
3. To access **My eLab** at any time, go to http://mybookshelf.pearsonerpi.com. **Bookmark this page for quicker access.**

Access to My eLab is valid for 12 months from the date of registration.

STUDENT ACCESS CODE

RA06ST-FZZZZ-HAIRY-ATMAN-CENTO-RISES

WARNING! This book CANNOT BE RETURNED if the access code has been uncovered.

Note: Once you have registered, you will need to join your online class. Ask your teacher to provide you with the class ID.

TEACHER Access Code

To obtain an access code for My eLab, please contact your Pearson ELT consultant.

1 800 263-3678
assistance@pearsonerpi.com

@HelpPearsonERPI

W135228 (A36730)

1326

JULIA WILLIAMS

leap advanced

READING AND WRITING

Learning English for Academic Purposes

PEARSON

Montréal

Managing Editor
Patricia Hynes

Project Editor
Linda Barton

Proofreader
Mairi MacKinnon

Coordinator, Rights and Permissions
Pierre Richard Bernier

Text Rights and Permissions
Jocelyne Gervais

Art Director
Hélène Cousineau

Graphic Design Coordinator
Lyse LeBlanc

Book and Cover Design
Frédérique Bouvier

Book Layout
Interscript

The publisher thanks the following people for their helpful comments and suggestions:

Susan A. Curtis, University of British Columbia
Joanna Daley, Kwantlen Polytechnic University
Kristibeth Kelly Delgado, Fanshaw College
Michelle Duhaney, Seneca College
Joan Dundas, Brock University
Linda Feuer, University of Manitoba
Carleen Gruntman, Université Laval
Brianna Hilman, University of Calgary
Marcia Kim, University of Calgary
Izabella Kojic-Sabo, University of Windsor
Jennifer Layte, University of Manitoba
Catherine Lemay, Université Laval
Brooke Mills, Kwantlen Polytechnic University
Tania Pattison, Trent University
Karen Rauser, University of British Columbia, Okanagan Campus
Cyndy Reimer, Douglas College
Tanya Seredynska, HEC Montréal

ERPI publishes and distributes PEARSON ELT products in Canada.

1611 Crémazie Boulevard East, 10th Floor
Montréal, Québec H2M 2P2
Canada
Telephone: 1 800 263-3678
Fax: 514 334-4720
information@pearsonerpi.com
pearsonerpi.com

Registration of copyright – Bibliothèque et Archives nationales du Québec, 2013
Registration of copyright – Library and Archives Canada, 2013

Printed in Canada 6789 SO 18 17 16
ISBN 978-2-7613-5228-4 135228 ABCD OF10

Dedication

To Wayne
For Sam and Scott

Text Credits

Chapter 1, pp. 6–11 Excerpts from *Principles of Macroeconomics, 5th Edition* by N. Gregory Mankiw, Ronald D. Kneebone & Kenneth J. McKenzie © 2011 Nelson Education Ltd. Reproduced by permission. pp. 17–19 Excerpts from *Labour Force Survey: 2011 Year-End Review* by T. Wannell & J. Usalcas © Statistics Canada. pp. 23–25 Excerpt from *Macrowikinomics: New Solutions for a Connected Planet* by D. Tapscott & Anthony D. Williams reprinted by permission of Penguin Group (Canada), a division of Pearson Education Canada.

Chapter 2, pp. 28–31 "Young Millionaires 2010" by J. Wang, J. Ankeny & J. Holland reprinted with permission of Entrepreneur Media, Inc. © 2005 by Entrepreneur Media Inc. All rights reserved. pp. 34–37 Excerpts from *Business* by R.W. Griffin, R.J. Ebert, F.A. Starke & M.D. Lang, originally published as *Business, 7th Edition* by R.W. Griffin & R.J. Ebert © 2004. Reprinted by permission of Pearson Education, Inc., Upper Saddle River, New Jersey. pp. 44–50 Excerpts from "Towards an Explanation of the Growth in Young Entrepreneur Activities: A Cross-Country Survey of Work Values of College Students" by S. Mboko © North American Business Press.

Chapter 3, pp. 56–59 Excerpts from "Tough Love for Renewable Energy" by J. Ball © Jeffrey Ball. pp. 62–65 Excerpts from "Rooftop Power" by Wendy Priesnitz reprinted with permission of the author. pp. 69–73 Excerpts from "Gather the Wind" by D. Castelvecchi © 2012 Scientific American, a division of Nature America, Inc. All rights reserved.

Chapter 4, pp. 77–81 Excerpts from "Dr. Sustainability: Environmental Scientist of the Year" by T. Taylor © Timothy Taylor. pp. 82–86 "China's Green Building Future" by C. Nelson reprinted with permission of the author. pp. 90–95 Excerpts from *Green Building Trend: Europe* by Jerry Yudelson © 2009 Jerry Yudelson. Reproduced by permission of Island Press, Washington, DC.

Chapter 5, pp. 103–106 Excerpts from *Public Relations and the Social Web: How to Use Social Media and Web 2.0 in Communications* by R. Brown © 2009 Rob Brown / Kogan Page. pp. 109–112 Excerpts from *New Media: An Introduction, Canadian Edition* by T. Flew & R. Smith © Oxford University Press Canada 2011. Reprinted by permission of the publisher. pp. 121–123 "Consumer Activism and Corporate Responsibility: The Power of One" by J. Izzo reprinted with permission of the author.

Chapter 6, pp. 128–130, 135–137 Excerpts from *Net Smart: How to Thrive Online* by H. Rheingold © 2012 Howard Rheingold by permission of the MIT Press. pp. 139–144 Excerpts from "Creative 'Communities': How Technology Mediates Social Worlds" by S. O'Hear & J. Sefton-Green © Free Association Books.

Chapter 7, pp. 152–156 Excerpts from *Performance-Enhancing Drugs* by L.K. Egendorf © Reference Point Press. pp. 158–160 Excerpts from "Some Performance-Enhancing Drugs Should Be Legalized" by B. Kayser, A. Mauron & A. Miah, originally published as "Viewpoint: Legalisation of Performance-Enhancing Drugs," *The Lancet*, Dec. 1, 2005 © 2005, Elsevier (text) and © 2009 Gale, a part of Cengage Learning, Inc. reproduced by permission (introduction). pp. 163–167 Excerpts from *An Introduction to Drugs in Sport: Addicted to Winning?* by I. Waddington & A. Smith © 2009 Routledge, New York. Reproduced by permission of Taylor & Francis Books UK.

Chapter 8, pp. 174–178 Excerpts from "Pharmaceuticals May Be Poisoning America's Drinking Water" by Patricia Frank, originally published as "The Next Drug Problem," *American City & County*, June 1, 2007 Penton Media © 2013 Penton Media, Inc. 97360:213FO (text) and © 2011 Gale, a part of Cengage Learning, Inc. reproduced by permission (introduction). pp. 180–182 "Talking Substance about Detection … or Naming the Substances We Detect?" by E. Callaway, L. Macpherson & J. Simpson © 2010 Craig Kelman & Associates Ltd. All rights reserved. pp. 188–191 Excerpts from "Environmental Fate of Microconstituents and Removal during Wastewater Treatment: What Do We Know, What Do We Still Need to Find Out?" by S. Sathyamoorthy & A. Reid © 2010 Craig Kelman & Associates Ltd. All rights reserved.

INTRODUCTION

LEAP Advanced: Reading and Writing is premised on the same process-type approach to EAP teaching as you'll find in the previous *LEAP* books. You'll recognize many of the same features, plus a new one.

Familiar features are Warm-Up Assignments, positioned mid-chapter, which scaffold the Final Assignments. The Warm-Up Assignment structure incorporates a process approach to writing and ample opportunity to provide feedback before students attempt the Final Assignment.

Academic writing must be informed by reading content, and you'll note that the readings are by Canadian, European, African and American authors, and from academic sources. For this advanced level book, the readings are longer (and the content more challenging) than in previous *LEAP* books. The Focus on Reading and Focus on Writing sections offer explicit instruction in strategies to help students succeed, as do the Academic Survival Skill sections.

There is an emphasis on building vocabulary skills. Each chapter presents forty to sixty words; those on the Academic Word List (AWL) are highlighted. Discipline-specific words, collocations and idiomatic expressions are included where appropriate.

As this is an advanced level textbook, the reading and writing assignments encourage students to observe patterns of organization in the readings and combine them to suit their own writing purpose. For example, the Final Assignment in Chapter 8 is a problem-solution text, and within that larger structure, students will write texts with process, compare-contrast and persuasive characteristics.

As in other *LEAP* books, the chapter topics are paired. They are presented this way to promote recycling of vocabulary and key concepts. New in this book are Critical Connections sections located at the end of every second chapter. These sections require students to apply skills learned in one chapter to the content of the other to promote critical thinking and content synthesis.

LEAP Advanced: Reading and Writing provides a wealth of opportunities for students to think critically and encourages them to express this thinking in academically appropriate ways. To this end, writing strategies focus on the vocabulary and in-text positioning required to express critical thoughts.

ACKNOWLEDGEMENTS

I would like to acknowledge the following people for their support and influence over the years of writing the *LEAP* books.

Colleagues at the University of Waterloo: Judi Jewinski, Tanya Missere-Mihas, Pat Skinner, Stefan Rehm, Christa Schuller, Nancy Oczkowski, Maggie Heeney, Elizabeth Matthews, Dara Lane, Keely Cook, Christine Morgan and Margaret Wardell. Colleagues at Carleton University, whom I warmly remember and who had such a strong influence on the formative stages of the *LEAP* books. Dr. Wayne Parker, my advisor on matters of emerging contaminants. Dr. Ken Beatty, who continues to enthusiastically write the *Listening and Speaking* books in this series.

And thanks to my editors, Patricia Hynes and Linda Barton, who have edited and encouraged with constant good cheer and skillful suggestion. Thanks also to the rest of the Pearson team who work to make the *LEAP* books successful.

HIGHLIGHTS

The **overview** outlines the chapter objectives and features.

The **Gearing Up** section stimulates students' interest by activating prior knowledge.

Each chapter contains three **reading** texts from a variety of sources, including textbooks, newspapers, magazines and Web resources. Pre- and post-reading activities and questions focus on content and meaning.

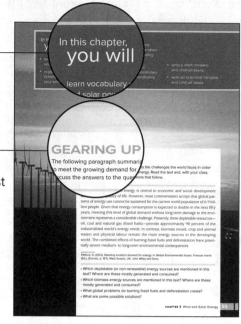

The shorter **Warm-Up Assignment** prepares students for the Final Assignment. Each chapter focuses on a different academic writing task.

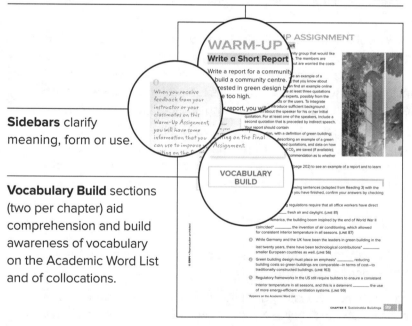

Sidebars clarify meaning, form or use.

Vocabulary Build sections (two per chapter) aid comprehension and build awareness of vocabulary on the Academic Word List and of collocations.

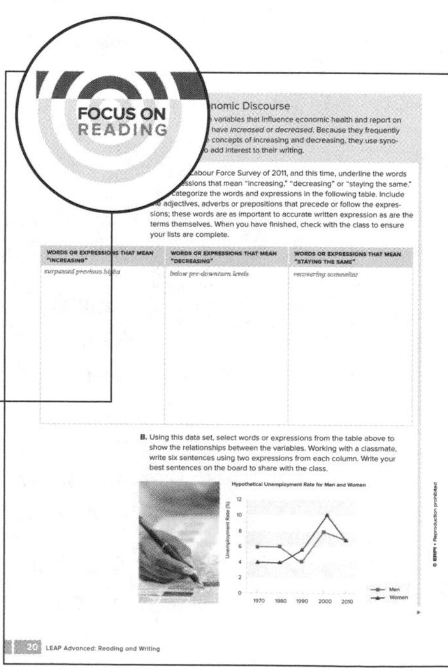

Focus on Reading develops specific skills students need to fully understand the content and structure of academic texts.

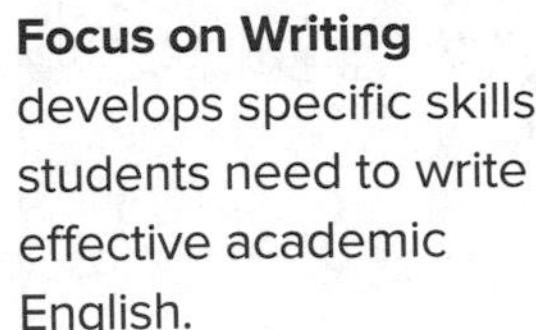

Focus on Writing develops specific skills students need to write effective academic English.

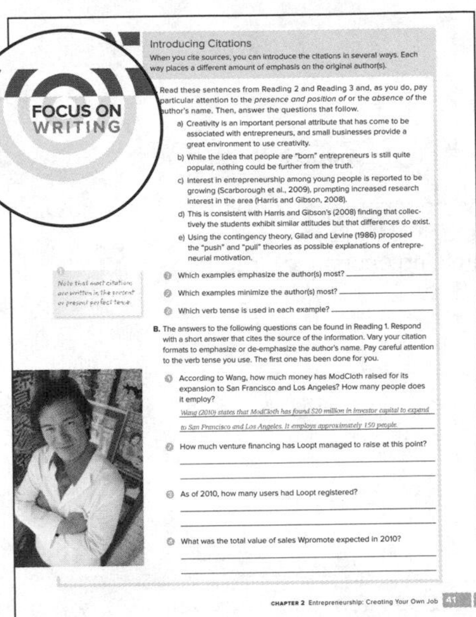

Academic Survival Skills help students improve essential skills for academic coursework.

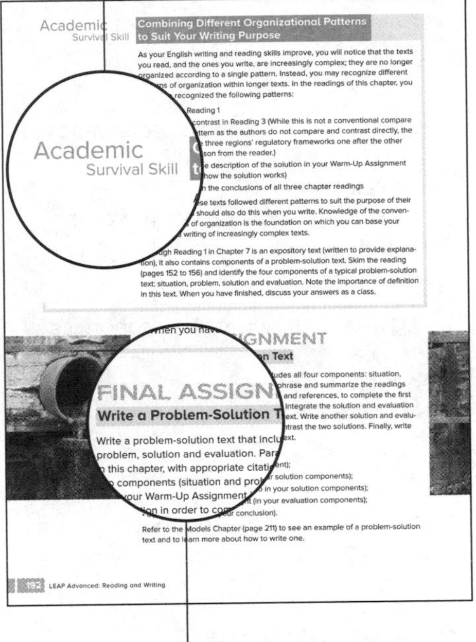

The **Final Assignment** synthesizes the chapter content and theme in an in-depth writing task. Each chapter focuses on a different academic writing format.

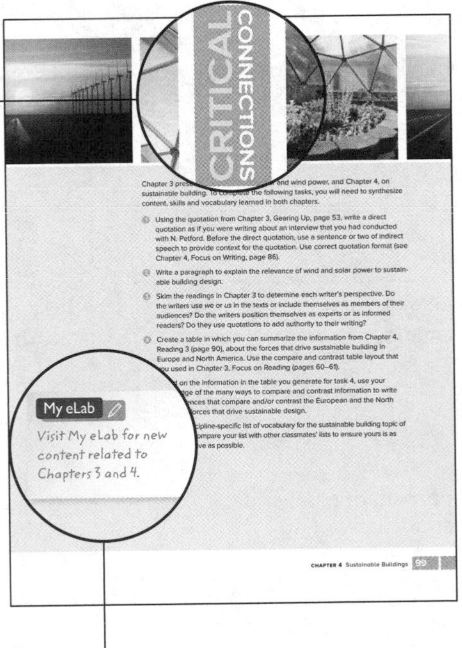

Critical Connections sections appear at the end of every second chapter and require the application of skills from one chapter to the content of another to promote critical-thinking skills, such as synthesizing.

References to **My eLab** point students toward additional content, practice and support.

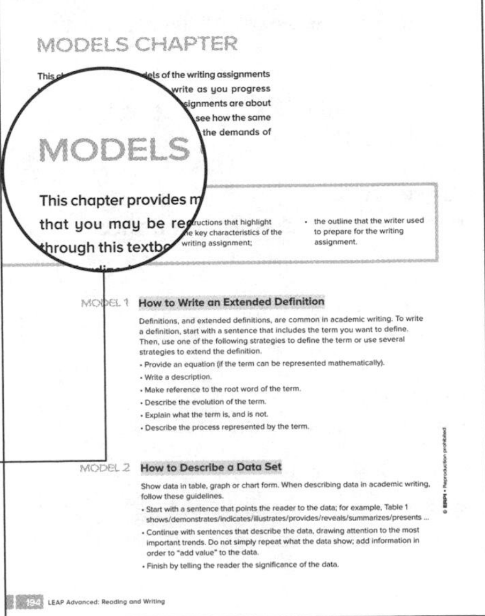

The **Models Chapter** provides students with instructions and models for the different types of writing assignments in the textbook.

SCOPE AND SEQUENCE

CHAPTER	READING	WRITING
CHAPTER 1 **NATURAL UNEMPLOYMENT** SUBJECT AREAS: business, economics	• Reading for comprehension (strategies, text organization) • Examining economic discourse	• Writing definitions
CHAPTER 2 **ENTREPRENEURSHIP: CREATING YOUR OWN JOB** SUBJECT AREAS: business, economics	• Reading journal articles	• Introducing citations
CHAPTER 3 **WIND AND SOLAR ENERGY** SUBJECT AREAS: engineering, technology	• Organizing information into tables	• Working toward variety in comparing and contrasting
CHAPTER 4 **SUSTAINABLE BUILDINGS** SUBJECT AREAS: architecture, engineering	• Identifying writer perspective in a text	• Using direct quotations and indirect speech
CHAPTER 5 **NEW MEDIA: ADVANTAGES AND DISADVANTAGES** SUBJECT AREAS: communication, technology	• Identifying paraphrases and summaries	• Using indicators that signal shifts in verb tense and voice
CHAPTER 6 **ONLINE COLLABORATIVE ENVIRONMENTS** SUBJECT AREAS: communication, creativity, technology	• Comparing original and paraphrased writing	• Using metaphor and simile in writing
CHAPTER 7 **PERFORMANCE-ENHANCING DRUGS** SUBJECT AREAS: ethics, sport, pharmacology	• Identifying and learning collocations through reading	• Analyzing text structure and organization
CHAPTER 8 **EMERGING CONTAMINANTS** SUBJECT AREAS: environmental science, pharmacology	• Discovering the organization of a problem-solution text	• Analyzing critical expression

ACADEMIC SURVIVAL SKILL	ASSIGNMENTS	CRITICAL THINKING
• Identifying reliable sources of information	• Writing a definition for a key economics term (one paragraph) • Writing a description of a data set (two to three paragraphs)	• Assessing information for reliability • Selecting reading strategies to increase reading speed • Relating chapter content to previous knowledge • Predicting text organization based on genre
• Knowing how and what to cite and reference	• Writing a short process essay (four to five paragraphs) • Writing an extended process essay (content determines length)	• Relating organizational structure to writing purpose • Assessing when citations are required • Evaluating secondary purposes for citations
• Building discipline-specific vocabulary knowledge	• Writing a short compare and contrast essay (five paragraphs) • Writing an extended compare and contrast essay (content determines length)	• Comparing and contrasting information • Designing tables to suit information and writing purpose • Assessing suitability of compare/contrast structures for writing outcomes
• Observing text features to learn about language	• Writing a short report (five to six paragraphs) • Writing an extended report (content determines length)	• Assessing the sustainability of buildings • Assigning headings to content • Integrating quotations or indirect speech • Inferring writer perspective • Analyzing the forces driving sustainable building • Making recommendations based on fact
• Using techniques to paraphrase and summarize	• Writing a paraphrase and a summary (one paragraph) • Writing a persuasive essay (content determines length)	• Evaluating the impact of new media • Applying concepts to previous knowledge • Analyzing time indicators and verb tense • Assessing sentence structure • Constructing an argument
• Synthesizing information in writing	• Writing a summary (four short paragraphs) • Writing an explanatory synthesis essay (content determines length)	• Comparing original and paraphrased texts • Applying metaphor and simile • Synthesizing information • Illustrating reading concepts with examples
• Expressing critical thoughts	• Revising an essay to add academic characteristics (revise a six- to seven-paragraph essay) • Writing a persuasive essay (content determines length)	• Expressing critical thinking in academic writing • Analyzing text organization • Revising an essay to add academic characteristics • Constructing an argument to persuade
• Combining different organizational patterns to suit your writing purpose	• Describing and evaluating a solution for a problem-solution text (two paragraphs) • Writing a problem-solution text (content determines length)	• Analyzing critical expression • Discovering the organization of a problem-solution text • Combining organizational patterns

TABLE OF CONTENTS

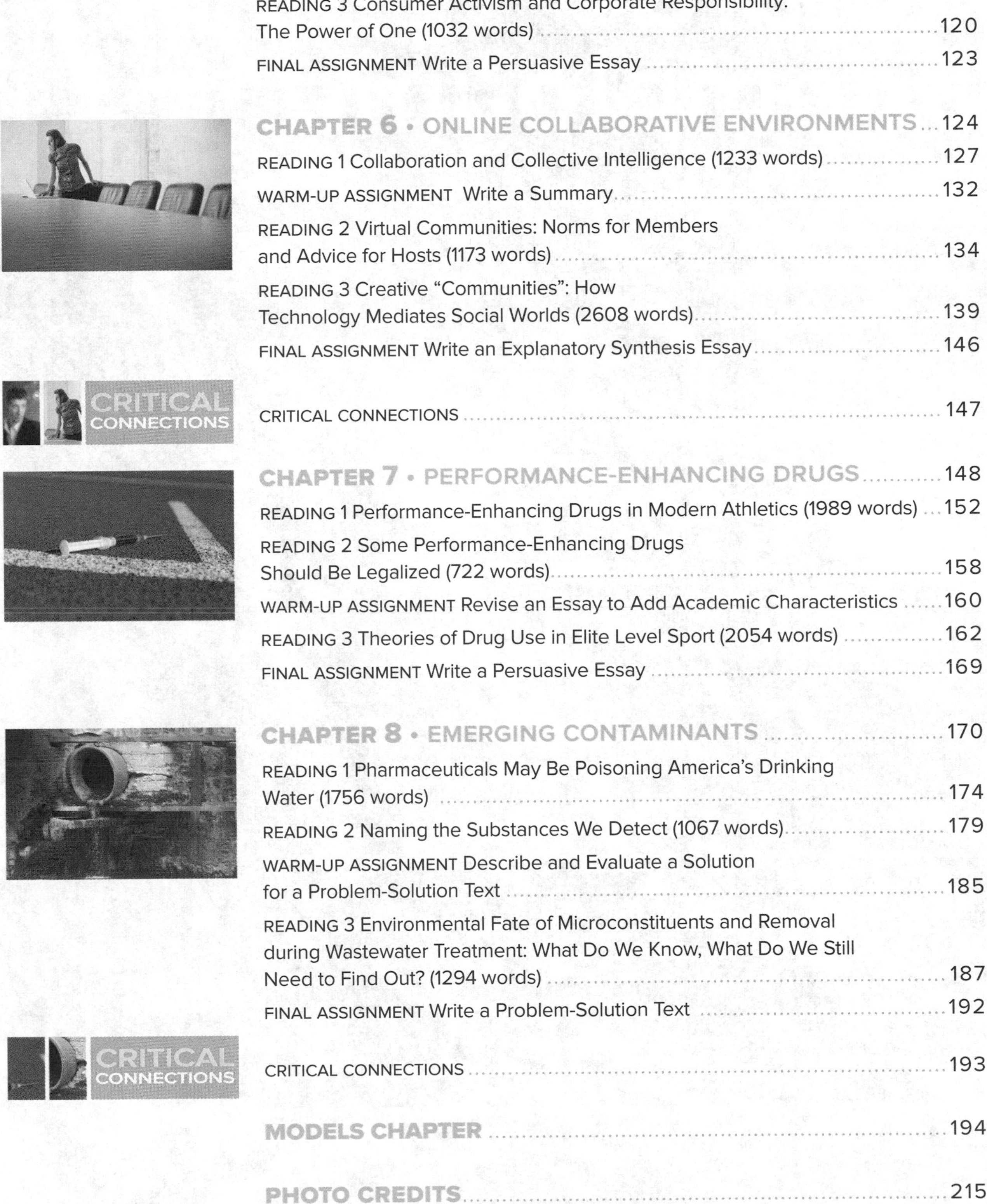

CHAPTER 1

Natural Unemployment

Unemployment is an important issue in every country and often affects youth more than other demographic groups. The unemployment rate not only influences the quality of life in a country; joblessness may also have severe impacts on individual finances and psychological well-being. Is it possible to eliminate unemployment completely? To answer this question, people turn to the field of macroeconomics, which defines unemployment and natural unemployment and explains the root causes.

In this chapter, you will

- learn vocabulary and collocations to help you express economics concepts;
- learn the conventions of writing definitions;
- identify reliable sources of academic information;
- recognize and write about key aspects of economic discourse;
- write a definition of an economics term;
- write a description of a data set that includes your definition.

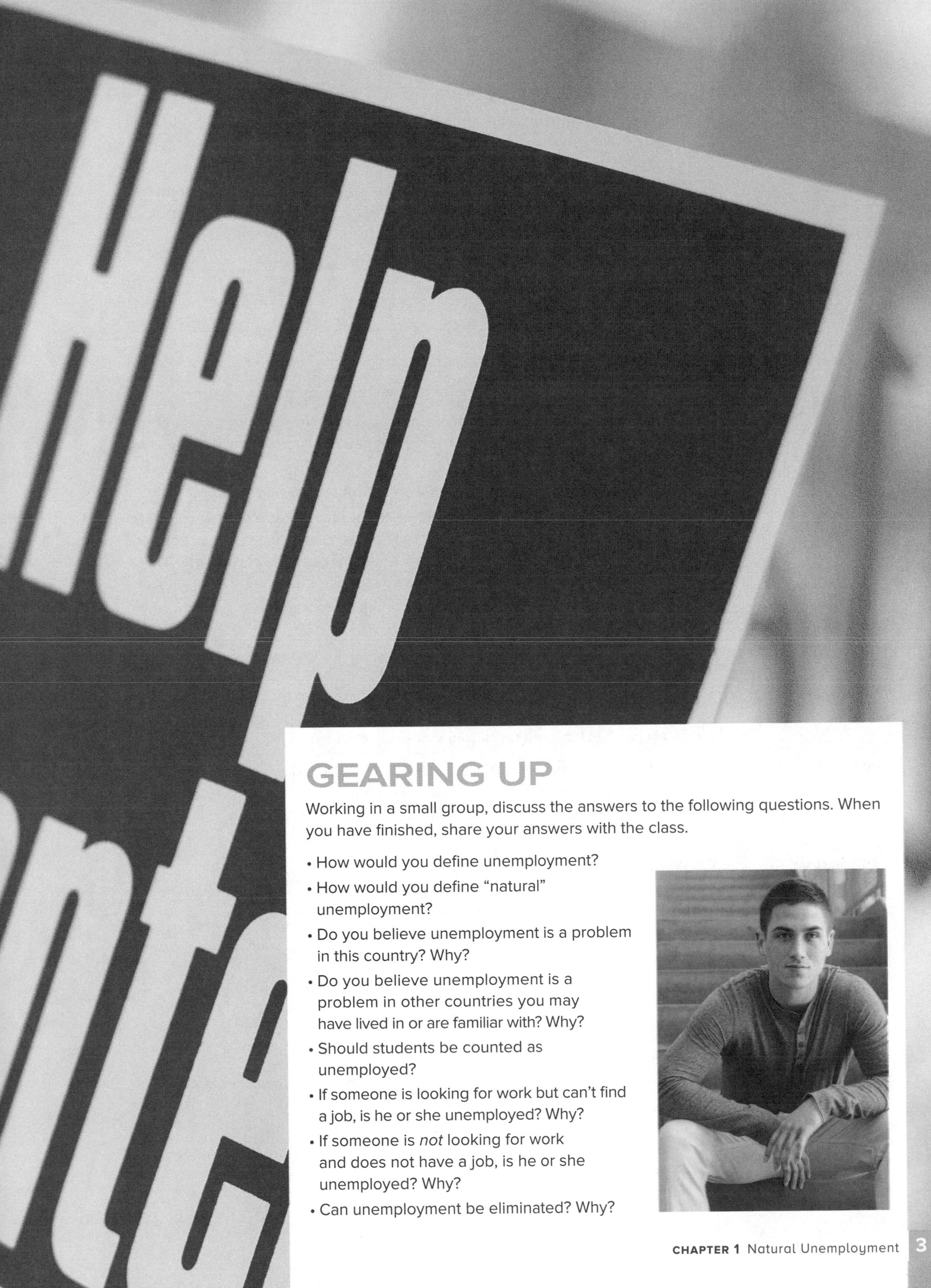

GEARING UP

Working in a small group, discuss the answers to the following questions. When you have finished, share your answers with the class.

- How would you define unemployment?
- How would you define "natural" unemployment?
- Do you believe unemployment is a problem in this country? Why?
- Do you believe unemployment is a problem in other countries you may have lived in or are familiar with? Why?
- Should students be counted as unemployed?
- If someone is looking for work but can't find a job, is he or she unemployed? Why?
- If someone is *not* looking for work and does not have a job, is he or she unemployed? Why?
- Can unemployment be eliminated? Why?

Reading for Comprehension

Reading in a language other than your first can be challenging, but you can apply certain strategies to read with greater comprehension and speed.

A. With your classmates, discuss what you can do to make reading in this additional language easier. Ask one of your classmates (or your instructor) to write the best reading strategies on the board. Copy the list here.

I skim the text before I read in detail.

____

____

____

____

B. To help you read in an additional language, here are some steps that other students have found helpful. These steps can help you with almost any type of text.

- Skim a reading to get a sense of the content, length and text type.
- Consider how the content relates to what you already know or what you want to know. This step is important because you learn new information better if you connect it to previous knowledge, or if it is information you are interested in.
- Use your knowledge of the text type to predict the organization of the information. The following table summarizes common text types and their organization.

TEXT TYPE	ORGANIZATION OF INFORMATION
TEXTBOOK	• Logical presentation of information, from simple to complex • Organized by chapter and headings • Main points in topic and concluding sentences of paragraphs
REPORT	• Starts with a summary or highlights section that lists the main points • Body is usually divided into sections with headings • Often presents information through charts, tables or graphs • May conclude with recommendations for action
ACADEMIC ESSAY	• Follows a formal structure • Thesis (presented at the end of the introduction) previews the content • Paragraphs present content in the order indicated by the thesis • Closing statement in conclusion summarizes the content
NEWSPAPER AND MAGAZINE ARTICLES	• Short paragraphs • Main points (who, what, where, when, why, how) presented in initial paragraphs • Details and elaboration of points follow • Direct quotations from experts may be included
JOURNAL ARTICLE	• Content previewed in the abstract • Generally organized into sections with headings: abstract, introduction, methods, results and conclusion
WEBSITE	• Information presentation varies depending on writer's purpose • Information is usually previewed in menus across top and down left-hand side • Related information is directly linked to key words in the text for fast access

- Divide a reading into sections and write a heading that reflects the content of each section. If a reading has already been divided into sections, use the writer's headings.
- If you were not given a set of questions to answer, develop a set yourself by turning each heading into a question.
- Read each section carefully to find the answer to the question you have generated. If the information is complex, write notes in the margin or on a separate sheet of paper. Answer the questions as completely as you can.
- Reflect on the content of a reading when you have finished. What did you learn that was new, interesting or important? What do you not understand or need to ask someone about? What opinion (if any) do you have about the information in the text?

C. Which strategies are new to you and/or your classmates?

____

____

____

____

____

D. With your classmates, discuss how these strategies help when reading in your additional language.

READING 1

Unemployment and Its Natural Rate

This reading is an excerpt from a popular macroeconomics book that you might read for a first-year university course. Use the steps in the Focus on Reading to help you read quickly with good understanding.

A. Skim Reading 1 to find the answers to questions 1 through 5.

1. a) What is the topic of the reading? ______________________

   b) How long is it? ______________________

   c) Which type of text is it? ______________________

2. What do you already know about the topic? Your discussion from Gearing Up may help you answer this question.

   ____

   ____

   ____

   ____

3. Based on the text type, how will the content most likely be organized?

   ____

   ____

   ____

4. This reading is already divided into sections. List the five section headings.

Unemployment and Its Natural Rate

____

____

____

____

5. Turn the first two headings into questions. (The last three headings are already questions.)

____

____

____

B. Now, read the text more closely and answer the questions that follow.

Unemployment and Its Natural Rate

An obvious determinant of a country's standard of living is the amount of unemployment it typically experiences. People who would like to work but cannot find jobs are not contributing to the economy's production of goods and services. Although some degree of unemployment is inevitable in a complex economy with thousands of firms and millions of workers, the amount of unemployment varies substantially over time and across countries. When a country keeps its workers as fully employed as possible, it achieves a higher level of GDP than it would if it left many of its workers idle.

... The problem of unemployment is usefully divided into two categories—the long-run problem and the short-run problem. The economy's *natural rate of unemployment* refers to the amount of unemployment that the economy normally experiences. *Cyclical unemployment* refers to the year-to-year fluctuations in unemployment around its natural rate and is closely associated with the short-run ups and downs of economic activity. ... In this chapter, we will discuss the determinants of an economy's natural rate of unemployment. As we will see, the term *natural* does not imply that this rate of unemployment is desirable. Nor does it imply that it is constant over time or impervious to economic policy. It merely means that this unemployment does not go away on its own even in the long run.

We begin the chapter by looking at some of the relevant facts that describe unemployment. In particular, we examine three questions: How does the government measure the economy's rate of unemployment? What problems arise in interpreting the unemployment data? How long are the unemployed typically without work?

We then turn to the reasons why economies always experience some unemployment and the ways in which policy-makers can help the unemployed. We discuss [three] explanations for the economy's natural rate of unemployment: job search, minimum-wage laws and unions. As we will see, long-run unemployment does not arise from a single problem that has a single solution. Instead, it reflects a variety of related problems. As a result, there is no easy way for policy-makers to reduce the economy's natural rate of unemployment and, at the same time, to alleviate the hardships experienced by the unemployed.

Identifying Unemployment

We begin this chapter by examining more precisely what the term *unemployment* means. We consider how the government measures unemployment, what problems arise in interpreting the unemployment data, how long the typical spell of unemployment lasts and why there will always be some people unemployed.

How Is Unemployment Measured?

In Canada, measuring unemployment is the job of Statistics Canada. Every month, Statistics Canada produces data on unemployment and on other aspects of the labour market, such as types of employment, length of the average workweek and the duration of unemployment. These data come from a regular survey of about 50,000 households, called the Labour Force Survey.

Based on answers to survey questions, Statistics Canada places each adult (aged fifteen and older) in each surveyed household into one of three categories:

- employed
- unemployed
- not in the labour force

A person is considered employed if he or she spent some of the previous week working at a paid job. A person is unemployed if he or she is on temporary layoff or is looking for a job. A person who fits neither of the first two categories, such as a full-time student, homemaker or retiree, is not in the labour force. Figure 9.1 shows this breakdown for 2009.

Figure 9.1: The Breakdown of the Population in 2009

Statistics Canada divides the adult population into three categories: employed, unemployed and not in the labour force.

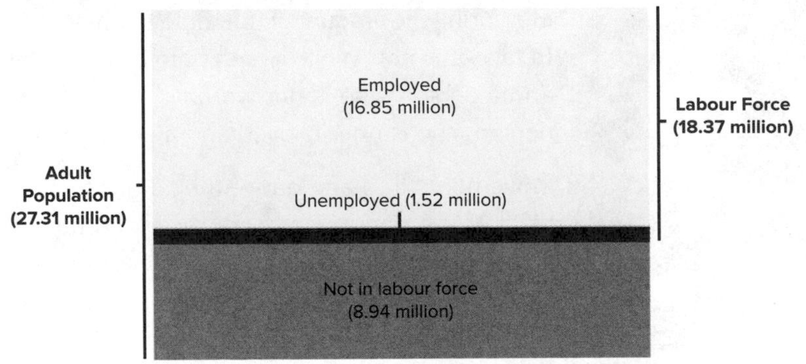

Source: Statistics Canada, CANSIM III Table 2820002.

Once Statistics Canada has placed all the individuals covered by the survey in a category, it computes various statistics to summarize the state of the labour market. Statistics Canada defines the **labour force** as the sum of the employed and the unemployed:

labour force: *the total number of workers, including both the employed and the unemployed*

$$\text{Labour force} = \text{Number of employed} + \text{Number of unemployed}$$

Statistics Canada defines the **unemployment rate** as the percentage of the labour force that is unemployed:

unemployment rate: *the percentage of the labour force that is unemployed*

$$\text{Unemployment rate} = \frac{\text{Number of unemployed}}{\text{Labour force}} \times 100$$

Statistics Canada computes unemployment rates for the entire adult population and for more narrowly defined groups—young, old, men, women and so on.

Statistics Canada uses the same survey to produce data on labour-force participation. The **labour-force participation rate** measures the percentage of the total adult population of Canada that is in the labour force:

labour-force participation rate: *the percentage of the adult population that is in the labour force*

$$\text{Labour-force participation rate} = \frac{\text{Labour force}}{\text{Adult population}} \times 100$$

This statistic tells us the fraction of the population that has chosen to participate in the labour market. The labour-force participation rate, like the unemployment rate, is computed both for the entire adult population and for more specific groups.

To see how these data are computed, consider the figures for 2009. In that year, 16.85 million people were employed, and 1.52 million people were unemployed. The labour force was

$$\text{Labour force} = 16.85 + 1.52 \text{ million} = 18.37 \text{ million.}$$

The unemployment rate was

$$\text{Unemployment rate} = (1.52/18.37) \times 100 = 8.3 \text{ percent.}$$

Because the adult population was 27.31 million, the labour-force participation rate was

$$\text{Labour-force participation rate} = (18.37/27.31) \times 100 = 67.3 \text{ percent.}$$

Hence, in 2009, two-thirds of Canada's adult population was participating in the labour market, and 8.3 percent of those labour-market participants were without work.

...

Does the Unemployment Rate Measure What We Want It To?

Measuring the amount of unemployment in the economy might seem straightforward. In fact, it is not. While it is easy to distinguish between a person with a full-time job and a person who is not working at all, it is much harder to distinguish between a person who is unemployed and a person who is not in the labour force.

Movements into and out of the labour force are, in fact, common. More than one-third of the unemployed are recent entrants into the labour force. These entrants include young workers looking for their first jobs, such as recent university and college graduates. They also include, in greater numbers, older workers who had previously left the labour force but have now returned to look for work. Moreover, not all unemployment ends with the job seeker finding a job. Almost half of all spells of unemployment end when the unemployed person leaves the labour force.

Because people move into and out of the labour force so often and for such a variety of reasons, statistics on unemployment can be difficult to interpret. On the one hand, some of those who report being unemployed may not, in fact, be trying hard to find a job; for example, they might be on temporary layoff and are waiting to be recalled to work. Or perhaps they are calling themselves unemployed because they want to qualify for Employment Insurance or because they are actually working and being paid "under the table." It may be more realistic to view these individuals as out of the labour force or, in some cases, employed.

On the other hand, some of those who report being out of the labour force may, in fact, want to work. These individuals may have tried to find a job but have given up after an unsuccessful search. Such individuals, labelled **discouraged searchers** by Statistics Canada, do not show up in unemployment statistics, even though they are truly workers without jobs. Similarly, some workers may be working part-time when in fact they want to work full-time. Although such workers are working less than they want to and so are underemployed, they do not show up in unemployment statistics.

discouraged searchers: *individuals who would like to work but have given up looking for a job*

The bottom part of Table 9.2, which provides 2009 data, shows the official unemployment rate for Canada as well as several alternative measures of labour underutilization calculated by Statistics Canada. The table shows that these alternative measures can paint quite a different picture of the unemployment situation. In the end, it is best to view the official unemployment rate as a useful but imperfect measure of joblessness.

This table shows various measures of joblessness for the Canadian economy. The data are averages for 2009. Figures may fail to sum exactly due to rounding.

TABLE 9.2: ALTERNATIVE MEASURES OF LABOUR UNDERUTILIZATION

MEASURE AND DESCRIPTION	PERCENTAGE OF THE LABOUR FORCE
Unemployed 1 to 4 weeks	2.8%
Unemployed 5 to 13 weeks	2.4%
Unemployed 14 to 25 weeks	1.4%
Unemployed 26 to 52 weeks	2.0%
Unemployed more than 52 weeks	0.4%
Official Unemployment Rate	**8.3%**
Discouraged searchers	0.2%
Those awaiting recall	0.5%
Involuntary part-time workers	1.8%
Official rate + discouraged searchers + those awaiting recall + involuntary part-time workers	10.8%

Sources: Statistics Canada, CANSIM II Tables 2820048 and 2820086, and authors' calculations.

...

Why Are There Always Some People Unemployed?

We have discussed how the government measures the amount of unemployment, the problems that arise in interpreting unemployment statistics and the findings of labour economists on the duration of unemployment. You should now have a good idea about what unemployment is.

This discussion, however, has not explained why economies experience unemployment. In most markets in the economy, prices adjust to bring quantity supplied and quantity demanded into balance. In an ideal labour market, wages would adjust to balance the quantity of labour supplied and the quantity of labour demanded. This adjustment of wages would ensure that all workers are always fully employed.

natural rate of unemployment: *the rate of unemployment to which the economy tends to return in the long run*

Of course, reality does not resemble this ideal. There are always some workers without jobs, even when the overall economy is doing well. Figure 9.4 shows Canada's observed unemployment rate and an estimate of Canada's natural unemployment rate. The **natural rate of unemployment** is what economists judge to be the rate of unemployment to which the economy tends to return in the long run. The exact value of the natural unemployment rate is unknown, but most economists estimate the rate in Canada to be currently 6 to 8 percent. Economists form estimates of the natural unemployment rate based on those variables they believe are the underlying determinants of the natural rate of unemployment. We will discuss these underlying determinants in the remainder of this chapter.

The values of the natural unemployment rate shown in Figure 9.4 represent the authors' opinions. Because the natural unemployment rate is only an estimate, there may be some disputes about the level of the rate at any particular time. However, the movements shown in the figure represent a fairly widespread view among economists about what has happened to Canada's natural unemployment rate since 1966. During the 1970s and 1980s, the natural unemployment rate roughly doubled, from about 4 percent to over 8 percent, and began falling in the mid-1990s. Most economists would agree that by 2005, the natural rate had fallen to between 6 percent and 7 percent. The recession that is identified as having started in Canada at the end of 2008 is believed to have pushed the natural unemployment rate back up. Our guess is that it is now near 7 percent.

Figure 9.4: Observed and Natural Unemployment Rates, 1996–2005

Most economists agree that the natural unemployment rate increased during the 1970s, stabilized at about 8 percent in the 1980s and has followed a slow downward path since the mid-1990s. The difference between the observed unemployment rate and the natural unemployment rate is the cyclical unemployment rate.

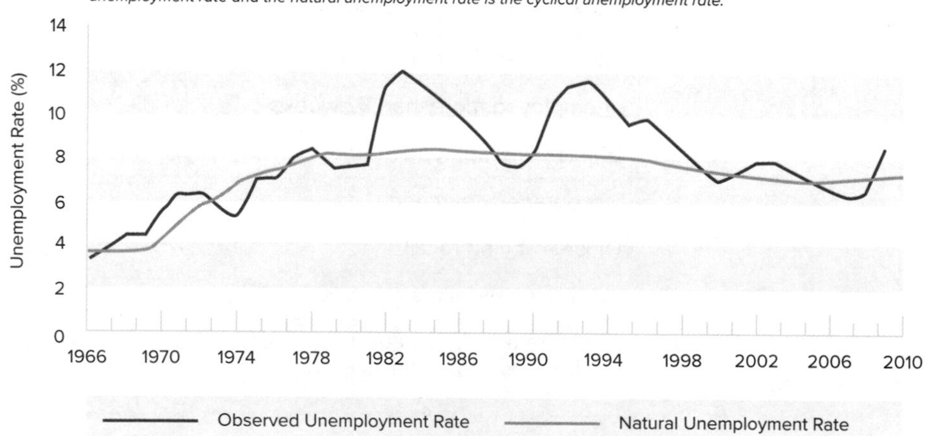

Sources: Statistics Canada, CANSIM II Series V691799, and authors' assumptions.

cyclical unemployment: *the deviation of unemployment from its natural rate*

Figure 9.4 also shows that the observed unemployment rate fluctuates around the natural rate. The observed unemployment rate differs from the natural rate due to the existence of **cyclical unemployment**. Cyclical unemployment arises due to the short-run economic fluctuations …

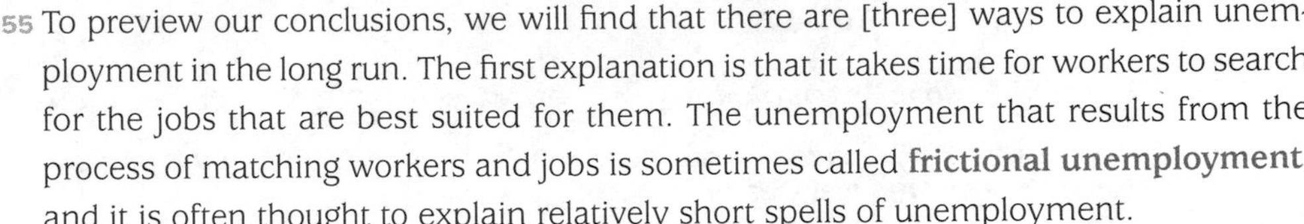

To preview our conclusions, we will find that there are [three] ways to explain unemployment in the long run. The first explanation is that it takes time for workers to search for the jobs that are best suited for them. The unemployment that results from the process of matching workers and jobs is sometimes called **frictional unemployment**, and it is often thought to explain relatively short spells of unemployment.

frictional unemployment: *unemployment that results because it takes time for workers to search for the jobs that best suit their tastes and skills*

The next [two] explanations for unemployment suggest that the number of jobs available in some labour markets may be insufficient to give a job to everyone who wants one. This occurs when the quantity of labour supplied exceeds the quantity demanded. Unemployment of this sort is sometimes called **structural unemployment**, and it is often thought to explain longer spells of unemployment. As we will see, this kind of unemployment results when wages are, for some reason, set above the level that brings supply and demand into equilibrium. Later in this section, we will examine [two] possible reasons for an above-equilibrium wage: minimum-wage laws and unions. (2027 words)

structural unemployment: *unemployment that results because the number of jobs available in some labour markets is insufficient to provide a job for everyone who wants one*

Mankiw, N. Gregory, Kneebone, Ronald D., & McKenzie, Kenneth J. (2011). *Principles of macroeconomics* (5th Canadian ed., pp. 191–201). Toronto, ON: Nelson Education.

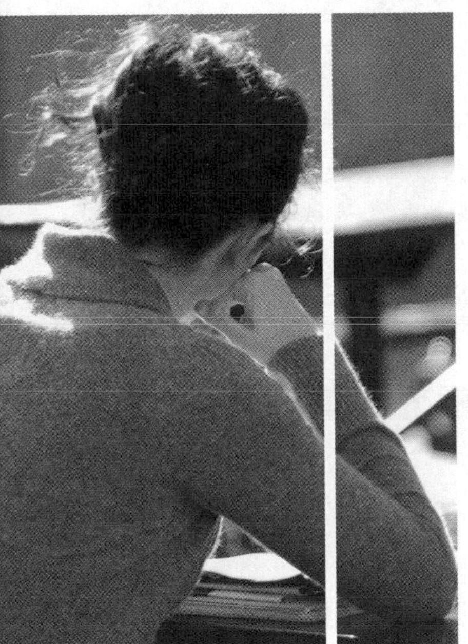

C. On a separate sheet of paper, answer the five questions: two that you converted from statements and three from the reading headings.

D. When you have finished, think about the reading. What did you learn that was new, interesting or important? What do you want to learn more about?

____

____

____

____

____

____

____

____

E. Compare your answers with those of your classmates.

VOCABULARY BUILD

As your vocabulary knowledge improves, you can further increase your fluency by learning words in combinations or in the small groups in which they are often used. These word combinations or groups are called *collocations*. Becoming aware of and using collocations will help build your reading and writing (and listening and speaking) fluency.

On the following page, key vocabulary from Reading 1 is divided into two tables. Table A contains vocabulary from the Academic Word List (AWL); Table B contains vocabulary related to the field of economics and general vocabulary.

For each word and phrase, read the definition (or quiz yourself on the definition if you think you know it already). Then, locate the word or phrase in Reading 1 by matching the line number, and write the collocations in the last column.

Table A

WORD	DEFINITION	COLLOCATIONS
aspects* (n.) LINE 48	parts of a situation, plan, idea, that has many parts	*other aspects*
cyclical* (adj.) LINE 14	occurring in periods of predictable, repeated increases and decreases	
deviation* (n.) LINE 153	noticeable difference from what is expected	
duration* (n.) LINE 49	length of time that something continues	
fluctuations* (n.) LINES 15, 154	changes in price, amounts, levels	
labour* (n.) LINES 48, 51, 72, 128	work or total number of workers available	
policy* (n.) LINES 26, 34	officially agreed-upon way of doing something	
precisely* (adv.) LINE 42	exactly and correctly	
structural* (adj.) LINE 163	related to how parts of a system connect	

*Appears on the Academic Word List

Table B

WORD/PHRASE	DEFINITION	COLLOCATIONS
alleviate (v.) LINE 39	make something less painful	*alleviate the hardships*
determinant (n.) LINES 2, 20, 138	strong influence or cause	
equilibrium (n.) LINES 166, 167	relatively stable balance between competing groups	
frictional (adj.) LINE 158	describes the unemployment that results from people taking time to find the job they want	
GDP (Gross Domestic Product) (n.) LINE 8	market value of all final goods and services produced within a country in a given period of time	
impervious (adj.) LINE 25	not influenced by something	
recession (n.) LINE 148	period of time of reduced purchase, trade and economic activity in a country	
spell (n.) LINE 44	period of time of a particular type of activity	

Writing Definitions

In Reading 1, some key economics terms are defined in the margin. While not all definitions are so conveniently highlighted in academic readings, it is true that definitions of key terms are often found in academic texts. Definitions are important to note as these are often tested in exams. Furthermore, when you include definitions in your own writing, it takes on this characteristic of academic discourse.

The following table includes economics definitions from Reading 1, as well as some definitions from other academic subjects, so that you can compare how these are written across disciplines.

Look closely at the definitions in the table that follows and find ...

1. the term that is defined by an equation ______________
2. the most descriptive definition ______________
3. the definition that starts with a reference to a word root ______________
4. the definition that describes the evolution of the term ______________
5. the definition that describes what the term is and what it is not ______________
6. the definition that describes a process ______________

DISCIPLINE	TERM	DEFINITION
COMPUTER SCIENCE	hypertext transfer protocol (HTTP)	The conventions that govern this dialogue [between web servers and individual computers] constitute the hypertext transfer protocol (HTTP). A protocol is a list of rules that define an agreed way of exchanging information. In HTTP, the browser first opens a connection, specifying the address of the desired server. Then, it makes its request. After delivering the response, the server closes down the connection. Once the transaction is complete, that is the end of the matter. (Witten, Gori, & Numerico, 2007)
ECONOMICS	unemployment rate	This rate represents the percentage of the labour force that is unemployed: $\text{Unemployment rate} = \frac{\text{Number of unemployed}}{\text{Labour force}} \times 100$
	structural unemployment	Structural unemployment is the kind of unemployment that results because the number of jobs available in some labour markets is insufficient to provide a job for everyone who wants one. (Mankiw, Kneebone, & McKenzie, 2011)
ECOLOGY	boreal forest	The boreal forest or taiga is a world of wood and water that covers over 11 percent of the Earth's land area. On the surface, the boreal forest is the essence of monotony. However, if you pay attention, you are rewarded with plenty of variety. In places, the trees stand so close together you can barely walk through them. Elsewhere, so many trees have been toppled by wind that you can walk on their piled trunks, one to two metres above the ground, for many kilometres. In still other places, the forest is open and you can wander wherever you like on its soft floor of needles and duff. A trek through a boreal forest eventually leads to the shore of a lake or river, where shade and cover give way to light and space. (Molles, 2008)

DISCIPLINE	TERM	DEFINITION
ENGINEERING	engineer	The term *engineer* comes to English from the Latin word *ingenium*, meaning "talent," "genius" or "native ability." Its first use was to describe those who had an ability to invent and operate weapons of war. Later, the word came to be associated with design and construction as in ships, roads, canals and bridges, and the people skilled in these fields were non-military, or civil, engineers. (Andrews, Aplevich, Fraser, & MacGregor, 2009)
HUMAN RESOURCE MANAGEMENT	employment equity program	An employment equity program is a detailed plan designed to identify and correct existing discrimination, redress past discrimination and achieve a balanced representation of designated group members in the organization. (Dressler & Cole, 2011)
PHYSICS	mass	In the International System of Units (SI), mass is measured in kilograms. Unlike the metre, the kilogram is not based on any natural physical quantity. By convention, the kilogram has been defined as "the mass of a particular platinum-iridium alloy cylinder" by the International Bureau of Weights and Standards in Sèvres, France. Weight and mass are quite different quantities, even though they are often confused in everyday language. Mass is an intrinsic, unchanging property of an object. Weight, in contrast, is a measure of the gravitational force acting on an object, which can vary depending on the object's location. For example, if you are fortunate enough to travel to Mars someday, you will find that your weight is less than on Earth, though your mass is unchanged. (Walker, 2010)

It is too simple to say that definitions are all written the same way, or even that definitions within a single discipline are all written the same way. For example, there are definitions in engineering and physics that are presented as equations. And in some disciplines, it is appropriate to use the second-person *you* in the definition. (See the definitions for ecology and physics.) However, the strategies listed are all methods you can use to write definitions.

References

Andrews, G., Aplevich, J.D., Fraser, R., & MacGregor, C. (2009). *Introduction to professional engineering in Canada* (3rd ed., p. 1). Toronto, ON: Pearson Prentice Hall.

Dressler, G., & Cole, N. (2011). *Human resources management in Canada* (11th Canadian ed., p. 41). Toronto, ON: Pearson Canada.

Mankiw, G., Kneebone, R., & McKenzie, K. (2011). *Principles of macroeconomics* (5th Canadian ed., p. 201). Toronto, ON: Nelson Education.

Molles, M.C. (2008). *Ecology: Concepts and applications* (4th ed., p. 36). New York, NY: McGraw Hill Higher Education.

Walker, J. (2010). *Physics* (4th ed., p. 3). San Francisco, CA: Pearson Addison-Wesley.

Witten, K., Gori, M., & Numerico, T. (2007). *Web dragons* (p. 64). San Francisco, CA: Elsevier.

Academic Survival Skill

Identifying Reliable Sources of Information

When you communicate in an academic environment, you must base your factual statements on reliable information. How do you know what sources are reliable? In almost all cases, reliable information is information that has been reviewed by a number of people with expertise in the area. Therefore, when you are searching for information, it is useful to know how the findings were produced. Here are a few common sources of academic information with notes on how it is generated.

DICTIONARIES: Published dictionaries have been written and reviewed by experts. Online dictionaries may not have been reviewed. To get the convenience of an online dictionary with the reliability of a published dictionary, look for a dictionary on CD-ROM that you can install on your computer or electronic device.

TEXTBOOKS: Published textbooks have been written and reviewed by experts. They are reliable sources of information.

JOURNAL ARTICLES: Journal articles have been written and reviewed by experts. They are also reliable sources of information.

NEWSPAPERS AND MAGAZINES: Newspaper and magazine articles are as reliable as the organizations that produce them. Generally, larger or well-known organizations produce reliable information. If you use a newspaper or magazine article as a source of information, it is useful to have that information confirmed by an alternate source. If you are not sure whether a newspaper or magazine article is a reliable source of information, don't use it.

WEBSITES: Websites are as reliable as the organizations or people who produce them. Some are produced by large organizations, like Statistics Canada, which meet high standards of review before information is posted. Others are produced by individuals or organizations with specific perspectives or opinions. These websites may provide only the information that supports the opinions of their creators. In these cases, the information is not reliable.

Students often ask about the reliability of information on *Wikipedia*. Currently, information on *Wikipedia* is reviewed but not necessarily by experts. *Wikipedia* is a good place to begin your search for information, but it is best to confirm that information with an alternate or original source.

Before you base your academic work on information from other sources, consider their reliability. Ask yourself:

- Who are the authors or creators of the information?
- Do they have a specific purpose or opinion that might influence the reliability of the information?
- Was the information reviewed by experts?

For this exercise, your instructor will present you with a set of texts. You may be able to supplement this set by adding textbooks or articles that you are carrying with you.

A. With a partner, review the texts and determine which ones are reliable sources of information and which ones are not.

B. Discuss your reasons for your selections with the class.

> If you are having trouble identifying reliable sources of information, your instructor or a librarian can help you.

WARM-UP ASSIGNMENT

Write a Definition for a Key Economics Term

Working with a partner, write a one-paragraph definition for one of the key terms at the end of Reading 1 (lines 167–168): *minimum wage* or *unions*. Review the models of definition writing below or in the Focus on Writing (page 13) to determine which models will work best for your term. You may want to use more than one model to extend your definition to a full paragraph.

- Equation
- Process description
- Reference to the word root
- Description of the evolution of the term (over time)
- Description of what the term is and what it is not
- Detailed description

When you receive feedback from your instructor or your classmates on this Warm-Up Assignment, you will have some information that you can use to improve your writing on the Final Assignment.

Include the name of your term in your definition, and write in the third-person objective perspective. Consult reliable sources of information to help you with your definition. However, for this assignment, do not use quotations from outside sources. State the definition in your own words so you do not plagiarize. (Refer to the Academic Survival Skill on paraphrasing techniques in Chapter 5, page 116.)

Refer to the Models Chapter (page 194) to see an example of a definition and to learn more about how to write one.

READING 2

Labour Force Survey: 2011 Year-End Review

Use the steps you learned in the Focus on Reading (pages 4–5) to read this excerpt from the Labour Force Survey of 2011 produced by Statistics Canada.

A. Skim Reading 2 to find the answers to questions 1 through 5.

1. a) What is the topic of the reading? ______________________

   b) How long is it? ______________________

   c) Which type of text is it? ______________________

2. What do you already know about the topic?

____
____
____
____
____

3. Based on the text type, how will the content most likely be organized?

____
____
____
____
____

4. This reading is already divided into sections. List the five section headings.

5. Working with a classmate, turn the section headings into questions. The first one has been done for you. Compare your questions with those of your classmates. Are they all the same? Discuss why they might be different.

What are the highlights of this report?

B. Now, copy your questions onto a separate sheet of paper. Read the text more closely and then answer the questions.

Highlights

- The labour market continued to recover through most of 2011, but there were signs of weakness toward the end of the year. Employment and aggregate actual hours of work surpassed previous highs, while the employment rate remained below pre-downturn levels.
- Employment growth was entirely in full-time jobs, with the greatest absolute employment gains in Alberta (99,000) and Ontario (85,000).
- Employment growth was concentrated among prime-age and older workers. Employment fell for youth and youth unemployment remained stubbornly high—ending the year at 14.1 percent.
- Employment grew strongly for landed immigrants who had been in Canada at least ten years, but their unemployment rate edged up to 7.1 percent due to higher participation in the labour market. Just the opposite occurred for immigrants who had landed in the previous five years: employment fell by 6.0 percent, but a decreasing participation rate also led to a drop in the unemployment rate.
- In 2011, the employment rate among Aboriginal peoples increased by 2.7 percentage points after declining 5.6 percentage points from 2008 to 2010. Employment rates increased for all age groups except for those fifty-five and over in 2011, with the largest absolute increase among prime-age Aboriginal peoples.
- Overall, job growth in the service sector (1.4 percent) outpaced the goods sector (0.2 percent), but there were pockets of strength and weakness in each sector.

Strong Start, Weaker Finish

The labour market continued to recover through most of 2011, but there were signs of weakness toward the end of the year. Employment increased by 1.3 percent from December 2010 to September 2011, then fell by 0.3 percent before recovering somewhat in December 2011, for a twelve-month increase of 1.1 percent. This represented a net gain of 190,000 jobs over December 2010, all in full-time employment. As more people found employment in the first three quarters of 2011, the unemployment rate fell steadily from 7.6 percent in December 2010 to 7.2 percent in September 2011—its lowest point since December 2008. The rate subsequently increased by 0.3 percentage points to end the year at 7.5 percent, just under its December 2010 level. Despite employment increases over the year, the employment rate remained the same as in December 2010, at 61.7 percent. This is because employment growth kept pace with population growth (1.1 percent).

While employment surpassed its pre-downturn level in January, actual hours worked did not reach this milestone until July. Actual hours grew by 1.9 percent from December to August and then remained essentially flat through the end of the year as small gains in the average number of hours per worker offset small decreases in employment.

...

Population Age Fifty-Five and Over Grows by 282,000, Driving Workforce Aging

Population aging continues to be a driving force in the labour market. The largest cohorts of the baby boom generation are starting to enter the fifty-five-and-over age range, concentrating population growth in a group with lower participation rates. The aging of the population will thus have a depressing effect on the overall participation rate unless the participation rate of those fifty-five and over increases enough to offset this compositional effect. In fact, the participation rate of older Canadians edged up in 2011, entirely attributable to gains among older women.

Employment continued to grow among those fifty-five and over, almost entirely as a result of population growth of about 282,000 in this group. After fifteen years of increases, the employment rates for men and women fifty-five and over ended the year very close to where they started. Employment rate declines among sixty-five- to sixty-nine-year-old men and sixty- to sixty-four-year-old women offset small gains among other older age groups.

Workforce Age Twenty-Five to Fifty-Four Also Increases

The employment rate of prime-age workers increased from 80.6 percent to 81.1 percent, December to December. The increase was mainly among prime-age women as their

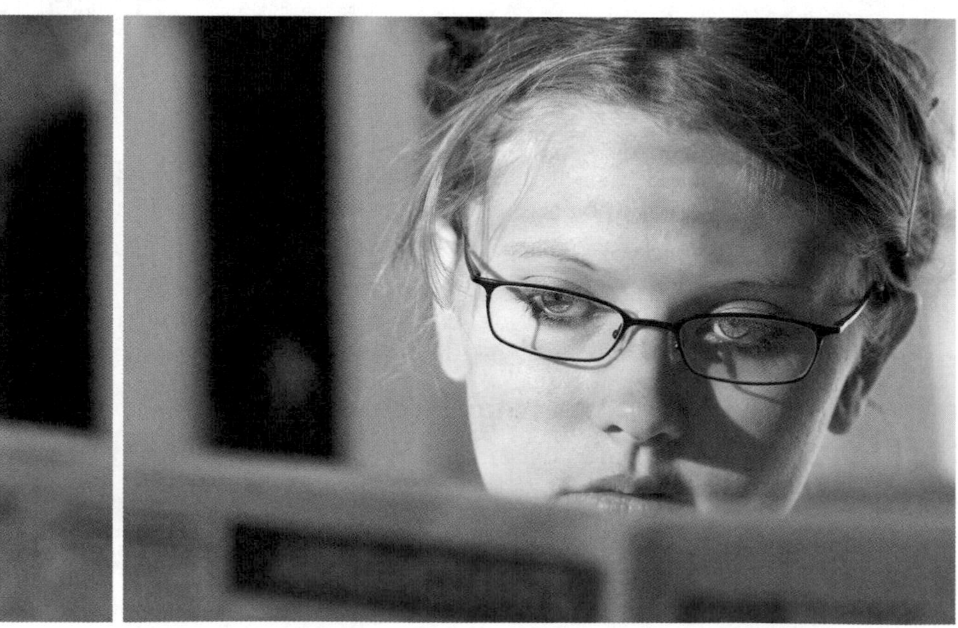

employment rate increased by 0.8 percentage points, while the rate for men edged up by 0.2 percentage points. Both rates remain below their pre-recession highs, by about 1 point for women and 2.5 points for men.

Recovery Stalls for Youth

Youth have much more ground to make up to regain their pre-recession employment rate. Their employment rate fell by 0.3 percentage points over the year and remained more than 5 percentage points below their pre-recession high. As a result, the unemployment rate for youth from fifteen to twenty-four increased from 14.0 percent in December 2010 to 14.4 percent in March 2011, before easing back to 14.1 percent in December 2011. With the slack labour market conditions for youth, the proportion of fifteen- to twenty-four-year-olds attending school increased from 59.8 percent in the fall of 2008 to 61.8 percent in the fall of 2011.

Chart C: Youth unemployment high, but lower than in most of 1990s

Unemployment rate (%), age 15 to 24

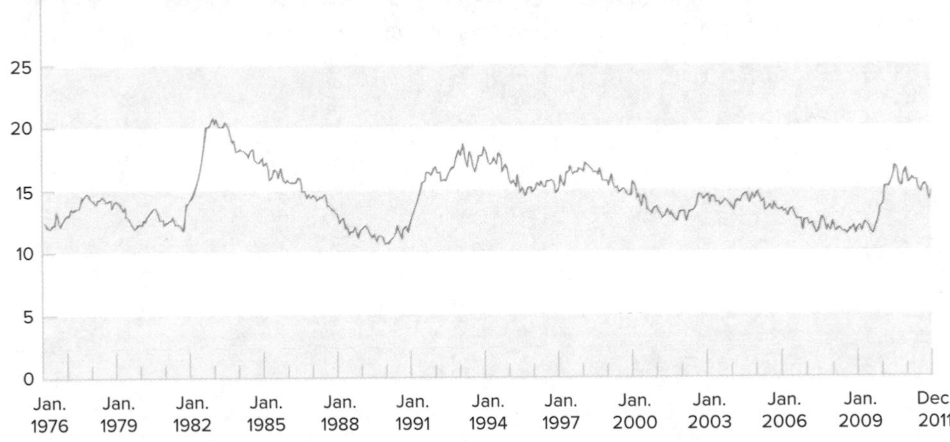

Source: Statistics Canada, Labour Force Survey, January 1976 to December 2011, seasonally adjusted data.

The persistence of youth unemployment following the downturn is not unprecedented. Current levels of youth unemployment are similar to those three years after the onset of the 1980s recession but remain well below persistently high levels of youth unemployment experienced through most of the 1990s. (827 words)

Wannell, T., & Usalcas, J. (2012, March 23). *Labour force survey: 2011 year-end review* (pp. 3–7). Statistics Canada. Retrieved from http://www.statcan.gc.ca

C. What did you learn that was new, interesting or important? What do you want to learn more about?

Examining Economic Discourse

Economists measure variables that influence economic health and report on how those variables have *increased* or *decreased*. Because they frequently need to express the concepts of increasing and decreasing, they use synonyms extensively to add interest to their writing.

A. Reread the Labour Force Survey of 2011, and this time, underline the words and expressions that mean "increasing," "decreasing" or "staying the same." Then, categorize the words and expressions in the following table. Include the adjectives, adverbs or prepositions that precede or follow the expressions; these words are as important to accurate written expression as are the terms themselves. When you have finished, check with the class to ensure your lists are complete.

WORDS OR EXPRESSIONS THAT MEAN "INCREASING"	WORDS OR EXPRESSIONS THAT MEAN "DECREASING"	WORDS OR EXPRESSIONS THAT MEAN "STAYING THE SAME"
surpassed previous highs	*below pre-downturn levels*	*recovering somewhat*
continued to recover	fell steadily	remained the same
growth	pre-downturn	
grew strongly	pre-recession	
growth kept pace	easing back	

B. Using this data set, select words or expressions from the table above to show the relationships between the variables. Working with a classmate, write six sentences using two expressions from each column. Write your best sentences on the board to share with the class.

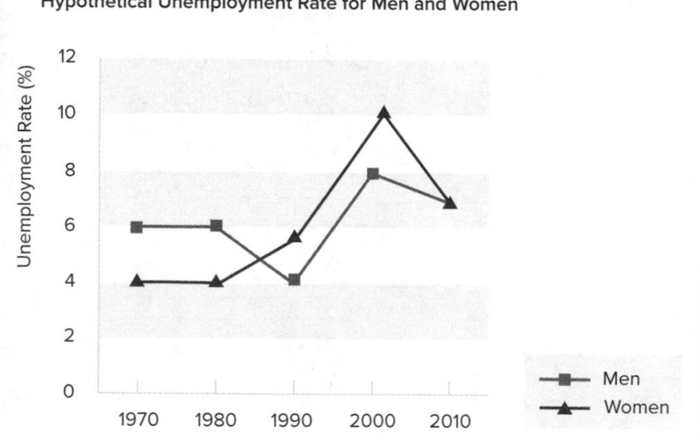

Example: The unemployment rate for women surpassed the rate for men in 1990.

1. ______________________________
2. ______________________________
3. ______________________________
4. ______________________________
5. ______________________________
6. ______________________________

VOCABULARY BUILD

Reading 3 is an excerpt from a book written for the mass market. As a result, there are fewer academic words in the text and more idiomatic expressions.

A. Read the definition of each academic word or quiz yourself on the definition if you think you know it already. Then, locate the word in Reading 3 by matching the line number, and write the collocation in the last column.

ACADEMIC WORD	DEFINITION	COLLOCATION
ideology* (n.) LINE 45	set of beliefs that strongly influence how people behave	*social ideology*
norms* (n.) LINE 31	generally accepted standards of social behaviour	
policies* (n.) LINE 30	ways of doing something that have been officially agreed upon by an organization	
priority* (n.) LINE 54	what is most important and requires attention before anything else	
prospects* (n.) LINE 14	possibilities that something will happen	
violate* (v.) LINE 15	disobey, or do something against an official agreement	

*Appears on the Academic Word List

B. In the following table, the key words or phrases in the first column are from Reading 3. Match each word or phrase to its definition.

WORD/PHRASE	DEFINITION
1 baby boom echo (n.)	6 reduce
2 baby boomers (n.)	______ be in a situation where something bad could happen to you
3 bearing the brunt of (v.)	______ actions taken by the government to deal more strictly with a problem
4 catalyst (n.)	______ increased numbers of people in a defined age group
5 culminated (v.)	______ ended
6 cut back on (v.)	______ people born post-World War II, between 1946 and 1964
7 demographic bulge (n.)	______ type of protest in which people refuse to work or study until their demands have been considered
8 dire (adj.)	______ begin something new
9 government crackdowns (n.)	______ increase
10 jack up (v.)	______ number of people who vote in an election (If the number is low, it is a sign that people are not participating in the political future of their country.)
11 kick start (v.)	______ children of the baby boomers
12 radicalization (n.)	______ slowly developing anger without showing it very much
13 run the risk of (v.)	______ something (or someone) that causes an important event to happen more quickly
14 simmering (adj.)	______ extremely serious or terrible
15 sit-ins (n.)	______ definition or establishment of a group of people in opposition to government policy
16 voter turnout (n.)	______ receiving the worst part of an attack or criticism

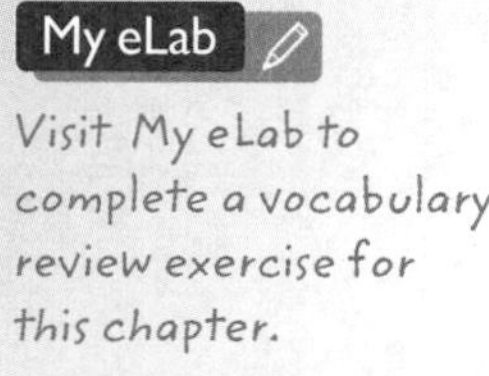
My eLab
Visit My eLab to complete a vocabulary review exercise for this chapter.

READING 3

The "Jobless Recovery"

Use the steps from the Focus on Reading (pages 4–5) to read this excerpt from the mass-market book *Macrowikinomics*. The reading is short, so there is no need to divide it into headings. A set of questions has been provided. Answer the questions in task A as a class. Then, do tasks B and C individually. When you and your classmates have finished, discuss the answers together.

A. Skim Reading 3 to find the answers to questions 1 through 3.

1. a) What is the topic of the reading? youth unemploymant

   b) How long is it? 748 words ; 8 paragraphs , 62 lines

   c) Which type of text is it? Essay

2. What do you already know about the topic?

   ____

   ____

   ____

   ____

3. Based on the text type, how will the content most likely be organized?

   ____

   ____

   ____

B. After you have read the text, demonstrate your understanding of it by indicating whether each of the following statements is true or false.

STATEMENTS	TRUE	FALSE
1 High youth unemployment was a catalyst for the revolutions in Tunisia and Egypt.	☑	☐
2 Society's unspoken agreement with young people is that if they study and work hard, they will find a job and become productive citizens.	☐	☐
3 Once youth unemployment is solved, the rest of our problems will be solved.	☐	☐
4 The unhappiness that unemployed youth are experiencing today has a precedent in the radicalization that occurred fifty years ago.	☐	☐
5 As there are so few young people today, they do not have much power.	☐	☐
6 Poor voter turnout among young people suggests that they are not involved in the political processes in their countries.	☐	☐
7 Youth do not have the ability to work together or become informed.	☐	☐
8 The author suggests that young people should pay higher tuition fees.	☐	☐
9 If youth remain unemployed and uninvolved in society, they will rebel against the older generation.	☐	☐
10 The author of this text is a young person. How do you know this? ______________________	☐	☐
11 This reading tries to make readers take action to change things. How do you know this? ______________________	☐	☐

A common thread to the revolutions in Tunisia and Egypt and protests elsewhere in the Middle East and North Africa is the soul-crushing high rate of youth unemployment. Twenty-four percent of young people in the region cannot find jobs. To be sure, protesters were also agitating for democracy, wanting the full rights of citizenship and not to be treated as subjects. But non-existent employment opportunities were a powerful catalyst.

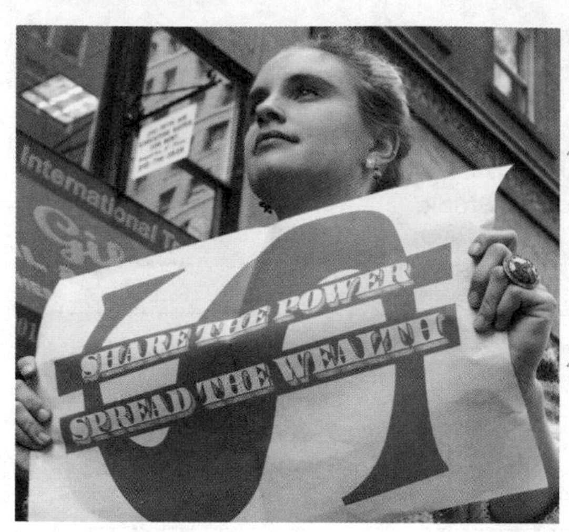

Youth unemployment is similarly dire in other parts of the world. In Spain, more than 40 percent of young people are unemployed. In France, the rate is more than 20 percent, and in the United States, it's 21 percent. In country after country, many young people have given up looking for work. A recent survey in the UK revealed that more than half of the eighteen- to twenty-five-year-olds questioned said they were thinking of emigrating because of the lack of job prospects.[1]

Such high rates of unemployment violate the unspoken agreement society has with young people: If they are industrious, law-abiding and diligent students, their lives will be prosperous. That's why it's hardly surprising that unemployed young people are fueling a growing protest movement around the world. To make matters worse, widespread youth unemployment is just one sign of a deeper failure. The society we are passing to today's young people is seriously damaged. And as we explain in *Macrowikinomics*, many institutions that have served us well for decades, even centuries, seem frozen and unable to move forward. The global economy, our financial services industry, governments, health care, the media and our global problem-solving institutions like the UN are all struggling.

Young people are bearing the brunt of our failures. Full of enthusiasm and relatively free of responsibilities, youth are traditionally the generation most inclined to question the status quo and authority. Fifty years ago, baby boomers had access to information through the new marvel of television, and as they became university-age and delayed having families, many had time to challenge government policies and social norms. Youth radicalization swept the world, culminating in explosive protests, violence and government crackdowns across Europe, Asia and North America.

In Paris in May 1968, protests that began as student sit-ins challenging the Charles de Gaulle government and the capitalist system culminated in a two-week general strike involving more than eleven million workers. Youth played a key role in the so-called Prague Spring in Czechoslovakia that same year. In West Germany, the student movement gained momentum in the late '60s. In the United States, youth radicalization began with the civil rights movement and extended into movements for women's rights and other issues and culminated in the Vietnam War protests.

Young people today have a demographic influence similar to that of their once-rebellious parents. In North America, the baby boom echo is larger than the boom itself. In South America, the demographic bulge is huge and even bigger in Africa, the Middle East and Asia. Approximately 52 percent of the world population is under the age of thirty and a whopping 27 percent under the age of fifteen.[2]

The '60s baby boomer radicalization was based on youthful hope and social ideology. Protesters championed the opposition to war, a celebration of youth culture and the possibilities for a new kind of social order. Today's simmering youth radicalization is much different. It is rooted not only in unemployment but personal broken hopes, mistreatment and injustice. Young people are alienated; witness the dropping young voter turnout for elections. They are turning their backs on the system. And we shouldn't forget that today's youth have at their fingertips the most powerful tools ever for finding out what's going on, informing others and organizing collective responses.

We need to make the creation of new jobs a top priority. We need to reinvent our institutions—everything from the financial industry to our models of education and science—to kick-start a new global economy. We need to engage today's young people, not jack up tuition fees and cut back on retraining. We need to encourage their drive, passion and expertise. We need to help them take advantage of new web-based tools and become involved in making the work more prosperous, just and sustainable. If we don't take such measures, we run the risk of a generational conflict that could make the radicalization of youth in Europe and North America in the 1960s seem insignificant in comparison. (748 words)

Notes

1. *The Economist.* (2011, July 5). The outsiders: Where the financial crisis has hit hardest. *The Economist.* Retrieved from http://www.economist.com/blogs/dailychart/2011/07/youth-unemployment

2. US Census Bureau, 2011.

Tapscott, D., & Williams, Anthony D. (2012). *Macrowikinomics: New solutions for a connected planet* (pp. xiv–xvi). Toronto, ON: Portfolio Penguin.

C. What did you learn that was new, interesting or important? What do you want to learn more about?

FINAL ASSIGNMENT

Write a Description of a Data Set

Write a description of a data set that matches the definition you wrote in the Warm-Up Assignment. Use what you know about reliable information sources to find a data set, and cite your sources, following the examples in this chapter.

For example, if you wrote a definition for *minimum wage*, find a data set that shows minimum wages in Canada (or in a single Canadian province) or in another country or region. If you wrote a definition for *unions*, find a data set that shows the impact unions have on wages in a specific country, region or industry.

- Begin with your Warm-Up Assignment definition.
- Continue with a description of the data that matches your definition.
- Use your knowledge of economic discourse to describe the increases and decreases in the data.
- Finish with a recommendation for steps we need to take to reduce youth unemployment in the future.

Refer to the Models Chapter (page 194) to learn more about how to describe a data set and to see an example of one (page 196).

CHAPTER 2

Entrepreneurship: Creating Your Own Job

In a recession, finding a job can be difficult, but you can increase your chances of finding employment by becoming better educated, building a network of friends, professors and supervisors, and developing job search documents like cover letters and resumés. You might also think about creating your own job. With an innovative idea and some entrepreneurial skills, you may even end up creating jobs for others.

In this chapter, **you will**

- learn vocabulary related to entrepreneurship and job creation;
- learn how to use different citation styles;
- discover the organizational pattern of academic journal articles;
- write a process essay to explain the success of a young entrepreneur;
- write a process essay about a young entrepreneur and include citations.

GEARING UP

A. Working in a small group, read the description of an entrepreneur and discuss the methods of definition used. (See the Focus on Writing, page 13.)

The term *entrepreneur* is a French word that means someone who "takes on" or starts something. In English, an entrepreneur is someone who starts a new business, usually involving financial risk. Successful entrepreneurs change the way products, goods or services are created, sold and/or delivered and may be credited with revolutionizing a product category or even initiating social change. Entrepreneurs are distinct from "small business owners" who may be content to make enough money to support their families. An entrepreneur is driven to create lasting and far-reaching change.

B. Based on this description, discuss characteristics a successful entrepreneur might have. List your group's top five for each category. Then, compare answers with another group.

ESSENTIAL	NICE TO HAVE	NOT IMPORTANT
hard-working		

READING 1 Young Millionaires 2010

Reading 1 is a magazine article about four young entrepreneurs who found success.

launch (v.):
start something new (You can launch a career, launch a website, launch a ship, launch a rocket, launch an investigation and launch a business. Check the collocations listing for this verb in your dictionary to see all the things you can launch.)

A. Work in groups of four. Each group member will read about one of the entrepreneurs and his or her experience and take notes on a separate sheet of paper. Write down

- the characteristics of the entrepreneur;
- the entrepreneurial idea that became successful;
- how the entrepreneur raised the money (resources) to **launch** the business.

B. When you have finished, work with members of other groups who have read about the same entrepreneur. Confirm your information and understanding of the content. Then, return to your original group and exchange information with your group members. Take notes on each of the entrepreneurs so you have notes on all four.

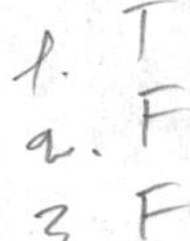

Here's how four ultra-successful twentysomethings leveraged their brilliant ideas into major businesses online. And how you can, too.

Out of Her Closet, a $50 Million Business by Jennifer Wang

Susan Gregg was seventeen and heading off to Carnegie Mellon University, and she had a problem: a closet overstuffed with one-of-a-kind vintage shoes and dresses. The solution? Open an online boutique.

ModCloth.com was headquartered in her dorm room and run with the help of her high school sweetheart, Eric Koger. The two drove from Pittsburgh to their South Florida hometown several times throughout college to haul up stock. By the end of their senior year in 2006, ModCloth was getting 60,000 visitors a month, and plenty of them were asking for more.

Gregg—a double major in German and business and now married to Koger—knew what to do. First, she raised the capital: $50,000 in credit card debt, plus loans from Koger's uncles, student loans and a second mortgage. Then she hired designers to create an original, vintage-inspired collection. "I googled, 'Where can I buy wholesale clothing?'" Gregg-Koger recalls. She found the Magic Trade Show in Las Vegas, wandered the booths, asked questions and found her designers.

These days, as co-founder and chief creative officer, Gregg-Koger, twenty-five, still handpicks all the clothes, shoes and accessories featured on the site (most sell for less than $100) and seeks out designers who fit ModCloth's aesthetic. Koger, the CEO, oversees the technical side. The site gets around two million visitors every month and is on track to surpass $50 million in sales this year. They've raised $20 million in new funding to open up offices in San Francisco and Los Angeles this summer, and employee numbers are close to 150 and rising.

Gregg-Koger says ModCloth's biggest advantage is the fact that she is ModCloth's ideal customer: "Other companies might say, 'We need to get on this social networking stuff,' whereas it was intuitive for us. If I have a Facebook account, and my friends do, my business should."

ModCloth's future is "social commerce," she adds. That is, in developing a site that involves customers, even if they're not actually buying. ModCloth recently introduced a "Be the Buyer" program, which lets customers choose which styles go into production, and a "Name It and Win It" contest. The idea is to leverage crowdsourcing and encourage customers to share and comment—and get excited about clothes that will be available in a few months.

"But that's like version 0.5," she says. "There's a lot more coming."

The Patriarch of Mobile Location by Jason Ankeny

Loopt is a quintessential expression of a generation shaped by mobility, interactivity and constant connectivity. In other words, it's the kind of innovation that could only spring from a mind as youthful as Sam Altman's. "People often try to build things for themselves first," says Altman, Loopt's twenty-five-year-old co-founder and CEO. "I built this for my friends."

The social-mapping service Altman created when he was a sophomore at Stanford University offers users a real-time virtual lifeline to nearby friends, their present whereabouts and activities. The mobile app's utility is bolstered by details about local attractions and events, including travel directions and reviews from content partners such as Zagat and Citysearch. Loopt also instantly shares status updates with Facebook and Twitter contacts and even lets users browse profiles of potential new friends within a given area.

Altman is a veteran of the mobile social networking revolution: founded in 2005, Loopt predates Foursquare, Gowalla and Brightkite by several years. And in what is now a hotly competitive realm, Loopt's focus is product innovation: in June, the Mountain View, California, company launched Loopt Star, a game that awards users coupons, music downloads and perks in exchange for their checking in to the service from specific destinations. Altman compares Star to a virtual loyalty card that lets retailers connect directly with customers while they're shopping or looking for a place to eat. The user with the most check-ins at a specific site is the "Boss" of that location, further driving repeat business.

Loopt has garnered more than $17 million in venture financing so far. The company doesn't disclose financial figures, but sales come from content partners and retailers, along with local advertising—which is where the biggest growth opportunity lies.

The Loopt app is available as a free download on more than a hundred mobile handset models offered by all four major US providers, including the iPhone. The Loopt network now connects more than four million registered users, with hundreds of thousands more signing up each month. Altman expects Loopt to continue to grow at a significant rate throughout 2010.

"Now that mobile phones are a fundamental communications device, the concept of place is becoming increasingly important," he says. "Smartphones are transformational things."

Marketing Guru for the Digital Age by Joel Holland

Michael Mothner was on the last round of interviews for a coveted job as an analyst at Goldman Sachs in New York City. The managing director looked over his resumé and noticed a company called Wpromote, which Mothner said he had started and had some success with as a sophomore at Dartmouth in 2001. "To call my bluff, he asked why I would want to work for Goldman if my company had been successful," says Mothner, now twenty-nine. "That was a defining moment for me. I stood up and said, 'You know what? You're right. I don't think this job is right for me.'"

After recovering from the shock, he began building Wpromote, a search engine marketing company that then offered a cheap platform for submitting websites to multiple search engines. This was 2004, and Google was just coming on—but Mothner foresaw its dominance. "I was having a lot of success using Google's pay-per-click (PPC) services to drive traffic to my company," he says. "So I came to the conclusion that there was a market for helping consult and manage these PPC campaigns for other people."

Wpromote did just that, launching a tiered service that helped people create PPC campaigns, choose keywords and manage bids. In the process, Mothner and his team were learning a lot about what elements helped websites get better Google rankings, so Wpromote offered a search engine optimization (SEO) service, too.

The strategy paid off: Wpromote rocketed from $500,000 in sales in '04 to $2.8 million in '05 and $6.2 million by 2007. Then the economy went south, but Mothner barrelled ahead anyway.

Today Wpromote, based in El Segundo, California, has sixty-two employees providing PPC, SEO, web development and social media advertising to 2,300 clients, including Hewlett-Packard. It had $8.5 million in sales for 2009 and expects to book at least $12 million to $13 million this year. Plus, Mothner plans to run Wpromote as if he will own it forever: "I think it is dangerous when people build companies with the sole intention of selling them."

The New Food Democracy

There's a Spanish proverb that says, "The belly rules the mind," but sometimes the two operate in perfect harmony. Just ask Emily Olson. While working as a brand manager for The Fresh Market, a gourmet supermarket chain, she saw how artisanal food start-ups struggled to land on retailers' shelves.

"Just because something tastes awesome, doesn't mean it can make it into stores," Olson says. "So I started thinking 'How do we democratize this?' "

Olson, now twenty-six, teamed up with Rob LaFave, twenty-seven, and Nik Bauman, twenty-six—friends who shared entrepreneurial ambitions dating back to their time at Virginia Tech. Their search for alternative distribution models led online, a natural progression for twentysomethings raised in the Amazon.com era. The result, inspired by the crafts site Etsy, is Foodzie, a web marketplace that connects small vendors with shoppers across the US. Foodzie offers small producers a free platform—a virtual farmer's market—to promote and distribute their meats, cheeses, produce, snacks and sweets. Vendors can set up their online storefronts, complete with photos and the philosophies behind their products. Foodzie processes all transactions, even sending sellers prepaid shipping labels once a purchase is complete.

"Our products come from people who are passionate about what they're making—often there's a story behind what they're doing, like a family recipe," Olson says. "We want products with a personal connection. And we want them to be delicious, not mass-produced."

She and her fellow Foodzies developed the model under the auspices of the Boulder, Colorado, incubator TechStars. Their mentor, Jeff Clavier, founder and managing partner of SoftTech VC, later spearheaded a $1 million seed investment in the San Francisco-based platform, which went live in December 2008.

Foodzie hosts nearly four hundred sellers nationwide and claims a 20 percent cut of all purchases made through the site. Though Foodzie doesn't disclose revenue, Olson says midway through 2010, Foodzie is on track to quadruple its 2009 sales. Top sellers include the Skillet Bacon Jam ($37) and Cheesecakes in a Jar ($36.45).

Now Olson and company are exploring ways to help vendors distribute their products both online and in stores—and not limiting Foodzie to being a direct-to-consumer distributor.

"Our mission is to help smaller food producers become bigger businesses," she says. "There is growing consumer awareness that you can still support small producers without breaking your budget. More than ever, people really care about where their food comes from."

(1558 words)

Wang, J., Ankeny, J., & Holland, J. (2010, September). Young millionaires 2010. *Entrepreneur*. Retrieved from http://www.entrepreneur.com/article/217183

VOCABULARY BUILD

A. You might already be familiar with the meanings of the words in the following table; however, you may need to be attentive to the changes in form that result when the words change from nouns to verbs or to adjectives or adverbs.

Change the form of each word to match the part of speech in the column heading. Line numbers are given for words from Reading 2.

AWL	NOUN	VERB	ADJECTIVE	ADVERB
*	LINE 48: ______	LINE 16: ______	assumed	
	LINE 57: ______		LINE 58: ______	capably
	LINE 56: ______	compete	LINE 80: ______	competitively
*	LINE 14: ______	LINE 4: ______	creative	creatively
*	LINE 15: ______		environmental	LINE 76: ______
	entrepreneur		LINE 16: ______	
*	finances	finance	LINE 92: ______	LINE 98: ______

*Appears on the Academic Word List

B. Read the sentences (adapted from Reading 2) in the first column. From the words or phrases given in the box below, choose the best meaning for each word or phrase in bold and write it in the second column. When you have finished, compare your answers with those of a classmate.

businesses	follow	~~left~~	means	possible
eliminate	gain financial benefit	likely	parts of a system	promising
first	knowledge	makes up	parts of industry	

WORDS/PHRASES IN CONTEXT	MEANING
❶ If a business is not expected to make a profit for a number of years, it cannot be reasonably **abandoned*** in the short term.	abandoned (v.): *left*
❷ A competitive advantage exists when **potential*** customers see the product or service as being better than that of a competitor.	potential (adj.):
❸ Many successful managers in large organizations in both the public and private **sectors*** also exhibit similar entrepreneurial characteristics.	sectors (n.):
❹ Estimating market demand requires an **initial*** understanding of who the customers are.	initial (adj.):
❺ Lacking a competitive advantage or developing one that is not sustainable **constitutes*** two fatal flaws of many new businesses.	constitutes (v.):
❻ The Heritage Foundation assesses the extent to which entrepreneurs have freedom to **pursue*** new business opportunities.	pursue (v.):
❼ Approximately half of all new business ideas come from **insights*** gained or skills learned at a previous job.	insights (n.):
❽ The faster you can **weed out** the “dead-end” venture ideas, the more time and effort you can devote to the ones that remain.	weed out (v.):

WORDS/PHRASES IN CONTEXT	MEANING
9 As employees, **prospective*** entrepreneurs are familiar with the product or service and with the customers, suppliers and competitors.	prospective (adj.):
10 Typically, generating ideas **involves*** abandoning traditional assumptions about how things work and how they ought to be.	involves (v.):
11 Most new **ventures** do not emerge from a deliberate search for **viable** business ideas but from events relating to work or everyday life.	ventures (n.):
	viable (adj.):
12 The entrepreneur must identify a business opportunity and access the resources needed to **capitalize** on it.	capitalize (v.):
13 We will focus our attention on understanding the three key **elements***—the entrepreneur, the opportunity and the resources.	elements (n.):

*Appears on the Academic Word List

READING 2 Entrepreneurship

Use the steps in the Focus on Reading, pages 4–5, to help you read quickly with good understanding.

A. Skim Reading 2 to find the answers to the following questions.

1 a) What is the topic of the reading? ______

b) How long is it? ______

c) Which type of text is it? ______

2 What do you already know about the topic?

______

______

______

3 Use your knowledge of the text type to predict the organization of the reading.

______

______

______

B. The authors have used headings to divide the content of this reading into sections. Write your own set of questions, on a separate sheet of paper, by converting the reading headings. Check your questions with a classmate to make sure they are relevant before you answer them.

C. This text contains seven definitions. Highlight each defined term and, in the margin, identify the method of definition used. (See the Focus on Writing, page 13, for the list of how authors define terms.)

! Remember, definitions are important in academic writing.

D. Find and highlight lines 28–30, 41–42, 44–46 and 70–71 in Reading 2.

1 Then, identify

a) where the sentences are located in each paragraph;

______

______

b) what the sentences have in common.

____

____

2 Which three key elements of the entrepreneurial process are discussed in this reading?

____

____

In this reading, the authors use a different system of citing sources from the system most often used in this book. Both systems are correct. (See the Academic Survival Skill, on page 38.)

Entrepreneurship

Entrepreneurship is the process of identifying an opportunity in the marketplace and accessing the resources needed to capitalize on that opportunity. "An entrepreneur is someone who perceives an opportunity and creates an organization to pursue it."[1] For example, Mark Zuckerberg created the website Facebook, and just a few years later it had close to forty million active users. By 2008, Zuckerberg was widely thought to be the richest person in the world under the age of twenty-five, with a net worth of over $1.5 billion. It takes more than a good idea to be successful. Zuckerberg worked long hours, and he is constantly tailoring the website to suit its expanding audience.[2]

...

Each year, the Heritage Foundation publishes an index of economic freedom, which assesses the extent to which entrepreneurs have freedom to pursue new business opportunities. In 2009, the top three countries were Hong Kong, Singapore and Australia ... Canada ranked seventh ... and North Korea ranked last.[3]

Creativity is an important personal attribute that has come to be associated with entrepreneurs, and small businesses provide a great environment to use creativity.[4] But do not assume that only small business owners exhibit entrepreneurial characteristics. Many successful managers in large organizations in both the public and private sectors also exhibit similar characteristics.[5] Entrepreneurship is evident in a wide range of contexts: in small or new firms, in old firms, in large firms, in firms that grow slowly, in firms that grow rapidly, in non-profit organizations and in the public sector.[6]

...

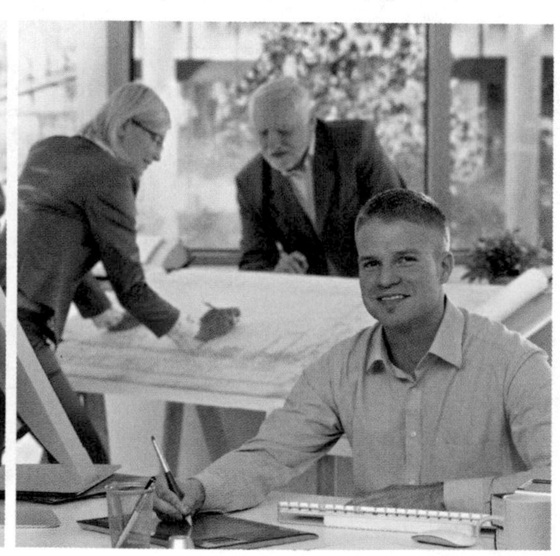

The Entrepreneurial Process

The entrepreneurial process is like a journey. To get to the destination (the start-up of a new venture), the entrepreneur must identify a business opportunity and access the resources needed to capitalize on it. Along the way, social, economic, political and technological factors in the broader environment will have an influence, but we will focus our attention on understanding the three key process elements—the entrepreneur, the opportunity and the resources—and how they interact.

...

The Entrepreneur

Since the entrepreneur is at the heart of the entrepreneurial process, researchers have paid considerable attention to identifying the personal characteristics of entrepreneurs ... Some are behavioural (for example, high energy level), others are personality traits (for example, independence) and still others are skills (for example, problem solving).[7]

While the idea that people are "born" entrepreneurs is still quite popular, nothing could be further from the truth.[8] In fact, entrepreneurial characteristics are widely distributed in the population.[9] We also know that personal characteristics often have less impact on a person's actions than the situation a person is in.[10] What is really important is not who the person is but what the person *does*.[11] The two main things that entrepreneurs need to do are identify an opportunity and access resources.

Identifying Opportunities

Identifying opportunities involves generating ideas for new (or improved) products, processes or services, then screening those ideas so that the one that presents the best opportunity can be developed, and then developing the opportunity.

Idea generation

Typically, generating ideas involves abandoning traditional assumptions about how things work and how they ought to be and involves seeing what others do not. If the prospective new (or improved) product, process or service can be profitably produced and is attractive relative to other potential venture ideas, it might present an opportunity.

Where do ideas come from? Most new ventures do not emerge from a deliberate search for viable business ideas but from events relating to work or everyday life.[12] Approximately half of all new business ideas come from insights gained or skills learned at a previous job. As employees, prospective entrepreneurs are familiar with the product or service and with the customers, suppliers and competitors. They can relate those needs to their own personal capabilities and can determine whether they are capable of producing products or services that can fill the void.

Jay Hagan and Scott Gaidano learned how to recover data from damaged hard drives while working for a company that manufactured them. When that company went bankrupt, they started their own business and called it DriveSavers.

...

The next most frequent sources of venture ideas are a personal interest/hobby (16 percent) and a chance happening (11 percent).[13] A chance happening refers to a situation where a venture idea comes about unexpectedly. For example, while on vacation in another country you might try a new snack food that you feel would be in demand if introduced to the Canadian market.

Screening

Entrepreneurs often generate many ideas, and screening them is a key part of the entrepreneurial process. The faster you can weed out the "dead-end" venture ideas, the more time and effort you can devote to the ones that remain. The more of the following characteristics that an idea has, the greater the opportunity it presents.

The Idea Creates or Adds Value for the Customer. A product or service that creates or adds value for the customer is one that solves a significant problem or meets a significant need in new or different ways. Consider Sally Fox's idea for eliminating the dyeing process in textile operations.[14] By cross-breeding long-fibre white cotton and short-fibre coloured cotton, she developed Foxfibre, an environmentally friendly new cotton fibre that is naturally grown in several colours and is long enough to be spun commercially.

The Idea Provides a Competitive Advantage That Can Be Sustained. A competitive advantage exists when potential customers see the product or service as being better than that of competitors. Sustaining a competitive advantage involves maintaining it in the face of competitors' actions or changes in the industry. All other things being equal, the longer markets are in a state of flux, the greater the likelihood of being able to sustain a competitive advantage. Lacking a competitive advantage or developing a competitive advantage that is not sustainable constitutes two fatal flaws of many new ventures.[15]

To continue with Sally Fox's story, not too long after she sold her first crop she was running a $10 million business and had well-known companies like Levi's, L.L. Bean, Land's End and Esprit as customers. But Fox's journey turned out to be bumpy. She had to relocate twice in response to pressure from powerful cotton growers who were afraid that her coloured varieties would contaminate their own crops. Also, once spinning mills began moving to Southeast Asia and South America, Fox's cotton lost the financial advantage it had over traditional cotton. Because the overseas mills were unwilling or unable to process the relatively small quantities of cotton her farmers produced, she lost her big customers. Fox now concentrates on smaller mills and smaller customers, and she is rebuilding her business and her network of growers.

The Idea Is Marketable and Financially Viable. While it is important to determine whether there are enough customers who are willing to buy the product or service, it is also important to determine whether sales will lead to profits.[16] Estimating market demand requires an initial understanding of who the customers are, what their needs are, and how the product or service will satisfy their needs better than competitors' products will. It also requires a thorough understanding of the key competitors who can provide similar products, services or benefits to the target customer. For example, ten years ago few people thought that manufacturers of cellphones would be competitors of camera manufacturers in providing real-time photos through digital imaging.

...

The Idea Has Low Exit Costs. The final consideration is the venture's exit costs. Exit costs are low if a venture can be shut down without a significant loss of time, money or reputation.[17] If a venture is not expected to make a profit for a number of years, its exit costs are high, since the project cannot be reasonably abandoned in the short term. On the other hand, if the venture is expected to make a profit quickly, its exit costs will be lower, making the idea more attractive.

...

Financial Resources

There are two main types of financing—debt and equity. Briefly, debt financing refers to money that is borrowed. The borrower is obliged to repay the full amount of the loan in addition to interest charges on the debt. The most common sources of debt financing are banks (who provide personal loans), trust companies, co-operatives, finance companies, equipment companies, credit unions, government agencies and suppliers (who provide goods such as inventory to the entrepreneur with an agreement to bill the entrepreneur later).

Equity financing refers to money that the entrepreneur (or others) invests in a business in return for an ownership interest. Equity investors, as owners, are keenly interested in how any profit will be distributed. The most common sources of equity financing are personal savings (new venture founders draw heavily on their own finances to start their businesses), love money (investments from friends, relatives and business associates), venture capitalists (who loan money to promising new ventures in return for a share of ownership in the business) and private investors (also known as angels), who are financially well-off entrepreneurs who wish to recycle their wealth by investing in new businesses. (1843 words)

Notes

1. William D. Bygrave and C.W. Hofer, "Theorizing About Entrepreneurship," *Entrepreneurship Theory and Practice* 16, No. 2 (Winter 1991): 14.
2. Fred Vogelstein, "How Mark Zuckerberg Turned Facebook Into the Web's Hottest Platform." *Wired,* September 6, 2007, www.wired.com/techbuz/startups/news/2007/09/ff_facebook?currentPage=3.
3. 2009 Index of Economic Freedom, "Country Rankings." Last modified 2009. Accessed July 25, 2012, http://www.heritage.org/index/ranking.aspx.
4. Angela Dale, "Self-Employment and Entrepreneurship: Notes on Two Problematic Concepts," in *Deciphering the Enterprise Culture*, Ed., Roger Burrows (London, UK: Routledge, 1991): 45–48.
5. Donald Sexton and Nancy Bowman-Upton, *Entrepreneurship: Creativity and Growth* (New York, NY: MacMillan Publishing Company, 1991): 11.
6. Allan A. Gibb, "The Enterprise Culture and Education: Understanding Enterprise Education and Its Links with Small Business, Entrepreneurship and Wider Educational Goals," *International Small Business Journal* 11, No. 3 (1993): 13–34.
7. Donald F. Kuratko and Richard M. Hodgetts, *Entrepreneurship: Theory, Process and Practice*, 7th ed. (Mason, OH: Thomson South-Western, 2007): 118–125.
8. Jeffry A. Timmons and Stephen Spinelli, *New Venture Creation: Entrepreneurship for the 21st Century*, 7th ed. (Boston, MA: McGraw-Hill/Irwin, 2007): 19.
9. J.D. Kyle, R. Blais, R. Blatt and A.J. Szonyi, "The Culture of the Entrepreneur: Fact or Fiction," *Journal of Small Business and Entrepreneurship* (1991): 3–14.
10. J.C. Mitchell, "Case and Situation Analysis," *Sociological Review* 31, No. 2 (1983): 187–211.
11. W.D. Bygrave and C.W. Hofer, "Theorizing About Entrepreneurship," *Entrepreneurship Theory and Practice* 16, No. 2 (Winter 1991): 14.
12. Walter Good, *Building a Dream* (Toronto, ON: McGraw-Hill Ryerson, 1998): 40.
13. Wayne A. Long and W. Ed McMullan, *Developing New Ventures* (San Diego, CA: Harcourt Brace Jovanovich, 1990): 374–375.
14. "Sally Fox: Innovation in the Field," www. vreseis.com/sally_fox_story.htm.
15. Michael E. Porter, "Know Your Place," *Inc. 13*, No. 9 (September 1992): 90–93.
16. Howard H. Stevenson, H. Irving Grousbeck, Michael J. Roberts and Amarnath Bhide, *New Business Ventures and the Entrepreneur* (Boston, MA: McGraw-Hill/Irwin, 1999): 19.
17. Howard H. Stevenson, H. Irving Grousbeck, Michael J. Roberts and Amarnath Bhide, *New Business Ventures and the Entrepreneur* (Boston, MA: McGraw-Hill/Irwin, 1999): 21.

Griffin, R.W., Ebert, R.J., Starke, F.A., & Lang, M.D. (2011). *Business* (7th Canadian ed., pp. 108–118). Toronto, ON: Pearson Education Canada.

E. What did you learn that was new and interesting?

____

____

____

____

____

WARM-UP ASSIGNMENT

Write a Short Process Essay

When you receive feedback from your instructor or your classmates on this Warm-Up Assignment, you will have some information that you can use to improve your writing on the Final Assignment.

Select one of the descriptions of the young entrepreneurs in Reading 1 and write a short process essay explaining his or her entrepreneurial experience. Focus on the three key elements in the entrepreneurial process as described in Reading 2: the entrepreneur (his or her characteristics), the idea (how it was generated) and the resources (how it was financed).

Refer to the Models Chapter (page 196) to see an example of a process essay and to learn more about how to write one.

Academic Survival Skill

Knowing How and What to Cite and Reference

Citations and references give the reader access to information about sources cited in a text.

A citation is indicated in the text by either a number or an author-date combination; a reference provides complete information about a source and is found at the end of the text in a References or Works Cited section or in a Notes section (often with a Bibliography).

Citations

Citations provide information, in brief, about the source of the original material. There are two general types of citation systems: numbered and author-date.

- The citation system used in Reading 2 is a numbered system. Each number corresponds to a numbered entry in a Notes section at the end of the text.
- The citation system used in Reading 3 is an author-date system. Each citation corresponds to an entry in a References section at the end of the text.

A. Look at Reading 2 and Reading 3 to see examples of the two citation types.

References, Works Cited and Bibliography

A References or Works Cited section lists all the sources that are cited in a text. A Bibliography lists all the sources that are cited as well as those the writer used for background information but did not cite. A References, Works Cited or Bibliography contains more detailed information so that the reader can find the original source. Entries include the author's name, date of publication, title of the work, page number, publisher, location of publisher (if a book), issue and volume number (if a journal, magazine or newspaper article) or URL (if found on a website). Entries are listed in alphabetical order according to the author's last name.

Citation Styles or Systems

Within each citation system (numbered or author-date) there are a number of different citation styles, each of which uses slightly different formats for information order and punctuation. If you look closely at the citations in either Reading 2 or Reading 3, you will see that they each contain information arranged in a similar order for similar sources, with very specific punctuation and use of italics.

In some citation styles, the author-date citation includes the page number.

When you cite sources in your writing, you need to give information in the correct order and follow the rules of punctuation, according to the citation style you use.

The citation style will depend on your field of study or the preferences of your instructors. If you are not sure which citation style to use, ask your instructor or a librarian.

DISCIPLINE OR FIELD OF STUDY	CITATION STYLE	CITATION SYSTEM
MEDICINE, HEALTH, BIOLOGICAL SCIENCES	American Medical Association (AMA)	Numbered (as in Reading 2)
PSYCHOLOGY, EDUCATION, SOCIAL SCIENCES AND ENGINEERING	American Psychological Association (APA)	Author-date (as in Reading 3)
HISTORY (AND OFTEN USED IN NEWSPAPERS, MAGAZINES AND TEXTBOOKS)	Chicago Manual of Style (CMS)	Numbered *or* author-date
SCIENCES AND MATH	Council of Science Editors (CSE)	Author-date-page number
ELECTRICAL ENGINEERING	Institute of Electrical and Electronics Engineers (IEEE)	Numbered
LITERATURE, ARTS AND THE HUMANITIES	Modern Languages Association (MLA)	Author-page number
ALL DISCIPLINES	Turabian	Numbered *or* author-date-page number

B. Look through a textbook or journal article you have with you or one a classmate has. Which citation style is used? Survey your class to determine which citation styles seem to be used most in the textbooks and documents your classmates have.

Citation Formatting Made (Relatively) Easy

In the past, writing citation information accurately according to the citation style used in your discipline required great attention to detail. While that is still important, it is now relatively easy to generate accurate references. You can use one of the following methods.

- Citation Machine is available for free online. Click the citation style you wish to use, type in the identifying information, and the software will format the information for you.
- RefWorks and EndNote Web are two examples of citation management software packages that are available for free through your library's website. Ask the librarian for help.
- Library databases may provide a link to citation software when you search and find library items. Click on Cite and select your preferred citation style.
- Current versions of Microsoft Word help format citations. Find the Document Elements tab and click on References.
- The associations that have developed citation systems publish style manuals and style guides that provide examples of citations. Many of these are online, or the library will link to them through its website. There are also paper copies of these manuals available through the library.

MySearchLab can also generate citations in several different formats. Check it out!

What to Cite and Reference, and What Not to Cite

Citing sources allows readers to go to the original source in case they want further information on the subject. Knowing what information to cite will help you avoid *plagiarism*. Plagiarism is copying another writer's words or ideas without giving credit to the original author. So, what do you need to cite?

In most cases, you *do not* need to cite general or commonly known information in your discipline. For example, the following sentence does not need a citation.

> Entrepreneurs bring creativity and energy to the marketplace in hopes of making money.

This is a general statement about entrepreneurs that is well understood by a wide variety of people. However, this sentence from Reading 2 (lines 12–13) does need a citation.

> In 2009, the top three countries were Hong Kong, Singapore and Australia ... Canada ranked seventh ... and North Korea ranked last.

This is specific information; therefore, you must cite the original source so that the reader knows where the information comes from.

Sometimes, it's difficult to know what information is considered general or commonly known, but the more you study and write in your discipline, the more confident you will become about identifying information that requires a citation. If you're not sure, it's best to reference the information.

Writers must reference

- exact quotations;
- specific ideas;
- specific facts learned from another source of information;
- specific research results;
- specific statistics;
- specific examples discovered from another source of information.

C. Look at the references for Reading 2 on page 37. Then, return to the reading and identify why each piece of information was referenced by the authors. For example, citation 1, "An entrepreneur is someone who perceives an opportunity and creates an organization to pursue it," is an *exact quotation*. Complete the activity as a class discussion.

D. Some cited information in Reading 2 might be considered general or common knowledge and might not need a reference. Discuss with your class why the authors chose to reference this information.

Secondary Purposes of Citations

Although citations provide essential identifying information to readers about the sources of the text, writers also use citations to

- demonstrate how knowledgeable they are;
- show the reader that they can write like other writers in the discipline;
- show respect for other writers;
- support colleagues in the discipline.

E. Discuss with your class how important it is to provide citations for these purposes.

Introducing Citations

When you cite sources, you can introduce the citations in several ways. Each way places a different amount of emphasis on the original author(s).

A. Read these sentences from Reading 2 and Reading 3 and, as you do, pay particular attention to the *presence and position of* or the *absence of* the author's name. Then, answer the questions that follow.

a) Creativity is an important personal attribute that has come to be associated with entrepreneurs, and small businesses provide a great environment to use creativity.

b) While the idea that people are "born" entrepreneurs is still quite popular, nothing could be further from the truth.

c) Interest in entrepreneurship among young people is reported to be growing (Scarborough et al., 2009), prompting increased research interest in the area (Harris and Gibson, 2008).

d) This is consistent with Harris and Gibson's (2008) finding that collectively the students exhibit similar attitudes but that differences do exist.

e) Using the contingency theory, Gilad and Levine (1986) proposed the "push" and "pull" theories as possible explanations of entrepreneurial motivation.

! *Note that most citations are written in the present or present perfect tense.*

1. Which examples emphasize the author(s) most? ____________________
2. Which examples minimize the author(s) most? ____________________
3. Which verb tense is used in each example? ____________________

B. The answers to the following questions can be found in Reading 1. Respond with a short answer that cites the source of the information. Vary your citation formats to emphasize or de-emphasize the author's name. Pay careful attention to the verb tense you use. The first one has been done for you.

1. According to Wang, how much money has ModCloth raised for its expansion to San Francisco and Los Angeles? How many people does it employ?

   Wang (2010) states that ModCloth has found $20 million in investor capital to expand to San Francisco and Los Angeles. It employs approximately 150 people.

2. How much venture financing has Loopt managed to raise at this point?

   ____

3. As of 2010, how many users had Loopt registered?

   ____

4. What was the total value of sales Wpromote expected in 2010?

   ____

VOCABULARY BUILD

Working with a classmate, match each key word and phrase to its definition. When you have finished, confirm your answers with those of another pair of students.

WORD/PHRASE	DEFINITION
❶ abstract* (n.)	6 payment for services
❷ acknowledged* (v.)	______ establishment of an organization
❸ aggregate* (adj.)	______ very soon
❹ approach* (n.)	______ seen in a certain way
❺ collectivist (adj.)	______ admitted or recognized
❻ compensation* (n.)	______ short written statement containing only the main ideas of a text
❼ conduct* (v.) a survey	______ persuasive language
❽ consistency* (n.)	______ tendency
❾ founding* (n.)	______ describing a system in which the benefit of a group is prioritized over the benefit of the individual
❿ fulfillment (n.)	______ containing or describing the total amount
⓫ imminent (adj.)	______ searching
⓬ orientation* (n.)	______ method of doing something
⓭ perceived* (adj.)	______ state of always being the same or following the same model
⓮ prior* (adj.) research	______ carry out
⓯ propensity (n.)	______ general tendency
⓰ proposition (n.)	______ hypothesis
⓱ refinement* (n.)	______ aptitude or interest
⓲ rhetoric (n.)	______ feeling of happiness and satisfaction because your work is interesting and useful
⓳ seeking* (v.)	______ earlier
⓴ trend* (n.)	______ small improvement

*Appears on the Academic Word List

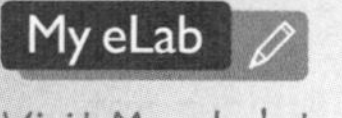

Visit My eLab to complete a vocabulary review exercise for this chapter.

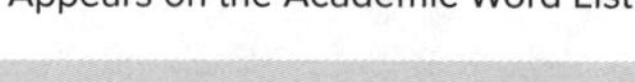

Reading Journal Articles

As you progress in your academic career, you will be required to read journal articles to get the most reliable and up-to-date information about a topic. Journal articles usually report the results of specific research and, even across disciplines, typically follow the same organizational structure: they are divided into predictable sections and each section has a specific purpose.

A. Working with a partner, skim Reading 3 and complete the first column to match the major sections of the journal article with their purposes. When you have finished, confirm your answers with the class.

B. Skim Reading 3 again, this time looking for elements common to journal articles, as shown in the SECTION PURPOSE column, and write the line numbers where each element is found. This will help you understand the structure of a journal article.

SECTION OF JOURNAL ARTICLE	SECTION PURPOSE	COMMON INDICATORS
ABSTRACT	• Summarizes the article to provide readers with enough information to decide if it will be useful to them. LINES ________	• Often not labelled with a heading, but inset from the rest of the text or in italics.
________	• Explains why this research is important. LINES ________ • Identifies a knowledge gap in the current research literature—something that is unknown. LINES ________ • Summarizes the research literature that is relevant to the problem the authors are trying to solve. LINES ________ • States the research question that will guide the researchers to find the missing knowledge. LINES ________	• Often introduced with a subordinate conjunction (although/while/despite). • Contains citations of other research.
________	• Describes the process the authors used to discover the information they are searching for. LINES ________	• May be written in the passive voice.
________	• Summarizes the results of the research and compares them to previous research. LINES ________	• Often written in the present tense. • Often contains citations.
________	• Explains the important contributions this research has made. LINES ________ • States the limitations of the research project and possible opportunities for further research. LINES ________	

READING 3

Towards an Explanation of the Growth in Young Entrepreneur Activities: A Cross-Country Survey of Work Values of College Students

Read the article closely and, when you have finished, demonstrate your understanding of it by indicating whether each of the following statements is true or false. Confirm your answers with your classmates and, as a class, rewrite any false statements to make them true.

STATEMENTS	TRUE	FALSE
1 In the abstract, the author, Mboko, states that the research provides an explanation for the growth in young entrepreneurship.	☐	☐
2 There have not been many research studies about entrepreneurship.	☐	☐
3 There have not been many research studies about what motivates young people to become entrepreneurs.	☐	☐
4 There have not been many research studies that compare student attitudes to entrepreneurship in developed and developing countries.	☐	☐
5 Gilad and Levine suggest that young people become entrepreneurs because they can't get employment elsewhere. This is the "pull" theory of entrepreneurial motivation.	☐	☐
6 Mboko believes that entrepreneurship meets the career aspirations of young people more than a job with an established organization.	☐	☐
7 Mboko uses an online survey to collect data.	☐	☐
8 The results show that business students in the US and SA generally have similar motivation to become entrepreneurs.	☐	☐
9 The differences in student attitudes toward entrepreneurship may be a result of culture, but this was not a major focus of this study.	☐	☐
10 The study connected student attitudes toward young entrepreneurship to the founding of businesses.	☐	☐

This short exploratory paper aims to study job attitudes of business college students with a view to contributing to the explanation of the reported global growth in young entrepreneur activities. Seven career attitude factors adapted from the theory of planned behaviour are used to conduct a comparative study of work attitudes of university business students in the United States and South Africa to establish if there are significant differences across nations. The results show similarity in what the students expect from their future careers but do not necessarily provide an explanation for the observed increase of young entrepreneurs.

Introduction

Entrepreneurship is an important career option. In the past few years, successive Results Reports from the Global Entrepreneurship Monitor have indicated that throughout the world entrepreneurs are pursuing new ventures out of both necessity and opportunity. Around the globe, public policy rhetoric in the area of job creation in different countries has pronounced a growing interest in undertaking actions to portray entrepreneurship

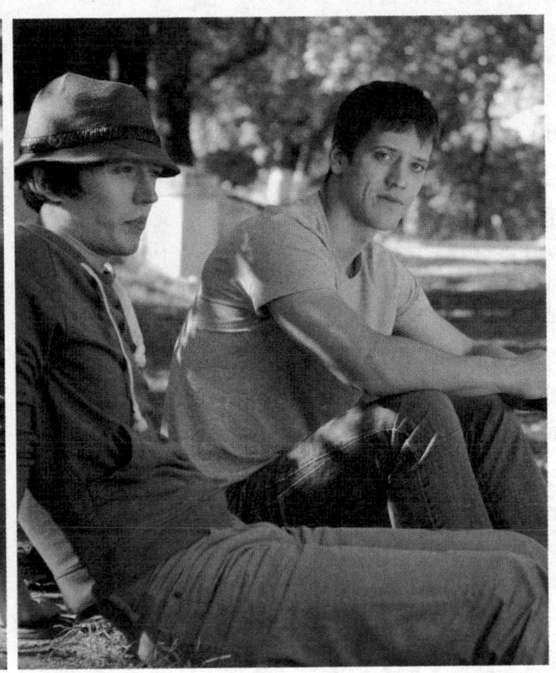

as an attractive alternative to organizational employment among students (Schwarz et al., 2009). Interest in entrepreneurship among young people is reported to be growing (Scarborough et al., 2009), prompting increased research interest in the area (Harris and Gibson, 2008). This paper aims to study job attitudes of business graduates with a view to contributing to the explanation of the reported global growth in young entrepreneur activities. Starting up a new venture is acknowledged to be an individual decision (Littunen, 2000). This makes the individual entrepreneur central in the investigation of entrepreneurial activities. Research has encouraged a continuous study and refinement of the entrepreneurial profile. In examining the global landscape, it is clear that some cultures produce many more entrepreneurs than others, and finding possible explanations continues to be of increasing importance in the global economy.

Although significant research has been conducted in the field of entrepreneurship, writers continue to emphasize that studies on entrepreneurial motivation are still limited (van Gelderen et al., 2008). Research on work values of young college graduates has shown that they desire work which provides a feeling of accomplishment, job security and the opportunity for advancement. Much of this research has been done in developed ... economies. Also, with the reported increase in entrepreneurial activity among young people, two further research questions that arise are whether the work values reported earlier still hold and whether there are differences across countries.

The objective of this exploratory comparative study is to contribute to entrepreneurship research through establishing the work attitudes of today's undergraduate college business students across countries. Seven employment attitude factors of job security, workload, social environment, responsibility, opportunity, job challenge and self-direction adapted, from the theory of planned behaviour, are used to conduct a comparative study of work attitudes of university business students in the United States of America (US) and South Africa (SA) to establish if there are significant differences across nations.

While entrepreneurship is important to all economies, businesses need employees. Some young people opting for entrepreneurship may actually have great potential as employees. A skilled, knowledgeable and committed workforce is an essential resource of successful businesses. Business leaders need to know today's young employee expectations and motivations. The results of this exploratory research make an important contribution in this regard.

...

Entrepreneurship research has attempted to identify the situational and environmental factors that predict entrepreneurial activity. Using the contingency theory, Gilad and Levine (1986) proposed the "push" and "pull" theories as possible explanations of entrepreneurial motivation. The "push" theory suggests that a person can opt for entrepreneurship as a result of unfavourable environmental conditions like job dissatisfaction, while the "pull" theory argues that people can find entrepreneurship attractive. Despite research indications that individuals become entrepreneurs mainly because of "pull" factors, college graduates and students are reported to be increasingly disenchanted with career prospects as organizational employees (Orham, 2001), seemingly suggesting a "push" factor scenario.

...

Methodology

The population is built from graduating students from two partner universities, one in South Africa and one in the US. Country selection is based on the need to have a developing and developed nation representation, and the two universities are chosen for ease of access. An existing partnership between the two universities made them a preferred good choice. The sample consists of undergraduate student subjects facing imminent career decisions.

Survey data is collected through a self-administered questionnaire, an approach found appropriate given the limited use of alternative methods of data collection, like online surveys in developing nations like South Africa, and the need for consistency.

... Our basic proposition is that a partial explanation for the increase in entrepreneurial activity among young people is that compared to organizational employment, entrepreneurship better meets the career aspirations of the young people of today and that this phenomenon cuts across nations ...

A basic survey analysis tool is used to generate the career preference patterns. The questions allow assessment of job attitudes along seven identifiable categories. The aggregate tables generated by the two data sets representing responses from the two universities studied are used to discuss the results along seven employment attitude factors of job security, workload, social environment, responsibility, opportunity, job challenge and self-direction. In the analysis, we use the overall rating average. For the overall rating average, given that in our scale 1 = agree and 3 = disagree, the smaller the overall rating average, the higher the extent of agreement with the statement and vice versa.

Results

... Participants were US students n = 71, South African students n = 33, and rating scale 1 = agree, 2 = neutral and 3 = disagree.

[Table 8, lines 1–2,] show the importance attached to job security. Overall attitude to job security is the average response to the two questions related to job security as shown [in line 3]. Job security is an important factor in career choice to both the US students (1.48), and South African students (1.44), with the South African students seemingly attaching more importance to job security than the US students.

[Lines 4–8] show scores for workload factors. The average score for workload factors [shown in line 9] is 1.99 for US students and 1.75 for South African students. For the US students surveyed, job simplicity has the lowest rating at 2.38. The results show a higher preference for fixed working hours for the South African students (1.48), compared to 1.93 for the US students. The respondents agree on their level of concern for leisure (1.73). The responses also show that for the South African students, job related stress, at 1.76, may be a concern in career choice.

[Lines 10 and 11] show the scores for work social environment. The social environment construct takes care of people as social beings. The overall ratings, ... [line 12,] for the groups are close at 1.8 and 1.9 and lean more toward being neutral than having a clear positive concern. Although the overall averages are close on the individual items, the

South African students show a higher concern to be part of the social environment (1.5) than the US students, with only 1.77 agreeing with the statement.

The responses [in lines 13–16] show the respondents disagreeing with statements suggesting avoiding responsibility as a factor in career choice, an average of 2.59 for US students and 2.57 for South African students.

[Lines 17–21] show results of responses to organizational human resources management practices of rewarding employees. From [line 18] it can be seen that opportunity as represented by promotional possibilities is 1.37 for US students and 1.33 for South African students surveyed. The South African students show a high concern for compensation based on merit, 1.24, against 1.66 for United States students.

Job challenge and interest are variables that address intrinsic rewards linked to job satisfaction. The results [in line 24] show an average overall rating closer to agreeing than neutral, 1.43 for US students and 1.23 for South African students.

The final set of variables addresses entrepreneurial orientation construct. They are about self-direction as represented by the freedoms associated with the entrepreneurship career. The results are summarized in [lines 25–29]. The overall rating for US students is 1.63, and for South African students is 1.52. The specific entrepreneurial area where the US students score highest is the desire to create something new (1.57). Results in the other three areas of evidence of being one's own boss, independence, choosing one's own tasks and exploiting personal creativity are close, averaging 1.65. For the South African students, the lowest score is in the area of choosing one's own tasks (1.76), with the other three areas very close at 1.45.

Table 8: Scores for all factors considered in choosing a career among US and SA students

	UNITED STATES				SOUTH AFRICA			
	AGREE (%)	NEUTRAL (%)	DISAGREE (%)	AV.	AGREE (%)	NEUTRAL (%)	DISAGREE (%)	AV.
JOB SECURITY	71.8	12.7	15.5	1.44	72.7	9.1	18.2	1.45
JOB STABILITY	63.4	21.1	15.5	1.52	72.7	12.1	15.2	1.42
OVERALL JOB SECURITY	67.6	16.9	15.5	1.48	72.7	10.6	16.7	1.44
NOT HAVING LONG HOURS	30.0	45.7	24.3	1.94	42.4	24.2	33.3	1.91
TO HAVE LEISURE	43.7	38.4	16.9	1.73	45.5	36.4	18.2	1.73
TO HAVE FIXED WORKING HOURS	35.2	36.6	28.2	1.93	60.6	30.3	9.1	1.48
NOT TO HAVE A STRESSFUL JOB	31.0	42.3	26.8	1.96	48.5	27.3	24.2	1.76
TO HAVE A SIMPLE JOB	11.3	39.4	49.3	2.38	36.4	36.4	27.3	1.91
OVERALL WORKLOAD INFLUENCES	30.2	40.7	29.1	1.99	46.7	30.9	22.4	1.75
PARTICIPATE IN SOCIAL ENVIRONMENT	39.4	43.7	16.9	1.77	60.0	30.0	10.0	1.50
BE MEMBER OF SOCIAL MILIEU	25.7	55.7	18.6	1.93	35.5	22.6	41.9	2.06
OVERALL SOCIAL ENVIRONMENT	32.6	49.7	17.8	1.85	47.8	26.3	26	1.78

	UNITED STATES				SOUTH AFRICA			
	AGREE (%)	NEUTRAL (%)	DISAGREE (%)	AV.	AGREE (%)	NEUTRAL (%)	DISAGREE (%)	AV.
AVOID RESPONSIBILITY	11.3	18.3	70.4	2.59	12.1	3.0	84.8	2.73
NOT TAKING ON TOO MUCH RESPONSIBILITY	8.5	23.9	67.6	2.59	9.4	25.0	65.6	2.56
AVOID COMMITMENT	11.3	19.7	69.0	2.58	18.8	21.9	59.4	2.41
OVERALL RESPONSIBILITY	10.4	20.6	69.0	2.59	13.4	16.6	69.9	2.57
OPPORTUNITY FOR CAREER PROGRESS	81.4	2.9	15.7	1.34	78.8	9.1	12.1	1.33
PROMOTION	78.9	5.6	15.5	1.37	78.8	9.1	12.1	1.33
ECONOMIC OPPORTUNITY	69.0	16.9	14.1	1.45	87.9	6.1	6.1	1.18
COMPENSATION BASED ON MERIT	49.3	35.2	15.5	1.66	81.8	12.1	6.1	1.24
OVERALL ECONOMIC OPPORTUNITY	65.7	19.2	15.03	1.49	82.8	9.1	8.1	1.25
CHALLENGE AND EXCITEMENT	67.1	21.4	11.4	1.44	84.8	3.0	12.1	1.27
INTERESTING AND MOTIVATING JOB	71.8	14.1	14.1	1.42	87.9	6.1	6.1	1.18
OVERALL JOB CHALLENGE	69.5	17.8	12.8	1.43	86.4	4.6	9.1	1.23
FREEDOM, INDEPENDENCE, OWN BOSS	49.3	38	12.7	1.63	69.7	12.1	18.2	1.48
ABILITY TO CHOOSE OWN WORK TASKS	47.9	36.6	15.5	1.68	54.5	15.2	30.3	1.76
CREATE SOMETHING NEW	54.3	34.3	11.4	1.57	69.7	18.2	12.1	1.42
TAKE ADVANTAGE OF CREATIVE NEEDS	47.9	40.8	11.3	1.63	68.8	21.9	9.4	1.41
OVERALL NEED FOR SELF-DIRECTION	49.9	37.4	12.7	1.63	65.7	16.9	17.5	1.52

SCALE: AGREE = 1 NEUTRAL = 2 DISAGREE = 3

...

In this final section we use results from responses to [all the] questions ... to show the top rated preferred career attributes. Top for the South African students is an interesting and motivating job (1.18), with promotional opportunities (1.18). These fall into two categories, the nature of the job and potential rewards from the job. In second place is economic opportunity (1.24). A close third position at 1.27 is the challenge and excitement associated with the job. This attribute, as with interest and motivation, is about the nature of the job. Fourth is opportunity for career progress (1.33), and the last in the top five is job security and stability both at 1.45.

As can be seen in Table 8, the responses from US students show a strong preference for opportunities in the career. In first place is opportunity for career progress (1.34), and second is promotion opportunity (1.37). In third place are two factors in different categories. The students are interested in a job that is interesting and motivational (1.42), a job characteristic factor, and job security (1.42). In fourth position, at 1.44, is challenge and excitement. Last in the top five preferences for the US students is the importance of economic opportunity (1.45). The following table is a summary of the top ranked preferred career attributes as found by this study of college students in the United States and in South Africa.

Top ranked preferred career attributes among US and SA students

RANK	UNITED STATES	SOUTH AFRICA
1	Opportunity for career progress	Promotion/Interesting and motivating job
2	Promotion	Economic opportunity
3	Interesting and motivating job/Job security	Challenge and excitement
4	Challenge and excitement	Opportunity for career progress
5	Economic opportunity	Job stability/Job security

Discussion

Analysis of the results of this exploratory study reveals two interesting patterns. First is the universality of the broad career expectations of today's young people, and second are the important differences in attitude in the South African and US students. This is consistent with Harris and Gibson's (2008) finding that collectively the students exhibit similar attitudes but that differences do exist.

...

This research makes three important contributions. First, it highlights what young business students expect from their careers. Second, it provides a comparative perspective of the career preferences of young people. The important role of entrepreneurship to any economy is widely acknowledged. Economic and community development hinges on growing business formation and growth. To encourage economic development in the form of new businesses it is necessary to have information on factors that exert a positive influence on attitudes toward self-employment. Information that helps enhance entrepreneurship should be of interest to a range of stakeholders including researchers, educators and policy makers. Understanding differences in work attitudes across nations will make a contribution toward explaining differences in rates of firm start-ups across nations which is an important consideration in this age of globalization.

Third, the research has a message for business leaders. There is a need for a paradigm shift if organizations are going to attract and retain top talent. Today's young people believe they can take a heavy workload provided it is exciting. They also have the propensity to look for alternative opportunities if the organization fails to meet their expectations. A possible contribution of this study is that in addition to the traditional rewards organizations should consider making the work environment an interesting place.

One limitation of this exploratory study is its cross-sectional nature. It does not provide a direct link between job attitude and active business founding. As such, conclusions linking job attitudes to levels of entrepreneurship are theoretically based. Another limitation is that because of the survey nature of the research, it has not been possible to make follow-up questions to uncover the reasoning behind the attitudes. The results suggest potentially interesting explanatory research to provide detailed information of the career intentions of today's business students and country differences as shown by this study and attempt to answer the questions raised in the discussion section above. It is also important to provide longitudinal studies in this area to follow the career paths of the respondents.

(2655 words)

References

Gilad, B., & Levine, P. (1986). A behaviour model of entrepreneurial supply. *Journal of Small Business Management,* 24, 45–51.

Harris, M.L., & Gibson, S.G. (2008). Examining the entrepreneurial attitudes of US business students. *Education + Training 50*(7), 568–581.

Littunen, H. (2000). Entrepreneurship and the characteristics of the entrepreneurial personality. *International Journal of Entrepreneurial Behaviour and Research, 6*(6), 295–301.

Orham, Scott D. (2001). Why women enter into entrepreneurship: An explanatory model. *Women in Management Review, 16*(5), 232–243.

Scarborough, N.M., Wilson, D.L., & Zimmerer, T.W. (2009). *Effective small business management: An entrepreneurial approach,* 9th ed. Toronto, ON: Pearson, Prentice Hall.

Schwarz, E.J., Wdowiak, M.A., Almer-Jarz, D.A., & Breitenecker, R.J. (2009). The effects of attitudes and perceived environment conditions on students' entrepreneurial intent: An Austrian perspective. *Education + Training, 51*(4), 272–291.

van Gelderen, M., Brand, M., van Praag, M., Bodewes, W., Poutsma, E., & van Gils, A. (2008). Explaining entrepreneurial intentions by means of the theory of planned behavior. *Career Development International, 13*(6), 538–559.

Mboko, S. (2011). Towards an explanation of the growth in young entrepreneur activities: A cross-country survey of work values of college students. *Journal of Marketing Development and Competitiveness, 5*(4), 108–118.

FINAL ASSIGNMENT

Write an Extended Process Essay

Find an example of a young entrepreneur. Search "profiles of young entrepreneurs" on the Internet, or use an example provided by your instructor. Write a longer process essay about this person, describing his or her entrepreneurial development. Include citations and references.

- Learn as much as you can about the background, education and experience of this entrepreneur. Remember to use reliable sources and to keep track of citations and referencing information.
- In the introduction to your essay, provide a definition of *entrepreneur, entrepreneurship* or *entrepreneurial education.*
- In your essay, discuss the entrepreneur's characteristics and defining experiences (including entrepreneurial motivation), the business idea (how the idea was generated) and the resources used (how the business was financed).
- As you will be citing multiple sources of information, use the citation style that you will use in your discipline. Follow the correct format for either numbered or author-date citations, and finish your essay with a corresponding reference section. On the front of your paper, write the citation style you are following so it is clear to your instructor.

Refer to the Models Chapter (page 196) to see an example of a process essay and to learn more about how to write one.

CRITICAL CONNECTIONS

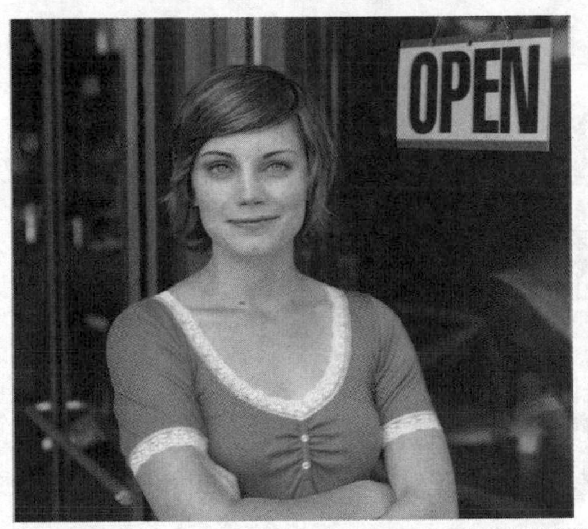

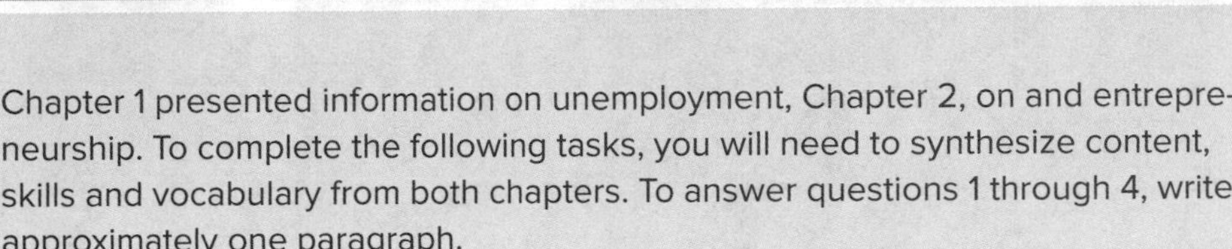

Chapter 1 presented information on unemployment, Chapter 2, on and entrepreneurship. To complete the following tasks, you will need to synthesize content, skills and vocabulary from both chapters. To answer questions 1 through 4, write approximately one paragraph.

1. Would a young entrepreneur be categorized by Statistics Canada as employed or unemployed? Explain your answer.
2. Why might a young entrepreneur consider
   a) encouraging a union for her employees?
   b) paying above minimum wage?
3. Write an extended definition for one or more of the following terms.
   a) social commerce
   b) social-mapping service
   c) venture financing (or seed money)
   d) pay-per-click services
   e) search engine optimization
   f) virtual farmer's market
4. Describe the process that Statistics Canada uses to determine the statistics for the Labour Force Survey each month.
5. Using the topic of unemployment, write a sentence that does not need a citation. Then, write a second sentence containing specific information from Chapter 1 that does need a citation.
6. Search your library's research databases for journal articles about unemployment. Use online citation tools to help you write bibliographic entries for five of them. Skim the journal articles to determine if they follow the same organization structure (abstract, introduction, methods, results and conclusion) as the journal article in Chapter 2, Reading 3.

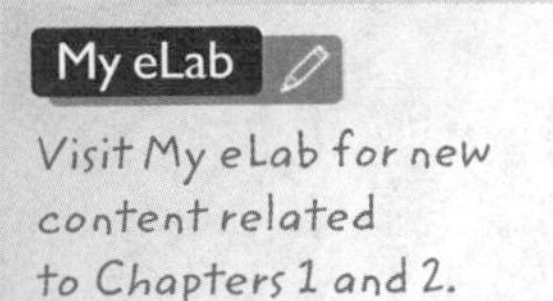

My eLab
Visit My eLab for new content related to Chapters 1 and 2.

CHAPTER 3

Wind and Solar Energy

How the world produces energy to feed its increasing hunger for power is one of the defining issues of our time. The vast majority of the power we consume is generated by burning fossil fuels: oil, coal or natural gas. However, the appeal of these energy sources is decreasing as scientists point to how they pollute our environment. This, and the threat of their eventual depletion, is the inspiration for innovation with renewable energy sources. When scientists and engineers talk about diversifying "the energy mix," they speak of how a combination of renewable energy

In this chapter,
you will

- learn vocabulary related to wind and solar power;
- organize information from readings into tables that reflect your writing purpose;
- use suitable expressions and grammatical forms when comparing and contrasting information;
- learn about building a discipline-specific vocabulary to leverage your vocabulary acquisition;
- write a short compare and contrast essay;
- write an extended compare and contrast essay.

GEARING UP

The following paragraph summarizes the challenges the world faces in order to meet the growing demand for energy. Read the text and, with your class, discuss the answers to the questions that follow.

In any society, access to energy is central to economic and social development and improved quality of life. However, most commentators accept that global patterns of energy use cannot be sustained for the current world population of 6.9 billion people. Given that energy consumption is expected to double in the next fifty years, meeting this level of global demand without long-term damage to the environment represents a considerable challenge. Presently, three depletable resources—oil, coal and natural gas (fossil fuels)—provide approximately 90 percent of the industrialized world's energy needs. In contrast, biomass (wood, crop and animal waste) and physical labour remain the main energy sources in the developing world. The combined effects of burning fossil fuels and deforestation have potentially severe medium- to long-term environmental consequences.

Petford, N. (2012). Meeting society's demand for energy. In *Global Environmental Issues*. Frances Harris (Ed.), (2nd ed., p. 167). West Sussex, UK: John Wiley and Sons.

- Which depletable (or non-renewable) energy sources are mentioned in this text? Where are these mostly generated and consumed?
- Which biomass energy sources are mentioned in this text? Where are these mostly generated and consumed?
- What global problems do burning fossil fuels and deforestation create?
- What are some possible solutions?

VOCABULARY BUILD

A. Below are key words and phrases used to describe wind and solar power generation. Underline any unfamiliar words and look them up in a dictionary.

battery storage	electricity meter	infrastructure*	solar panel*
blades	electromagnets	photovoltaic cells	transmission lines
coil of copper wire	grid	solar array	turbine

*Appears on the Academic Word List

B. Working with a partner, use the key words and phrases to explain briefly how wind and solar power are generated and transmitted to homes.

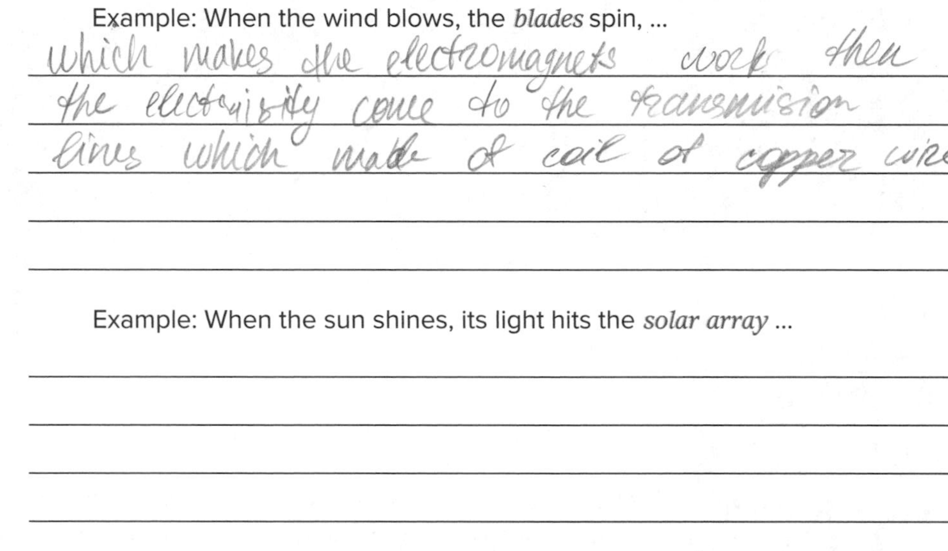

Example: When the wind blows, the *blades* spin, ...

Example: When the sun shines, its light hits the *solar array* ...

C. The key words in the following tables are from Reading 1 and Reading 2. Match each word to its synonym. When you have finished, check your answers with the class, and discuss strategies you could use to help you memorize the pairs of words (for example, *apex* and *peak* both have "pe" in them).

Table A

WORD	SYNONYM
1 aesthetic (n.)	_____ made of
2 allure (n.)	_____ local
3 apex (n.)	_____ acidic
4 appliances (n.)	_____ machines (or tools)
5 channels* (v.)	_____ peak
6 circumstances* (n.)	_____ expert
7 comprising* (v.)	_____ appeal
8 consultant* (n.)	_____ attractiveness
9 corrosive (adj.)	_____ funnels (or drains)

WORD	SYNONYM
10 devices* (n.)	________ situations
11 domestic* (adj.)	________ electrical equipment

Table B

WORD	SYNONYM
1 dormers (n.)	________ irregular
2 dramatically* (adv.)	________ balances
3 hobbyist (n.)	________ unheard of
4 inconsistent* (adj.)	________ part of a machine
5 jurisdictions (n.)	________ amateur
6 maintenance* (n.)	________ (high peaked) windows
7 mechanism* (n.)	________ regions
8 offsets* (v.)	________ significantly
9 range* (n.)	________ repair
10 strategic* (adj.)	________ planned (for a particular purpose)
11 unprecedented* (adj.)	________ extent (of variability)

*Appears on the Academic Word List

READING 1 So Fresh and So Clean

Use the approach to reading comprehension that you learned in Chapter 1 and practised in Chapter 2 to help you understand this text.

A. Skim Reading 1 to find the answers to questions 1 through 5.

1 a) What is the topic of the reading? ________________

b) How long is it? 115 lines

c) Which type of text is it? Scientific article for magazine

2 What do you already know about the topic?

____

____

____

____

3 Based on the text type, how will the content most likely be organized?

____

____

____

4. Reading 1 has been divided into sections, with section headings given below. Working as a class, choose the heading that best represents each section and write it in the space provided in the reading.

   Suggested headings:

   The Disadvantages of Wind and Solar Power

   The Place of Wind and Solar Power in the "Energy Mix"

   Challenges for Wind and Solar Power

   World Use of Renewable Energy and How Wind and Solar Power Work

   The Advantages of Wind and Solar Power

5. Working with a partner, turn the section headings into questions. Write your questions on a separate sheet of paper, and then compare them with those of your classmates. Do you all have the same questions? Why might you have different questions?

B. Now, read the text more closely and answer the questions that follow.

Section 1: ______________________________

The first step to adopting more … renewable power is to understand how the various technologies work and what challenges they face. Historically, most renewable electricity has come from hydroelectric dams, which now provide about 16 percent of the world's electricity. Today, the sources growing the fastest and receiving the most investor attention are wind and solar power.

Wind power, which generates about 1.4 percent of the world's electricity, is produced as pinwheel-style turbines spin atop towers that rise hundreds of feet above the ground. Solar power provides an even smaller share of global electricity: just 0.1percent. Techniques for generating it vary; the most popular uses panels containing wafers of silicon thinner than a fingernail to convert sunlight into electrical current. A few of these photovoltaic panels, as they are known, can be mounted directly on a building's roof, letting the occupants produce at least some of their own power. Or hundreds of panels can be grouped together on the ground in vast arrays that funnel power into the electrical grid—sprawling, centralized power plants of a new sort, some of which have been built in the American Southwest.

Section 2: ____________________

Although wind power is more widespread today, solar power is theoretically more attractive. The sun emits a nearly limitless supply of energy, and it does so during the daytime, when people use the most electricity. (Wind tends to blow most strongly at night.) Solar power also is easily distributed—panels can be placed on a streetlight or a soldier's backpack—whereas wind power is mostly a centralized energy source, requiring clumps of turbines to generate sizable amounts of power. But both wind and solar energy offer big advantages over fossil fuels. Wind and sunshine are clean, emitting neither the pollutants that cause smog nor the carbon dioxide that contributes to climate change. They are ubiquitous, providing a domestic energy source even in places with no indigenous fossil fuels. And they are essentially never-ending.

Section 3: ____________________

There are huge caveats to this rosy assessment, and they come down mostly to money. In most places, producing electricity from new wind and solar projects is more expensive than making it in new conventional power plants. Wind and solar power are younger technologies, with much work left to be done to wring out cost. The downsides of fossil fuels, notably their geopolitical and environmental risks, are not fully reflected in their market prices. And everything about the modern electrical system is predicated on the use of fossil fuels: the coal mines and gas fields that produce them; the railroads, pipelines and ships that transport them and the power plants that burn them. That system has been built up and its costs largely paid down over decades.

Wind and solar power enjoy no such entrenched infrastructure. The challenge of making and installing the wind turbines and solar panels is just the start. Massive new transmission lines must be built to move large amounts of renewable electricity from the out-of-the-way places where it is generated to the metropolitan areas where it is consumed. This new equipment costs money and it often stokes opposition from people who are not used to living near industrial-scale energy infrastructure of any sort. Along with other opponents, a group of landowners in Cape Cod, Massachusetts, for instance, has managed to delay the construction of an offshore wind farm that was proposed back in 2001. Even environmental activists often fight large renewable-energy projects, out of concern for local landscapes or animals. Last spring, the Obama administration temporarily halted construction on part of a solar project in the Mojave Desert because of concerns that it would harm endangered tortoises; the government later let the construction resume.

Section 4: ______

Taking wind and solar power mainstream will also require better ways to get it to consumers when they need it, since the times when wind turbines and solar panels generate the most electricity are not necessarily the times when people use electricity most. Power plants fired by natural gas can be dialed up or down to meet changing electricity demand, but the sun shines and the wind blows only at certain times. One potential solution is to stockpile renewable power—either in large-scale storage equipment, such as massive batteries, or in smaller-scale devices, such as people's plug-in hybrid cars. Other approaches include better technologies to predict gusts and rays and "smart" electrical-transmission grids that could tie together far-flung renewable-power projects. Both could help compensate in one place for … grey skies somewhere else. Scientists are working to bring down the cost of all these ideas. For now, in some places with dense concentrations of wind turbines, some of the power they could produce is wasted; the turbines are shut off when the wind is blowing so hard that the turbines would produce more power than the grid could handle.

Section 5: ______

Wind and solar power will not replace fossil fuels anytime soon—not by a long shot. The International Energy Agency (IEA) projects that by 2035, wind and solar could be producing 10 percent of global electricity, up from 1.5 percent now, and that renewables of all sorts could be generating 31 percent of the world's electricity, up from about 19 percent now. But even that expansion would require an increase in subsidies—"support that in some cases," the IEA notes, "cannot be taken for granted in this age of fiscal austerity." Some countries with particularly generous subsidies and high electricity prices have made wind and solar power big enough to matter. Denmark gets 18 percent of its electricity from wind, and Spain gets 2 percent from the sun—the world's leaders by share, according to the IEA's latest figures. But even that renewable electricity is backed up by fossil-fuel power plants. Last year, fully one-third of the new electricity-generating capacity brought on line in the United States came from wind and solar projects. Even so, given the vastness of the conventional energy system, wind and solar power remained relatively tiny, accounting for just 3 percent of the electricity the country actually produced. For the foreseeable future, renewable power is likely to supplement, not supplant, conventional energy …

Considering what renewable power is up against, the drive for it might seem a folly. But giving up now would be a mistake. As a result of recent technological improvements, the prospect of renewable power as an economically competitive part of the energy mix is no longer a pipe dream. Wind turbines and solar panels have gotten more efficient and less expensive ... Solar power remains more expensive than conventional power (except in a few sunny places with high power prices, such as Hawaii), but its costs, too, are falling rapidly. Now more than ever, sustained but strategic support could produce blockbuster innovations with the potential to meaningfully change the energy mix. (1129 words)

Ball, J. (2012, May/June). Tough love for renewable energy. *Foreign Affairs, 91*(3), 122–133.

C. On your separate sheet of paper, answer the five questions you generated from the reading headings.

D. What did you learn that was new, interesting or important? What do you want to learn more about?

____

____

____

____

Organizing Information into Tables

You may want to record the information you learn when you read so that you can refer to it when you write. An efficient way to do this is to write it—in point form—in a table. This is especially useful if the information is technical or complicated in some way or if it is extensive.

The table you create might look different depending on your purpose. If you want to write about information step by step, such as in a process, classification or definition essay, a useful table might look like this.

SOURCES	INFORMATION
Write citation information here. Keeping accurate references saves time when you write.	*Write what you want to remember here. The linear or step-by-step presentation of information clarifies its order.*

If you want to write about differences in characteristics, such as in a compare and contrast essay, your table might look like this.

CHARACTERISTICS FOR COMPARISON OR CONTRAST	ITEM TO COMPARE OR CONTRAST (E.G., SOLAR POWER)	ITEM TO COMPARE OR CONTRAST (E.G., WIND POWER)	SOURCES
CHARACTERISTIC 1: (E.G., AMOUNT OF ENERGY AVAILABLE)	*Write information about solar power here.*	*Write information about wind power here.*	*Write citation information here.*
CHARACTERISTIC 2: (E.G., EXPENSE OF EQUIPMENT)			

When you need to compare and contrast information (as you will in your written assignments for this chapter), a table like this one will help you organize and remember that information.

A. Reading 2 is about solar and wind power that can be generated on an individual's rooftop (as opposed to large wind or solar farms). Write the source at the top of the table. As you read, write key information in the appropriate row. The first few points have been done for you. When you have finished, check with your class to make sure you have included most of the important points. You will use this information as the basis for your Warm-Up Assignment, so include enough to support your writing effort.

SOURCE: ______________________________

____

CHARACTERISTICS FOR COMPARISON OR CONTRAST	SOLAR POWER	WIND POWER
CONDITIONS FOR USE	• *South facing* • *Sloped (or flat) roof* • *Space* • *Exposure (no trees, chimneys, dormers, vents to shade the panels)*	• *Exposure to wind*
POSSIBLE USES		
DESCRIPTION OF ENERGY SOURCE AND HOW IT GENERATES POWER		
ADVANTAGES AND/OR BENEFITS		

CHARACTERISTICS FOR COMPARISON OR CONTRAST	SOLAR POWER	WIND POWER
DISADVANTAGES		
WHERE ENERGY IS STORED AND HOW		
EXAMPLES OF NEW, INNOVATIVE TECHNOLOGY		

1. Are there any empty spaces in the table? Why?

   ____

   ____

   ____

2. Note that one of the characteristics for comparison and contrast is a description of each energy source. Why are these descriptions provided?

   ____

   ____

   ____

B. Add information from Reading 1 to supplement the information from Reading 2 in this table. Write it in a separate colour or underline or circle it. Why should you distinguish it from information from Reading 2?

____

____

READING 2 Rooftop Power

Renewable energy is taking hold in cities and their suburbs, with solar systems and wind turbines being installed on both homes and businesses at an unprecedented rate. The allure is great: to save electricity and reduce dependence on fossil fuels, as well as to create a visible symbol that we are doing our part to go green.

There are some successful installations that have proven themselves over the years, and some exciting experiments happening, both on multi-unit buildings and individual homes. However, mounting a wind turbine or solar system on your roof isn't as simple—or often as beneficial—as it might seem. And there is a major upfront investment, although the payback can be significant once the system is paid for. So let's examine the possibilities and the pitfalls.

Solar

Since renewable energy relies on natural sources, your property has to be exposed to that source—in this case, the sun. So you'll need an area of south-facing sloped roof—or a flat roof where panels could be installed facing south using a mounting mechanism to tilt them to the right angle—that measures at least 2 by 4 metres (or 6.5 by 13 feet). Ideally, the roof should receive full sun from 10 a.m. to 3 p.m. year round. Keep in mind development possibilities or growing trees that could block the sun in the future. Even chimneys, dormers and vents can shade your panels and reduce their efficiency. Your supplier will calculate the correct slope for your latitude.

There are two main ways to use the power of the sun to reduce energy costs in your home. You can use the heat from the sun's rays to heat your home or your domestic hot water, or to produce electricity to power lights and appliances …

In climates where temperatures rarely dip below freezing, a direct circulation system can be used, where pumps circulate household water through the collectors and into the home. In colder climates, an indirect circulation system is used, with pumps circulating a non-freezing, heat-transfer fluid through the collectors and a heat exchanger …

Most solar water heaters require a well-insulated storage tank. In two-tank systems, the solar water heater preheats water before it enters the conventional water heater. In one-tank systems, the backup heating system is combined with the solar storage in one tank.

Then, there is a solar electric system, using photovoltaic (PV) cells, which are semiconductor devices, usually made of silicon. Photons in sunlight are absorbed by the silicon and electrons are knocked loose from their atoms, allowing them to flow through the silicon to produce electricity.

Because they contain no liquids, corrosive chemicals or moving parts, PV cells require very little maintenance, don't pollute while in use, and operate silently. In a household

system, the cells are bundled together into solar panels, which have a sheet of glass on the front, allowing light to pass while protecting the cells from the elements. Panels are linked together in arrays to fit individual generation needs. You can add panels to your roof at any time after installation—given that you have the available space, of course—in order to increase power output ...

The energy generated by solar panels can be stored in batteries. But in some jurisdictions, your roof-mounted PV system will probably be grid-tied, meaning that any excess electricity generated is sent to the transmission grid. Net metering programs give these systems a credit for the electricity they deliver to the grid. This credit offsets electricity provided from the grid when the system cannot meet demand, effectively using the grid as a storage mechanism.

Due to the growing demand for solar energy, the manufacture of solar cells and PV arrays has been increasing by almost 50 percent a year recently. Technology has also been improving rapidly, decreasing the cost and making the cells smaller and more flexible.

A Philadelphia company, SRS Energy, has even developed a dark blue roof tile made from a high-performance polymer used in car bumpers that has flexible solar technology embedded inside. The tiles are lightweight, unbreakable and recyclable ... Additionally, a number of companies are introducing flexible, thin-film solar PV cells and modules that can be attached, via foil, directly to rooftops.

Wind

Wind power is the renewable energy technology that is growing most quickly, largely because it is one of the least expensive. Like solar, the cost of wind power has fallen dramatically over the last decade or so. However, some wind energy experts feel that wind is not suited to rooftop installation. But more about that later.

The blades on a wind turbine use lift the same way airplanes do. The wind passes over the blades and the lift created causes them to move. The moving blades turn a shaft, which in turn rotates a series of large electromagnets inside a tightly wound copper wire coil within the generator. The moving magnetic field between the coil and the magnets creates an electric current, which is drawn off and transmitted as electricity.

Wind turbines come in a variety of sizes and capacities from 300 watt (W) "mini" turbines that hobbyist homeowners can install themselves, to utility-scale turbines in the 3 to 5 megawatt (MW) range that can be over 120 metres (400 feet) tall. In optimum circumstances, a 6 kW turbine comprising a rotating blade and generator will produce around 15,000 kWh per year. This is enough to power a small office.

There are two main types of wind turbine: vertical axis and horizontal axis.

Home wind turbines that have a vertical axis are more suitable for rooftop mounting. They are impacted less by winds that change directions, work at lower wind speeds, can be quieter than horizontal axis units and can have a more pleasing aesthetic than other models. Some even look like roof vents …

Right now, the American Wind Energy Association (AWEA) estimates that just 1 percent of small wind turbines installed today are attached to roofs, and nearly 99 percent to a tower.

And many small wind experts feel that towers are where wind turbines belong. They say that there is too much turbulence and inconsistent flow of wind from trees and other buildings at the height of most roofs, and the turbines create too much noise and vibration.

Typical advice is that for proper operation, the rotor of a wind turbine should be situated at least 10 metres (33 feet) above anything within 100 metres (328 feet). A tower is usually supplied when you purchase a wind turbine, but many municipalities will not allow towers to be installed. With trees, one needs to take into account the height to which they will grow during the turbine's lifespan …

The Warwick Wind Trials Project in the UK confirmed poor performance and noise issues with roof-mounted wind turbines. Its 2009 report summarizes the finding of a trial covering almost 200,000 hours of operation of twenty-six building mounted wind turbines from five manufacturers across the UK during 2007 and 2008. Author and small wind expert Paul Gipe wrote on his blog that, "If further proof is needed that mounting wind turbines on rooftops is a bad idea, the final report on the Warwick Wind Trials is it."

Gipe particularly referred readers to this part of the report: "Of particular note is that turbines on our high rise sites … were able to generate as much energy in one month as other turbines in the trial did in one year. It is unfortunate that these high performing turbines had to remain switched off for the majority of the trial following complaints about noise from the building residents. The best performing turbine in the trial generated an average of 2.382 kWh per day when in operation, equivalent to 869 kWh in a full year. The poorest site generated an average of 41 kWh per day when in operation or 15 kWh per year, *which is less than the energy it consumed to run the turbine's electronics"* [emphasis added].

What everyone agrees on is that there are many companies and individuals happy to take advantage of a hot market for wind power and provide homeowners with what they want, rather than what will work. So buyer beware!

Fortunately, the challenges of rooftop wind have the inventor community hard at work. Two wind turbines have recently won awards for their innovation in addressing the issues of efficiency, noise and aesthetics.

Earlier this year, a Michigan-based company called WindTronics won a Gold Edison Award for its small rooftop Honeywell Wind Turbine. Designed by Imad Mahawili, a chemical engineer and long-time wind energy consultant, its gearless design eliminates mechanical resistance and drag, allowing it to generate power in wind speeds as low as an unprecedented two miles per hour and as high as forty-five miles per hour, without the typical noise, size, weight and vibrations associated with traditional wind turbines. Weighing 170 pounds and measuring 6 feet in diameter, the turbine can be mounted in several ways, including on a rooftop, a pole or a commercial mount …

A UK company has taken a different approach to rooftop wind with its RidgeBlade system, which won the Dutch Postcode's Green Challenge in 2009, providing its developers, The Power Collective, with funds to help bring the design to market. Designed by a former Rolls Royce turbine engineer, this elegantly simple micro-generation system employs discreetly housed cylindrical turbines positioned horizontally along the apex of a sloping roof. The slope of the roof naturally channels wind into the turbine chamber, meaning RidgeBlade can produce electricity under low or variable wind conditions. The company claims that this high efficiency means that the system could pay for itself within a few years.

The lure is strong to reduce electricity bills, reduce greenhouse gases and become more individually energy independent. And solar or wind can help in that regard. However, if your roof isn't suitable, remember that conservation can go a long way toward meeting those goals. (1660 words)

Priesnitz, W. (2010, September/October). Rooftop power. *Natural Life, 135*, 28–32.

Working toward Variety in Comparing and Contrasting

The English language seems designed to compare and contrast items; there are so many ways to express similarities and differences. These can be usefully categorized by grammatical function because if you are familiar with the grammar associated with the vocabulary, you will not only convey your meaning (comparing or contrasting), but also express your ideas in correct form (grammar). Given the wealth of compare and contrast expressions, you can select the one that best suits your needs and assures accurate use.

To express similarity or to make a comparison:

GRAMMATICAL OR LEXICAL CATEGORY	WORDS/PHRASES	EXAMPLES
COORDINATE CONJUNCTION	and	Both solar **and** wind power are renewable sources of energy.
SUBORDINATE CONJUNCTIONS	as just as	Solar power is a renewable source of energy **as** is wind power. Solar power is a renewable source of energy **just as** wind power is.
ADVERBIAL CONJUNCTIONS	likewise similarly	Solar power is a renewable source of energy; **likewise**, wind power is a never-ending source of energy.
EXPRESSIONS	is similar to is comparable to resembles	Solar power **is similar to** wind power because they are both sources of renewable energy.
	like	**Like** solar power, wind energy is renewable.
	as … as	Solar power is **as** renewable a source of energy **as** wind power.
	equally	Solar and wind power are **equally** renewable.

To express dissimilarity or to show a contrast:

GRAMMATICAL OR LEXICAL CATEGORY	WORDS/PHRASES	EXAMPLES
COORDINATE CONJUNCTIONS	but yet	It is relatively easy to install solar panels on a home rooftop, **but** it is harder to install a wind turbine.
SUBORDINATE CONJUNCTIONS	although even if though whereas while	**Although** it is relatively easy to install solar panels on a home rooftop, it is harder to install a wind turbine.
ADVERBIAL CONJUNCTIONS	however in contrast nevertheless	It is relatively easy to install solar panels on a home rooftop; **however**, it is harder to install a wind turbine.
EXPRESSIONS	it is ... than it is	**It is** easier to install solar panels on a home rooftop **than it is** to install a wind turbine.
	unlike in contrast to	**Unlike** solar panels, wind turbines are difficult to install on a home rooftop.
	on the other hand	Solar panels are easy to install on a home rooftop. **On the other hand**, it is more difficult to install a wind turbine.
	differs from is different from	Solar power **differs from** wind power because it is easier to install solar panels than a wind turbine.

Work with the information from the table you completed in the Focus on Reading (pages 60–61) and, on a separate sheet of paper, write at least five compare and contrast sentences. Use a variety of conjunctions and expressions to make your written work interesting. When you have finished, check your sentences with a classmate and write your best sentence(s) on the board. You will be able to use these sentences in your Warm-Up Assignment.

WARM-UP ASSIGNMENT

Write a Short Compare and Contrast Essay

Write a short compare and contrast essay about the similarities and differences between solar and wind power. Again, from the Focus on Reading table, select the characteristics of solar and wind power that will give you the most to write about. (You do not need to compare and contrast every characteristic.) Use a variety of conjunctions and expressions to show similarities and differences. Use the citation style that you would use in your discipline, where required, to cite information from Reading 1 or Reading 2.

!

When you receive feedback from your instructor or your classmates on this Warm-Up Assignment, you will have some information that you can use to improve your writing on the Final Assignment.

Refer to the Models Chapter (page 198) to see an example of a compare and contrast essay and to learn more about how to write one.

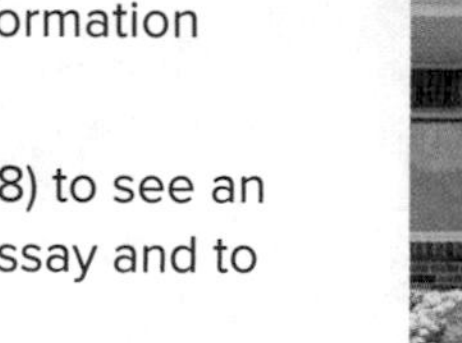

Academic
Survival Skill

Building Discipline-Specific Vocabulary Knowledge

As a language learner, you certainly know the importance of developing a strong vocabulary base. But did you know that the more vocabulary you know, the easier it is to learn new words? When you learn new words, chances are you remember them because they remind you of another word, sound or rhythm that you already know. So the more words you know, the easier it will be to learn new ones.

Although it can be hard to know where to start, there are a few good ways to build your vocabulary to leverage new vocabulary acquisition.

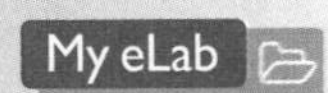

Visit My eLab Documents to find the AWL, with references to vocabulary used in LEAP.

To learn words that will be useful across a wide variety of disciplines, study the Academic Word List (AWL). AWL words are indicated with an asterisk (*) in this book and a complete list can be found on the Companion Website.

There are similar lists for specific disciplines, and researchers are working toward new lists every day. If you are studying in any of the following fields, you could learn the words on these lists to increase your discipline-specific vocabulary.

- Engineering Word List (Ward, 2009)
- Medical Academic Word List (Wang, Laing, & Ge, 2008)
- Newspaper Word List (useful if you like to read or listen to the news) (Chung, 2007)
- Science Word List (Coxhead & Hirsh, 2007)

You may be interested to know that research shows that English-language students who keep their own vocabulary lists and notebooks learn more vocabulary and are better at using new vocabulary in their writing than students who don't (Walters & Bozkurt, 2009).

Begin your own discipline-specific vocabulary notebook. If your discipline already has an established vocabulary list (as listed above), search in your library database (using the reference information below) until you find it. Each time you study the list, review twenty to thirty words, checking the words you know already, writing and learning definitions for words you don't. Review the words every two days for a week, then every week and finally, once a month.

If there is currently no vocabulary list for your discipline, start your own list by reading a textbook in your field and looking for discipline-specific words that occur frequently. Follow the same procedure as above for learning the new words. Learning twenty to thirty words a session is about right.

Bring your early lists to class to compare with those of classmates in the same discipline as you. You can double your vocabulary acquisition by learning each other's words.

References

Chung, T. (2009). The newspaper word list: A specialized vocabulary for reading newspapers. *JALT Journal, 31*(2), 159–182.

Coxhead, A., & Hirsh, D. (2007). A pilot science word list for EAP. *Revue Française de Linguistique Appliquée, XII*(2), 65–78.

Walters, J., & Bozkurt, N. (2009). The effect of keeping vocabulary notebooks on vocabulary acquisition. *Language Teaching Research, 13*, 403–423. doi:10.1177/13621168809341509

Wang, J., Liang, S., & Ge, G. (2008). Establishment of a medical academic word list. *English for Specific Purposes, 27*, 442–458. doi:10.1016/j.esp.2008.05.003

Ward, J. (2009). A basic engineering English word list for less proficient foundation engineering undergraduates. *English for Specific Purposes, 28*, 170–182. doi:10.1016/j.esp.2009.04.001

VOCABULARY BUILD

A. Match each of the energy-related words and phrases to its definition. Use the diagrams in Reading 3 to help you.

WORD/PHRASE	DEFINITION
1 compressed (adj.)	9 substance in which power can be held
2 dissolve (v.)	____ shallow lake of sea water
3 electrode (n.)	____ long, thin piece of metal that turns to generate power
4 ion (n.)	____ place where liquid is stored in a system
5 lagoon (n.)	____ under pressure
6 layer* (n.)	____ mix a solid with a liquid
7 reservoir (n.)	____ positively or negatively charged atom
8 shaft (n.)	____ small metal part to send electricity through a system
9 storage medium* (n.)	____ substance that covers a surface or that is in between two other things

*Appears on the Academic Word List

B. Complete the following sentences with synonyms for the words or phrases in parentheses. The first one has been done for you.

~~alternative~~	facilities*	permeability	recovered*	utilities
confronting	landfill	radical	remote	

*Appears on the Academic Word List

1. If the landscape is flat, the (different option) *alternative* to pumped hydro energy storage is a shallow sea-water lagoon.
2. To change how we store energy, a (new and large) ____________ redesign of batteries is required.
3. Multiple large-scale pumped hydro (rooms, equipment and services) ____________ can store about 2 percent of US power generation.
4. Many (companies that produce power) ____________ are located far from the cities where most electricity is consumed; therefore, significant infrastructure must be built to transmit the power to places where it is needed.
5. A wall can be built from (buried solid waste) ____________ to separate the lagoon from the sea.
6. Every power generation method results in some energy waste. In a recent study, the most efficient methods of electrical generation (got back what was lost) ____________ more than 80 percent of the energy.

7 The challenge (facing) ______________________ developers of any renewable energy source is to make it affordable.

8 Batteries are used to store energy in (distant) ______________________ regions of the world because batteries are easily portable.

9 Limestone is better than sandstone for air storage in a compressed hydro facility as limestone has reduced (ability for water or gas to flow through) ______________________.

Visit My eLab to complete a vocabulary review exercise for this chapter.

READING 3

Gather the Wind

Reading 3 presents three different ways of storing the excess energy that can be generated from solar and wind power. To summarize the information in a format that will prepare you to compare and contrast the storage methods, follow these steps.

A. On a separate sheet of paper, create a four-column table like the one in the Focus on Reading (pages 60–61). Label the four columns: CHARACTERISTICS FOR COMPARISON OR CONTRAST, PUMPED HYDRO ENERGY STORAGE, COMPRESSED AIR ENERGY STORAGE and ADVANCE BATTERY ENERGY STORAGE.

B. Read the text and, with a partner, decide which characteristics you will compare and contrast. Write these in the first column, creating one row for each. Leave enough room within each row to note the information from the reading. Write the citation information for Reading 3 at the top of the table.

C. Working individually, read the text for detail, transferring the information into the table in the appropriate row. Include enough detail to support your writing efforts for the Final Assignment.

D. When you have finished, compare your information with your partner.

If renewable energy is going to take off, we need good ways of storing it for the times when the sun isn't shining and the wind isn't blowing.

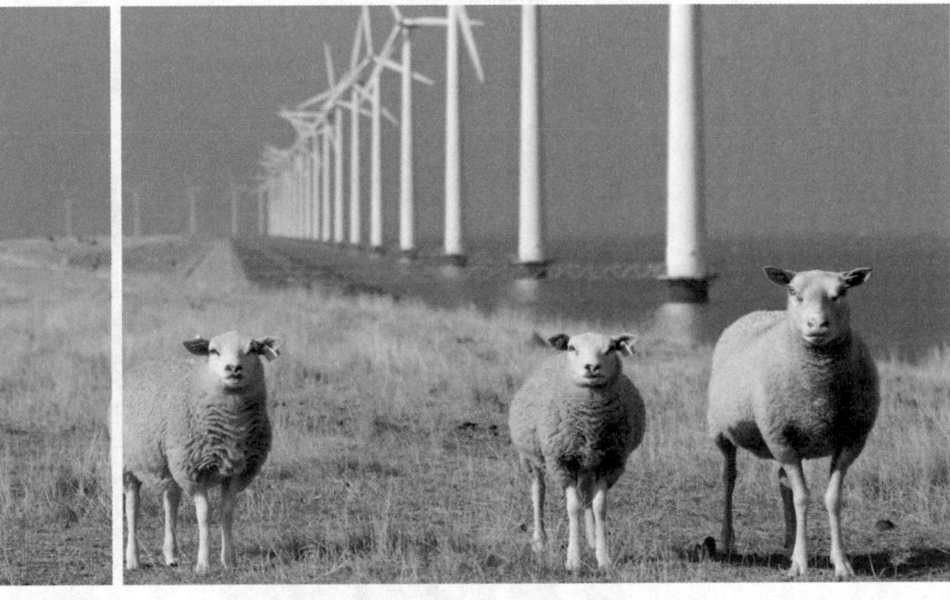

To see the big obstacle confronting renewable energy, look at Denmark. The small nation has some of the world's largest wind farms. Yet because consumer demand for electricity is often lowest when the winds blow hardest, Denmark has to sell its overflow of electrons to neighbouring countries for pennies—only to buy energy back when demand rises, at much higher prices. As a result, Danish consumers pay some of the highest electricity rates on the planet.

Utilities in Texas and California face a similar mismatch between supply and demand; they sometimes have to pay customers to take energy from their windmills and solar farms. On paper, wind and sun could supply the US and some other countries with all the electricity they require. In practice, however, both sources are too erratic to supply more than about 20 percent of a region's total energy capacity, according to the US Department of Energy (DOE). Beyond that point, balancing supply and demand becomes too difficult. What are needed are cheap and efficient ways of storing power, to be tapped later, that is generated when winds are howling and the sun is beating down.

Certain technologies such as superconducting magnets, super capacitors and advanced flywheels are too expensive for that purpose or cannot efficiently hold power for extended periods. But *Scientific American* has examined three technologies that might do the trick. Each of them could possibly store, for days, the amounts of energy needed to keep an entire metropolis humming …

… Each of the … contenders will require some kind of breakthrough, but the payoff could be huge. "Ten years from now, I expect that we will see a lot of energy storage on the grid," says Imre Gyuk, a physicist who manages the DOE's storage program.

Pumped Hydro

Several countries already store considerable power—about 20 gigawatts in the US—using pumped hydro. This century-old technique is essentially a hydroelectric dam that can operate in reverse. Excess electricity is used to pump water from a low reservoir to one higher uphill. When the water falls back down to the lower reservoir, it passes through turbine blades that turn a generator to create electricity. Round-trip efficiency—the energy that can be recovered, minus losses—can be as high as 80 percent.

In the US, thirty-eight pumped-hydro facilities can store the equivalent of just over 2 percent of the country's electrical generating capacity. That share is small compared with Europe's (nearly 5 percent) and Japan's (about 10 percent). But the industry has plans to build reservoirs close to existing power plants. "All you need is an elevation difference and some water," says Rick Miller, a senior vice president at HDR in Omaha. Enough projects are being considered to double existing capacity, he says.

Among the most ambitious plans is the Eagle Mountain Pumped Storage Project in southern California. It would carve two reservoirs out of an abandoned iron surface mine to store energy from regional wind and solar farms, and it could return 1.3 gigawatts of power—as much as a large nuclear power station. In Montana, Grasslands Renewable Energy's proposed hydro storage project would hold wind energy from the Great Plains in an artificial lake that would be built on top of a butte, with a drop of 400 metres.

Pumped hydro's growth is limited primarily by topography. Large, elevated basins must be flooded, which can damage the ecosystem. Some places, such as Denmark and the Netherlands, are just too flat. For those regions, Dutch energy consulting company Kema has come up with a radical "energy island" alternative: an artificial lagoon—in a shallow sea—with a circular wall that would be built from landfill. Excess electricity would pump seawater out of the lagoon and into the surrounding ocean. When energy is needed, water from the sea would flow back inside through tunnels in the wall, passing through turbines. The ocean acts as the "upper" reservoir ...

Compressed Air

Deep under the ground in rural Alabama, a cavern half as large as the Empire State Building holds what could be the quickest fix for the world's energy storage needs: air. Up on the surface, powerful electric pumps inject air at high pressure into the cavern when electricity supply exceeds demand. When the grid is running short, some of that compressed air is let out, blasting through turbines and spinning them. The facility, in McIntosh, Alabama, run by the PowerSouth Energy Cooperative, can provide a respectable 110 megawatts for up to twenty-six hours. It is the only

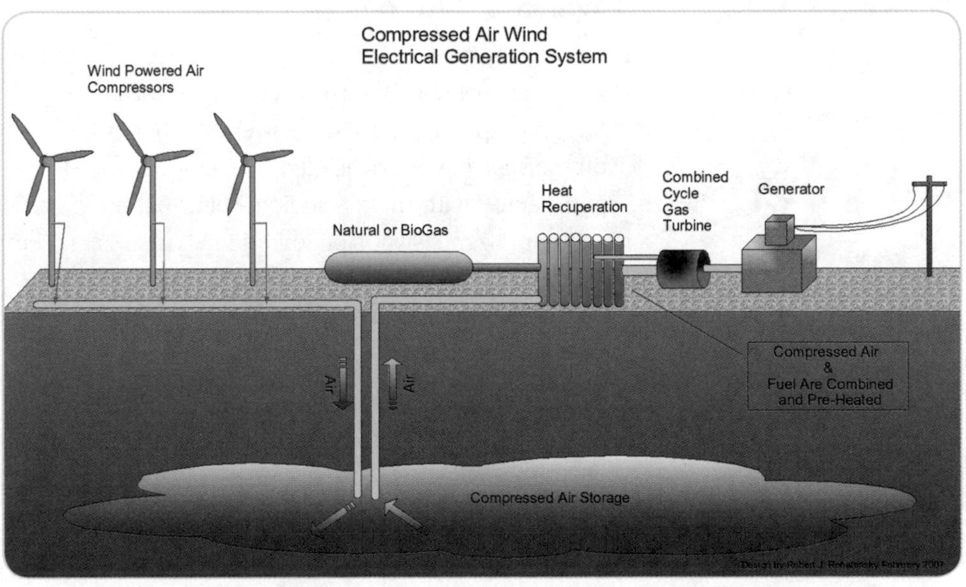

Source: Robert J. Rohatensky, February 2007, published under the Design Science License.

compressed-air operation in the US, but it has operated successfully for twenty years. German company E.ON Kraftwerke, based in Hannover, operates a similar plant in Huntorf in the state of Lower Saxony.

PowerSouth created the cavern by slowly dissolving a salt deposit with water, the same process that formed the US Strategic Petroleum Reserve caverns. Salt deposits are plentiful throughout the southern US, and most states have geologic formations of one kind or another, including natural caverns and depleted gas fields, that could hold compressed air.

Proposals for compressed-air projects have popped up in several states, including New York and California. Yet recently, a proposed $400-million Iowa Stored Energy Park near Des Moines was scrapped because detailed study showed that the permeability of the sandstone that would hold the air was unacceptable.

One practical hurdle is that air heats up when it is compressed and gets cold when it is allowed to expand. That means some of the energy that goes into compression is lost as waste heat. And if the air is simply let out, it can get so cold that it freezes everything it touches—including industrial-strength turbines. PowerSouth and E.ON therefore burn natural gas to create a hot gas stream that warms the cold air as it expands into the turbines, reducing overall energy efficiency and releasing carbon dioxide, which undermines some of the benefits of wind and solar power.

Because these complications limit the efficiency of compressed-air storage, engineers are devising countermeasures. One option is to insulate the cavern so that the air stays warm. The heat could also be transferred to a solid or liquid reservoir that could later reheat the expanding air.

SustainX, a start-up based in Seabrook, New Hampshire, sprays water droplets into the air during compression, which heat up and collect in a pool. The water is later sprayed back into expanding air, warming it. SustainX has demonstrated its process in above-ground tanks. General Compression in Newton, Massachusetts, is developing a similar approach for underground storage and is planning a large demonstration plant in Texas. "We don't need to burn gas, ever," says President David Marcus.

Advanced Batteries

Batteries may be the ideal storage medium for intermittent power sources, some experts say. They charge readily, turn on and off instantly and can be scaled up easily. For decades, utilities have provided backup power to remote recesses of the grid by stacking up racks of off-the-shelf batteries, including the lead-acid type found in cars. Some companies have experimented with molten sodium-sulfur batteries. Power company, AES, has installed more than 30 megawatts of lithium-ion batteries in Elkins, West Virginia, to back up its 98 megawatts of wind turbines. Yet if batteries are to compete for large-scale storage, their cost must drop considerably.

A battery's expense is driven by materials—the positive and negative electrodes and the electrolyte that separates them—as well as the process of manufacturing them into a compact package. Radical redesigns may have a better shot at sharply cutting costs than incremental improvements to common battery types.

Donald R. Sadoway, a chemist at the Massachusetts Institute of Technology, is developing one unusual design that he calls a liquid-metal battery. Its promise lies in its simplicity: a cylindrical vat kept at high temperature is filled with two molten metals, separated by a molten salt between them. The liquid metals are immiscible with the salt—"like oil and vinegar," Sadoway says—and have different densities, so they naturally stack on top of each other. When the two metals are connected via an external circuit, an electric current flows. Ions of each metal dissolve into the molten salt, thickening that layer. To recharge the battery, excess current from the grid runs the process in reverse, forcing the dissolved ions back into their respective layers ...

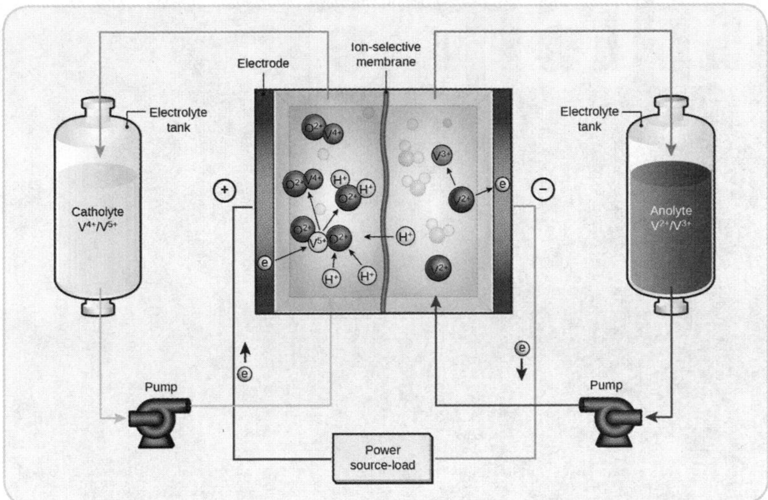

Source: Waterloo Global Science Initiative

A more tried-and-true design is the flow battery. A solid-state membrane inside a container separates two liquid electrodes, which can store a lot of energy ... The flow battery has several advantages. It operates at room temperature, unlike the liquid-metal battery, which must be heated. To scale up, just make larger electrodes or add more containers ...

Other companies are trying to improve on the idea by making the ion flow across the membrane more efficient. Mike Perry, a chemical engineer at United Technologies Corporation (UTC) in Hartford, Connecticut, says his company is investing millions of dollars and betting that within five years or so, flow batteries can become competitive with gas-fired plants used to satisfy peak utility demand. (1527 words)

Castelvecchi, D. (2012, March). Gather the wind. *Scientific American*, *306*(3), 48–53.

FINAL ASSIGNMENT

Write an Extended Compare and Contrast Essay

Write an extended compare and contrast essay to present the similarities and differences between solar and wind power and between the methods of storing excess power, presented in Reading 3.

- Use the body of the short compare and contrast essay that you wrote in the Warm-Up Assignment as the basis of this extended essay.
- Revise your introduction and thesis statement, as well as your conclusion, to indicate that this essay includes more information than did your shorter essay.
- Use information from the two tables you completed earlier, and remember to cite sources where required.

Refer to the Models Chapter (page 198) to see an example of a compare and contrast essay and to learn more about how to write one.

CHAPTER 4

Sustainable Buildings

In 1987, the United Nations received the *Report of the World Commission on the Environment and Development: Our Common Future*, written by Gro Brundtland. In this now famous report, Brundtland defined sustainability as "the ability to meet the needs of the present without compromising the ability of future generations to meet their own needs." This definition is now being applied to the building industry, which, in the past, destroyed vast tracts of land, used large amounts of materials and consumed huge quantities of energy. With a growing awareness that these building practices cannot be sustained, present-day architects, engineers and designers are using exciting new technology to create sustainable (or *green*) buildings, ones that have a net positive impact on the environment.

In this chapter, you will

- learn vocabulary related to sustainable building practices;
- recognize how direct quotations and indirect speech are integrated into texts;
- identify writer perspective in a text;
- observe common text features to achieve greater understanding of your additional language;
- write a short report on a sustainable building, integrating quotations from experts;
- write an extended report about the forces that are creating a demand for sustainable buildings.

GEARING UP

A. With your class, discuss the sustainability of the building you are in. Is the building sustainable or not? Which features of the building have a positive impact on the environment? Which features have a negative impact? To help you with this task, consider the following.

- How do you get to this building? Is the building near bus and bike routes or accessible by foot?
- Is there a parking lot that may have destroyed natural habitat?
- Is energy used to heat or cool the building?
- Is there water in the building? If so, where does it come from and where does the wastewater go?
- Can you open the windows?
- What is the orientation of the building? Do the windows in the room you are in face toward or away from the sun?
- What is the building made of? Are the building materials local? How much energy might it have taken to get the materials on-site?

B. After the class discussion, rate the building you are in on a scale from 1 (not sustainable) to 5 (very sustainable) and then explain why you gave the score you did.

____

____

____

____

____

VOCABULARY BUILD

A. For each word, read the definition (or quiz yourself on the definition if you think you know it already). Then, locate the word in Reading 1 by matching the line number, and identify the words that collocate with the key word. List the collocation(s) in the last column.

WORD	DEFINITION	COLLOCATIONS
administrative* (adj.) LINE 123	related to management of a company	*administrative staff*
altered* (adj.) LINE 43	changed	
commission* (n.) LINE 64	group of people who have been given the official job of finding out about something	
ethical* (adj.) LINE 146	related to the principles of right and wrong	
extraction* (n.) LINE 20	process of removal	
frameworks* (n.) LINES 57, 99	sets of ideas upon which decisions are based	
fundamentally* (adv.) LINE 78	in a way that is basic and important	
impending (adj.) LINE 81	anticipated in the future (unpleasant events)	
projections (n.) LINE 74	statements about what will happen in the future	

*Appears on the Academic Word List

B. Read the definition for each of the following words. Then, locate each word in either Reading 1 or Reading 2 by matching the line number. Write the meaning of each word in this context in the last column. Discuss with your class how the meanings of the words can change depending on their contexts.

WORD	DEFINITION	MEANING IN CONTEXT
dashboard (n.) READING 1: LINE 6	part of a car facing the driver and containing the controls	
sandboxes (n.) READING 1: LINE 96	boxes filled with sand for children to play in	
trump (v.) READING 2: LINE 20	do better than someone else in a competitive situation	

READING 1

Dr. Sustainability: Environmental Scientist of the Year

Use the approach to reading comprehension that you learned in Chapter 1 and practised in Chapters 2 and 3 to help you understand this text.

A. Skim Reading 1 to find the answers to questions 1 through 5. When you have finished, confirm your answers with the class.

1 a) What is the topic of the reading? ______________________

b) How long is it? ______________________

c) Which type of text is it? ______________________

2. What do you already know about the topic? Your discussion from Gearing Up may help you answer this question.

____

____

____

3. Based on the text type, how will the content most likely be organized?

____

____

4. This reading can be divided into seven sections. A heading for each section has been given below. Skim the reading and write the start and end line numbers for each section.

SECTION 1: Introduction to CIRS	LINES *4 to 24*
SECTION 2: Introduction to John Robinson	LINES ______
SECTION 3: John Robinson's Background	LINES ______
SECTION 4: Harm Reduction vs. Regenerative Sustainability	LINES ______
SECTION 5: The Role of Universities in Promoting Sustainability	LINES ______
SECTION 6: The Impact of CIRS	LINES ______
SECTION 7: The Future of Sustainability	LINES ______

5. Turn each heading into a question and write your questions on a separate sheet of paper.

B. Read the text more closely and answer the questions you have generated from the reading headings.

It's a bold claim, but Vancouver might just be home to the greenest building in the world. Meet the geography professor who brought it to life—Canadian Geographic's *environmental scientist of the year.*

The first thing you'll notice upon entering the University of British Columbia's brand-new Centre for Interactive Research on Sustainability on the school's Point Grey campus is that the building has a dashboard. You will also notice the building is referred to as "the greenest building in the world." Almost every interior space, for instance, is bathed in natural light. The corridors seem to breathe with unconditioned air, pleasantly scented with the pine that is the structure's most obvious material. It also has a lecture hall covered by a mounded green roof, which forms a hill of grass and shrubs between the two main wings of the building. But that dashboard—a wall-mounted flat-screen display showing the state of various building functions—just might capture and hold your attention the longest because of the crowd gathered around it.

That's all in a normal day at the Centre for Interactive Research on Sustainability (CIRS), which has been a magnet for attention since it opened late last year. At any given hour, even when one of the ongoing tours is not in progress, you'll find people standing in the lobby discussing the data on that dashboard, which shows, among other things, how much water has been recycled that day, the kilojoules count of harvested solar energy and the rate of thermal-heat extraction from the soil on which the building sits.

CIRS is more than a workspace for living things, as the dashboard and the animated conversation attest. It's a living thing itself. People engage with it as if it were of an order higher than architecture.

If that's your reaction, then John Robinson will be pleased. The man who almost single-handedly brought this building to life is committed not only to making structures green in the ecological sense ... but also to making them more humanly engaging. "CIRS is designed to be net positive in seven ways," says Robinson. "Ecologically net positive in energy, operational carbon, water and structural carbon. And also net positive for three human factors: health, productivity and happiness."

Robinson is executive director of the UBC sustainability initiative, an ambitious academic and operational approach to sustainability, and CIRS is its public face ... The $37 million, four-storey, 5,400-square-metre "living laboratory" offers a multidisciplinary space on campus for sustainability education and research and a physical structure in which sustainability ideas can be deployed and evaluated at scale ...

In addition to being an emblem of UBC's sustainability efforts, the building can also be looked at as a culminating statement about Robinson's influential career to date. Embedded in those pine timbers, and in details such as the skylight-mounted solar cells that double as energy collectors and providers of dappled shade, is a carefully built world view on sustainability that owes a lot to the route Robinson has taken through his professional life.

Originally interested in law (his father was a judge), Robinson found his vision of the future irrevocably altered when Monte Hummel—then head of Pollution Probe, later President of World Wildlife Fund Canada—came to speak to his grade-thirteen classroom in Port Hope, Ontario. "It was the first time I heard the word 'environment' used as a field or an issue," says Robinson ...

Robinson remembers the defining moment of Hummel's address to the students. "He showed us these cards. They ranged in colour from very light grey to very dark. He said, 'When you see smoke coming from an industrial smokestack, hold up these cards. If the smoke is darker than number three, phone the air management branch and report a violation.' " Robinson chuckles. "Such was the state of citizen science in 1970." Still, he was hooked.

Robinson went on to work on the committee opposing the Mackenzie Valley pipeline, which led to an interest in energy issues, which led to a geography degree from the University of Toronto, a master's in geography from Toronto's York University and a Ph.D. in the same field (thesis subtitle: An Investigation of Energy Policy and Conceptual Frameworks) from the University of Toronto in 1981. A professor in the University of Waterloo's Department of Environment and Resource Studies before moving on to UBC's Geography Department twenty years ago, Robinson has won several prestigious awards, including a share of the Nobel Peace Prize in 2007 for being a lead author in the last three assessments of the Intergovernmental Panel on Climate Change and a major award from BC Hydro in 2010 for advancing energy conservation in the province …

… [In 1987, the Brundtland Commission … helped create the understanding of "harm reduction" in relation to the environment.] "It's basically the concept of limits," he [Robinson] says. "It leads to strategies of harm reduction and mitigation. Reducing the bad things. That becomes the largest frame." And for two reasons, he passionately argues, this doesn't work. First, it's not enough. You can reduce emissions to zero, you can participate in Buy Nothing Day and other acts of personal constraint, but this won't address the social aspects of sustainability, such as poverty. "You can't ignore development," says Robinson, "because the two greatest causes of environmental damage are great wealth and great poverty."

Perhaps more important, he argues that approaches to sustainability based on limits and harm reduction—warnings and dire projections calling for constraint—simply don't create behavioural change. "The literature on motivation is very clear," says Robinson. "The information-deficit model doesn't work. The idea that we change our behaviour because we change our attitudes, because we change our values, because we get new information is just fundamentally wrong." Research has borne this out in multiple fields, which Robinson counts off on his fingers: health promotion, social psychology, energy efficiency, applied cultural anthropology, community-based social marketing …

If telling people about an impending climate-change disaster won't alter behaviour, then what will? Here is where the most recent evolution in Robinson's thinking, and the CIRS building of which it is an emblem, take shape. What we need, insists Robinson, is a program of "regenerative sustainability." We need to start living in a way that eliminates the damage we cause going forward—across ecological, social and economic lines—and also begins to improve the physical and social environments around us. Not only does this approach necessarily go further than mitigation, it more reliably attracts participation.

"It's exciting, and it's way more motivating. I've given talks on this a couple of dozen times. I've never had a point that resonates more, that people get more interested in, because it's positive. Can we have regenerative buildings?" Robinson eyes are alight with curiosity and enthusiasm. "How about transportation systems, cities, industrial processes? Could we be regenerative in steelmaking? I don't think we know, because we haven't examined those questions. And I think it's the job of universities and academics to really engage these questions."

Universities are the perfect "sandboxes," as Robinson puts it, for this kind of experiment and exploration. They are organically suited to the role. They're scaled to the size of neighbourhoods. They're owner-occupied. They're mandated to teach and do research. Bring on the policy-makers, he says, to consider the regulatory frameworks required. Bring on the private companies with ideas they'd like to test with a view to future commercialization. Bring on the public to tour the projects being tested and to get excited. And, perhaps most innovative of all, bring on the students, who within a couple of years should be able to get undergraduate minors in sustainability while working toward degrees in virtually every department at UBC, from engineering and computer sciences to dance and English.

There should be no specifically "green" jobs in Robinson's regenerative approach. Sustainability should be part of everybody's job. "We're training sustainability ambassadors," affirms Alberto Cayuela, associate director of the UBC sustainability initiative, as he tours a group of engineering students through the constructed wetland water-filtration system at the front of CIRS.

On clear days in Vancouver, the glass flanks of CIRS rise sparkling in the sun; on the city's frequent rainy days, its inner works rustle pleasantly with harvested water. One hundred percent of the building's water demand is satisfied by rain. Five hundred tonnes of carbon are sequestered in its building materials, more than were expended in its construction. Two hundred and seventy-five megawatt hours per year of surplus energy are produced from scavenged sources, including the energy harvested from a heat-leaky building next door. And as for the human factors, Cayuela says that the UBC Psychology Department currently has six different experiments under way to test the building's ability to change attitudes.

"Does being here make a person more likely to recycle?" he asks. "Do you learn better with skylights and displacement ventilation in the lecture hall?" The questions are open. And as if to immediately punctuate the confidence Cayuela projects, we are approached just then by one of his administrative staff, who apologizes for interjecting but feels she just has to share her own experience. A long-time sufferer of respiratory problems, she explains that her move across campus from one of the older library buildings six months ago has changed her life, literally. "The air in this building is clear," she says. "I can breathe."

It seems almost imaginary, the idea of buildings as net contributors to the environment in the ecological and human ways that comprise Robinson's "regenerative sustainability." ... "We don't want this world!" Robinson says, gesturing widely. "We want a different world that doesn't yet exist."

...

Robinson has to go. He has meetings to attend. He has projects under way. CIRS is a pinnacle accomplishment, but one suspects he has much more to come. Converting all of UBC to the regenerative model is a real objective for him. But then so, too, is "proselytizing" to other universities around the world, which should all, in Robinson's view, be embracing the same challenge.

In parting, he provides a working definition of sustainability that captures a long journey to this moment, to CIRS, to the strange combination of its practical and symbolic functions, to all that it represents. "Sustainability," says Robinson, "is the emergent property of a conversation about the kind of world we want to live in that's informed by some understanding of the ecological, social and economic consequences of different choices. It's not a scientific concept we can just give people. It's a normative, ethical judgment that people need to make."

He pauses. In other words, people have choices in this matter. They can embrace a regenerative vision of the future ...

Then he finishes: "But I'm very optimistic about our ability to make radical changes. That's why we built CIRS, to show people that it's possible. People have no idea it's even possible!"

Which is exactly what's going on among the people watching the CIRS dashboard: looking up with fascinated engagement at evidence of the building's inner workings. They're seeing what's possible. (1841 words)

Taylor, T. (2012, June 1). Dr. Sustainability: Environmental scientist of the year. *Canadian Geographic, 132*(3), 60–64. Retrieved from http://www.canadiangeographic.ca/

Watch the inspirational online video about this building. In your Internet browser, search "Centre for Interactive Research on Sustainability" at UBC.

C. What did you learn that was new, interesting or important? What do you want to learn more about?

____

____

____

____

____

____

____

China's Green Building Future

Reading 2 argues that sustainable building is a global concern. Like Reading 1, it is a magazine article.

A. After you have read the text, demonstrate your understanding of it by indicating whether each of the following statements is true or false.

STATEMENTS	TRUE	FALSE
1 According to Bisagni, the owners of the Naked Stables Private Reserve (a luxury hotel) used a green building approach because they felt a sense of moral responsibility to reduce environmental damage.	☑	☐
2 One of the biggest challenges to adopting a green building approach in the construction of new buildings is the belief that green buildings are more expensive to build.	☑	☐
3 Green buildings are cheaper to build and operate in the short term.	☐	☑
4 Green buildings save money in the long term through reduced energy usage.	☑	☐
5 Owners of green buildings must charge lower rents because people don't want to live in green buildings.	☐	☑
6 Green building practices are useful, but they don't reduce energy use enough to help China meet its energy reduction goals.	☑	☐
7 The purpose of paragraph 4 (lines 41 to 46) is to provide a definition of green building design.	☑	☐
8 Green building certification systems (like LEED and Three Star) make the public aware of sustainable building standards.	☑	☐

STATEMENTS	TRUE	FALSE
9 Most builders who have to choose between green building practices and lower labour and material costs choose lower costs.	☐	☐
10 An owner who builds a green building will never recover the costs.	☐	☐
11 Because builders don't live in the apartment buildings they build, they often don't see any value in using better insulation and windows.	☐	☐
12 The Chinese (PRC) government's own rating system for energy efficiency is mandatory for all new buildings.	☐	☐
13 While it is possible to rate the energy efficiency of a building, rating communities on the same basis is too complicated.	☐	☐
14 The centralized role the PRC plays in urban planning in China makes it easier to implement green design policies.	☐	☐
15 According to some experts, green building is going to succeed in China, whether the government supports it or not.	☐	☐

Green building makes up a small proportion of China's construction industry, but government targets may give sustainable building a boost over the next five years.

About sixty kilometres outside Hangzhou, the capital of Zhejiang province, is a luxury resort surrounded by the bamboo forest and tea plantations of Moganshan. The owners of Naked Stables Private Reserve—named for its stripped down, natural environment—aimed to make as minimal an impact on the surrounding environment as possible by reducing water and energy use and growing their own food on site. "[The owners] did all these things because they thought it was the right thing to do," says Alessandro Bisagni, founder and managing director of BEE Inc., a sustainable building consulting firm that works on projects in China and the United States.

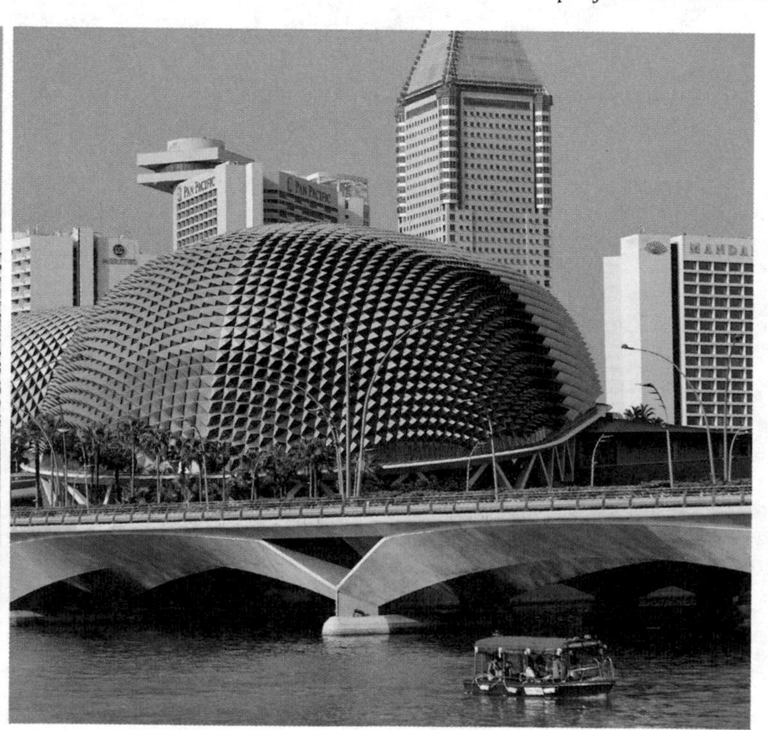

Since the first building in China was awarded a gold rating by the internationally recognized Leadership in Energy and Environmental Design (LEED) rating system in 2005, green building's popularity has grown in China. Green building still makes up a small proportion of building in the world's largest construction market, where maximizing profits and lowering building costs often trump sustainable design and energy efficiency considerations. Multinational companies, large Chinese companies, and an increasing number of hotels and resorts are currently the most likely green builders in China, but increasing environmental awareness and central government policies that set ambitious targets to reduce China's overall energy use may make green building practices more widespread in the coming years.

Green Building on the Rise

In 2011, developers in China started constructing 1.9 billion square metres of floor space and invested ¥6.2 trillion ($983 billion) in property development, according to the People's Republic of China [PRC] National Bureau of Statistics. At the same time, China's Twelfth Five-Year Plan (FYP, 2011–15) aims to reduce overall energy use by 16 percent per unit of gross domestic product (GDP) and reduce carbon dioxide emissions by 17 percent per unit of GDP by 2015. Because buildings account for roughly 25 percent of all energy consumed in China, regulators have focused on implementing green and energy-efficient practices in both new and established buildings. Beijing alone plans to build 35 million square metres of green buildings by 2015, according to the *People's Daily*.

In general, green building incorporates design, construction and operations practices that use sustainable materials in construction, achieve energy efficiency and water savings and improve indoor air quality, among other measurable targets. Green building developers also consider a building or project's location, selecting sites with exposure to sunlight and sites that are close to public transportation, grocery stores and other amenities.

Evaluating all buildings and development projects in China that take these strategies into account is difficult, but developers are increasingly applying for green building labels, such as LEED certification and China's own green building certification, the Green Building Design Label, also known as "Three Star." (The system assigns buildings one to three stars, with three stars being the highest rating.) In 2005, a PRC Ministry of Science and Technology office building in Beijing was awarded a LEED gold rating, the first building in China to receive LEED certification. The Beijing Olympic Village and other facilities for the 2008 Olympics followed, and by the end of 2011, more than 800 construction projects had been registered for certification while nearly 200 had been LEED certified. The Three Star system is newer and has fewer projects, but it has seen similar growth, increasing from ten projects certified in 2008 to eighty-three in 2010.

Challenges

Regardless of the certification system used, the green building concept does not always translate to the China market. According to a 2011 report by the China Greentech Initiative—a collaboration between more than one hundred organizations that focuses on identifying and developing green tech solutions in China—lack of understanding of green building and misaligned incentives have slowed the adoption of green building in China. Experts say construction decisions are often made based on short-term costs, such as material and labour costs, instead of considering the long-term savings from energy efficiency or green building techniques.

Bisagni says working on green building projects in the United States and China is like night and day because Chinese builders still prefer to cut costs in the short term. "The extent of solutions that you can propose in a project [in China] is limited in a way because of that payback and cost mentality," he says. "In China, there's still a large knowledge gap. In order to cross that, it takes a lot of effort."

Green building experts say that it is a myth that sustainable buildings are expensive to build. "A green building can pay for itself," says Yingchu Qian, head of sustainability business in Asia for Faithful + Gould, a construction consulting firm. Qian, who has worked on roughly 120 green building projects in China, says that the savings from energy-efficient practices and the premium developers can charge for green buildings help investors make back any additional money spent on construction. He said it usually takes five to ten years for a developer to make back the initial investment in a green building, but that in some cases it can take as little as two years.

Companies that chose to build green in China early on were not necessarily focused on cost. The early adopters in China have tended to be large, multinational corporations with a "sustainability vision" and those that see green building as a good marketing tool, says Jennivine Kwan, vice president of international operations at the US Green Building Council (USGBC), the organization that developed the LEED rating system. But now, more companies are considering operation costs, return on investment, higher tenant occupancy rates and a premium on rents. "Those things are real tangible financial reasons as to why people are building green buildings from an owner-developer point of view," she says.

Because developers in China may not see immediate cost savings, they often overlook the green features—such as better insulation and sealed windows—that could help the government meet its energy targets. This is especially true in the multi-family residential buildings that most people in urban China live in, say researchers at the US Department of Energy's Lawrence Berkeley National Laboratory (LBNL). "I think it also gets complicated because the tenants that live in the building didn't build it. The builder doesn't operate the building, so they are not motivated to invest in better insulation," says Nan Zhou, a scientist at LBNL's China Energy Group.

LBNL researchers have been working with the PRC government to improve energy efficiency initiatives and labelling standards, including the PRC Ministry of Housing and Urban-Rural Development's building energy efficiency label. This rating system ranks buildings from one to five stars. A building that receives a five-star rating is the most energy efficient—requiring an 85 percent reduction in energy use compared to buildings constructed in the 1980s. (Current building codes require that new buildings achieve a 50 percent reduction in energy use compared to the 1980s.) The energy efficiency label is still voluntary for most residential and non-residential buildings, but the government requires that certain buildings receive a star rating, including new government-owned and large public buildings, existing government-owned office buildings and large public buildings that apply for government energy retrofit subsidies.

Zhou says that because the green building and energy efficiency labels are still voluntary for the majority of buildings, such programs are not likely to reduce energy consumption in China on a large scale. "If there's a mandatory program ... then that can definitely reduce energy use," Zhou says.

Eco-Cities

While the PRC government implements energy labelling programs, provides subsidies for energy efficient technologies and releases policies to support carbon and energy reduction goals, China's push to develop more sustainable communities, or "eco-cities," may also influence green building's future in the country.

According to the Asian Development Bank, the PRC government began encouraging development of sustainable communities as early as the mid-1990s. Dozens of eco-cities are currently being developed, according to some estimates, but arguably the most high profile is the Sino-Singapore Tianjin Eco-City. The project is a collaboration between the governments of Singapore and Tianjin and promotes water and energy conservation, mixed-use development and comprehensive public transport for the city's expected 350,000 residents. The city's first residents began moving into apartments in mid-February, and the entire project is expected to be complete by 2020.

The PRC government's eco-cities initiative may be one reason China has the largest number of LEED certifications for neighbourhood development projects outside the United States, says USGBC's Kwan. These projects help local governments and developers design "communities that are a little more human scale, that are linked better to the outside environment and that provide that type of safe and healthy environment for all the people who live there," says Kwan. Like LEED for buildings, the LEED for neighbourhood development rating system evaluates an entire community. The rating system looks at whether the community has walkable streets and reduces residents' dependence on cars, and whether buildings and infrastructure are energy efficient, use renewable energy sources and reduce water use.

Compared to the United States or other developed countries, mixed-use development is already common in China, where many neighbourhoods feature all the services most people need within walking distance. The government's role in urban planning also makes it easier to create sustainable communities, Kwan says. "China is one of the few places in the world that actually decides where a city is going to happen. They actually build the city."

Green Building's Future in China

An analysis by LBNL researchers shows that China made the largest energy efficiency improvements in new construction and hit targets in energy management in government and large-scale public buildings during the Eleventh FYP (2006–10) period. However, China has not been as successful during the first year of the Twelfth FYP, says LBNL's Zhou, and she expects the PRC government to continue including energy and carbon reduction goals in future five-year plans. "This period will be very challenging because the first year has already ended and they did not meet the first year milestone," she says.

Whether green building will play a large role in meeting these goals remains to be seen, but advocates remain optimistic that the green building market will continue to grow in China. Still, some think the PRC government will have to implement stronger policies before mainstream developers build green projects on a larger scale. "The only way that can happen is from the top down," says Bisagni. "The government has to give direction about what green building has to be." (1768 words)

Nelson, C. (2012, April-June). China's green building future. *China Business Review*, 32–35.

B. What did you learn that was new, interesting or important? What do you want to learn more about?

____

____

____

____

____

____

Using Direct Quotations and Indirect Speech

Both Reading 1 and Reading 2 are magazine articles and both display the characteristics of this text type, including direct quotations and indirect speech. These elements integrate the viewpoints of the speakers (the people quoted) to present information and give authority to the text.

You will notice that there are no references for the quotations in these articles as there would be in a textbook or an academic journal. Magazines compensate for this by providing background information about the people quoted, either before the quotation or right after it.

A. Here are two examples, one from Reading 1 and one from Reading 2. In each example, highlight the background information that has been given about the speaker and then underline his quotation.

> If that's your reaction, then John Robinson will be pleased. The man who almost single-handedly brought this building to life is committed not only to making structures green in the ecological sense ... but also to making them more humanly engaging. "CIRS is designed to be net positive in seven ways," says Robinson. "Ecologically net positive in energy, operational carbon, water and structural carbon. And also net positive for three human factors: health, productivity and happiness."
>
> "[The owners] did all these things because they thought it was the right thing to do," says Alessandro Bisagni, founder and managing director of BEE Inc., a sustainable building consulting firm that works on projects in China and the United States.

B. Skim Readings 1 and 2 and underline the *first direct* quotations from the following speakers. Then, highlight the background information that is provided about them.

FROM READING 1: John Robinson and Alberto Cayuela

FROM READING 2: Alessandro Bisagni, Yingchu Qian, Jennivine Kwan and Nan Zhou

C. Following the models in Readings 1 and 2 and using a separate sheet of paper, combine the information below into a first direct quotation. Present the information in two ways: once with the speaker's background information before the quotation and once after.

QUOTATION: In just a few short years, the topic of sustainable development has moved from the sidelines to centre stage in discussions about climate change, social equity and economic prosperity—issues that will shape the very future of our planet.

SPEAKER: Richard Moe

BACKGROUND INFORMATION ABOUT THE SPEAKER: past president, National Trust for Historic Preservation

D. The following examples from Readings 1 and 2 show the mechanics of integrating quotations in a text. Look at the examples, and then on your separate sheet of paper, answer the questions that follow.

- "The air in this building is clear," she says. "I can breathe."
- "We don't want this world!" Robinson says, gesturing widely. "We want a different world that doesn't yet exist."
- "A green building can pay for itself," says Yingchu Qian, ...
- Then he finishes: "I'm very optimistic about our ability to make radical changes ..."
- "Sustainability," says Robinson, "is the emergent property of a conversation about the kind of world we want to live in ..."
- "We're training sustainability ambassadors," affirms Alberto Cayuela, ...
- Robinson chuckles. "Such was the state of citizen science in 1970."
- "It's exciting, and it's way more motivating. I've given talks on this a couple of dozen times. I've never had a point that resonates more ..."

1. Quotation marks show the start and the end of a quotation but also contain end punctuation. Is this punctuation located *inside* or *outside* the quotation marks?

2. Where is the speech tag (e.g., *she says*) located in the examples?

3. If the speech tag is located in the middle of a quotation, where is it inserted?

4. Although the verb *say* is used most often with a quotation, what other verbs can writers use to integrate quotations into texts?

5. Could a writer integrate a quotation *without* using one of these verbs? If so, when?

6. Once a speaker has been identified with background information and an initial quotation has been introduced, how does a writer introduce a subsequent quotation?

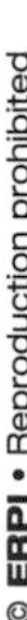

E. Practise the mechanics of quotations by adding punctuation to define the quotations in this paragraph. When you have finished, check your answers for tasks C, D and E with a classmate.

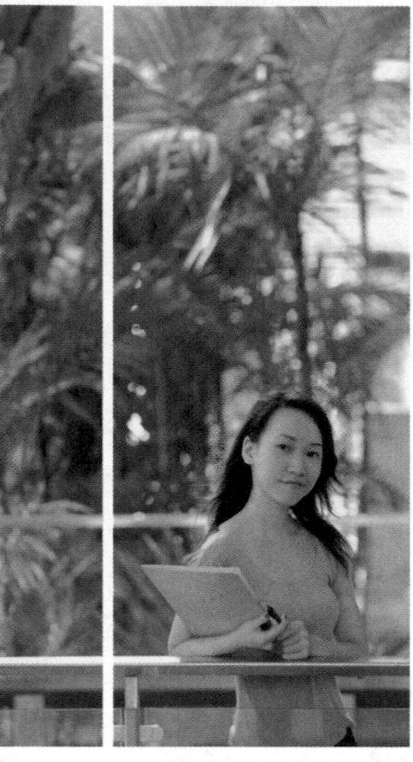

Scott Parker, director of the North American Sustainable Building Innovation Association (NASBIA), states Much more could be done to mitigate climate change in large cities. Green roofs and walls have been largely overlooked as an effective method to moderate internal building temperature and absorb CO_2 emissions. He points to projects in Europe and Japan, and emerging initiatives in Australia and New Zealand. Green roofs and walls he says are not the only solution to climate change challenges, but they can be implemented within the existing cityscape. He believes that green roofs and walls could be used to strategically alter city microclimates, creating spaces that are healthier for humans, plants and animals.

F. An indirect quotation, called *indirect* or *reported speech*, is often used to provide context for a direct quotation. Look at the following example from Reading 2. Underline the direct quotation. Consider the purpose of the first sentence and, on your separate sheet of paper, answer the questions that follow.

Bisagni says working on green building projects in the United States and China is like night and day because Chinese builders still prefer to cut costs in the short term. "The extent of solutions that you can propose in a project [in China] is limited in a way because of that payback and cost mentality," he says. "In China, there's still a large knowledge gap. In order to cross that, it takes a lot of effort."

1. The first sentence of the paragraph is an example of indirect speech. How is it similar to a direct quotation? How is it different?
2. What is the purpose of the indirect speech that comes before the direct quotation?
3. Why would the writer use indirect speech first and not a single, longer direct quotation?
4. Skim Readings 1 and 2 and highlight the indirect speech segments that precede direct quotations. (Use a different colour from the one used for task B.) Underline the direct quotations that follow the indirect speech.
5. For the indirect speech that you have highlighted, which verbs (other than *says*) do the writers use to introduce it?
6. Following the models in Readings 1 and 2, combine the information below into an indirect speech segment followed by a direct quotation.

   INDIRECT SPEECH: Zero net energy buildings operate only with energy generated on-site.

   DIRECT QUOTATION: This approach only addresses operating energy, not the energy required to construct the building.

   SPEAKER: Jean Carron

WARM-UP ASSIGNMENT

Write a Short Report

Write a report for a community group that would like to build a community centre. The members are interested in green design but are worried the costs will be too high.

In your report, you will include an example of a sustainable (green) building that you know about or have heard of (or you can find an example online or in the library). Integrate at least three quotations about the building from experts, possibly from the owners, the architects or the users. To integrate the quotations, introduce sufficient background information about the speaker for his or her initial quotation. For at least one of the speakers, include a second quotation that is preceded by indirect speech.

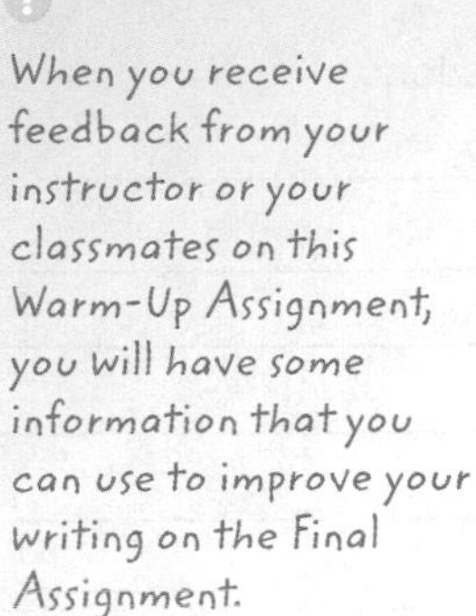
When you receive feedback from your instructor or your classmates on this Warm-Up Assignment, you will have some information that you can use to improve your writing on the Final Assignment.

Your report should contain

- an introduction, with a definition of green building;
- body paragraphs describing an example of a green building, with integrated quotations, and data on how much energy, water and $C0_2$ are saved (if available);
- a conclusion, with your recommendation as to whether or not to use green design.

Refer to the Models Chapter (page 202) to see an example of a report and to learn more about how to write one.

VOCABULARY BUILD

A. Complete each of the following sentences (adapted from Reading 3) with the correct preposition. When you have finished, confirm your answers by checking the line numbers.

1. In Europe, building regulations require that all office workers have direct access* ________ fresh air and daylight. (LINE 81)
2. In North America, the building boom inspired by the end of World War II coincided* ________ the invention of air conditioning, which allowed for consistent interior temperature in all seasons. (LINE 87)
3. While Germany and the UK have been the leaders in green building in the last twenty years, there have been technological contributions* ________ smaller European countries as well. (LINE 56)
4. Green building design must place an emphasis* ________ reducing building costs so green buildings are comparable—in terms of cost—to traditionally constructed buildings. (LINE 163)
5. Regulatory frameworks in the US still require builders to ensure a consistent interior temperature in all seasons, and this is a deterrent ________ the use of more energy-efficient ventilation systems. (LINE 99)

*Appears on the Academic Word List

B. In the following table are key words from Reading 3. Change the word endings to achieve the required word forms.

NOUNS	VERB	ADJECTIVES
adaptation* adaptability		
implementation* implement		
occupation*		

*Appears on the Academic Word List

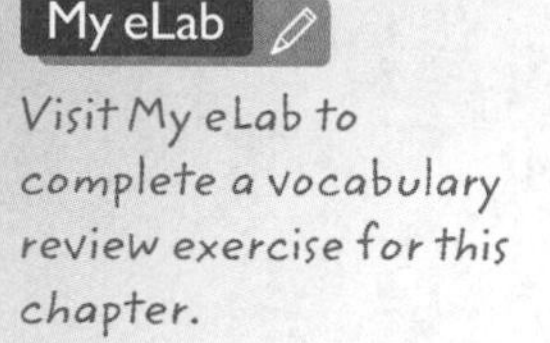
My eLab
Visit My eLab to complete a vocabulary review exercise for this chapter.

READING 3

European Green Buildings in Context

This reading provides insight into green building design in Europe.

A. Skim Reading 3 to find the answers to the following questions.

1. Which type of text is it? __________
2. What are the features of this type of text? __________
3. How many quotations are integrated into the text? __________
4. Are these direct quotations or indirect speech? __________
5. How are the quotations integrated differently in this reading compared to those in Reading 1 and Reading 2?

B. Read the text more closely and answer the questions that follow.

Although North American green building practices and technology have come a long way in the past fifteen years, it's realistic to say that Western European architects, engineers and builders are ahead of us in the widespread use of passive design techniques, integrating solar power into building design and producing low-energy buildings.

As an example of good European design, consider the Doxford Solar Office building, completed in 1998 by David Lloyd Jones and Studio E architects. This is a low-energy office building with the entire south-facing facade composed of building-integrated photovoltaics (BIPVs), generating 73 kilowatts (peak) of power, a design innovation not seen in the United States or Canada. The south facade is a completely integral system built in conjunction with a major German manufacturer. Expected annual net energy use of the 4,600-square-metre (49,500-square-foot) building is 115 kilowatt-hours per square metre (10.6 kilowatt-hours per square foot).

The Doxford Solar Office is located at a business park near Sunderland, in the United Kingdom. It was the first speculatively constructed office building to incorporate BIPVs, and the resulting solar facade was the largest constructed in Europe at that time.

This example of a highly integrated sustainable office building from more than ten years ago, developed for strictly commercial uses, raises some interesting questions. For example, what do Europeans know (and do) that we don't, and why? What are some fundamental differences in the way Europeans and Americans or Canadians approach sustainable design? When comparing the driving forces for sustainability in Europe and the United States, it's also instructive to consider the experiences and perspectives of leading practitioners, some of whom have practised in both places.

John Echlin is an American architect and former design principal of an architecture firm in Portland, Oregon, US, who worked in Switzerland for two firms over a period of seven years.

> What drives buildings in the US are free-market conditions and private development. There's no doubt that in Europe, what drives things are essentially culture and public benefit. In the US, we typically build buildings to last twenty years and don't really think much beyond that. But in Europe, the cultural norm is really to build permanently. Because of that, all building strategies relate to finding the most permanent solution. It tends to drive efficiency in operations and promote design approaches that make multiple uses out of single elements.[1]

Larry Malcic is director of design in London for the large international architecture firm HOK.

> In London, there has been a kind of constant theme of sustainability. Energy-responsible design is partially driven by the much higher energy prices in Europe, but also it's a kind of cultural attitude. Particularly starting with our work in the Netherlands and Germany, there's a real attitude that culturally says we have a custodial responsibility for where we live, for our buildings, our towns and our cities.
>
> On an island like the UK, there's a pretty clear consciousness that there isn't someplace else to move on to. That contrasts significantly with the American approach of "you build it, you use it" and then you move on because there's always someplace to move on to. Here, the landscapes are manmade: the parks are manmade. So there's a recognition that we have to deal carefully with what are, in fact, finite resources. I think that is a fundamental cultural difference.[2]

Does the extensive European use of sustainable building approaches result from specific climactic, cultural, political and economic factors that might not be found in the United States, making comparisons between the two continents difficult and lessons learned harder to extract? Let's take a look at the driving forces of sustainability in Europe.

Driving Forces in Europe

Climate

Many of the innovative European technologies come out of Germany and the United Kingdom, with a significant contribution from smaller countries and regions such as Switzerland, Austria, the Netherlands and Scandinavia. These countries tend to have cold winters and mild summers, with lower humidity than is found in much of the United States. In that respect, architects and engineers are designing mostly for a different climatic situation, one in which heating energy use is far more significant than cooling energy use. For example, European latitudes range from 47° in Zurich, to 50° in London and Frankfurt, to 59° in Oslo and Stockholm[3] … The counter to this notion of colder climates in Europe is the prevalence in North America of the fully sealed, all-glass high-rise office building, which needs air conditioning year-round for comfort in almost any climate.

The climate in the United Kingdom is quite mild, certainly by Central European standards, with no location more than sixty miles [ninety-six kilometres] from the ocean. In that respect, London's climate is quite similar to that of the coastal zone of the western United States, from San Francisco northward, except that those latitudes range from 38° in San Francisco to 48° in Seattle.

Culture

The lack of daylighting in most large-floorplate, open-plan offices in the United States would surprise and dismay most European engineers. Daylighting of all workspaces is pretty much a cultural norm in Europe, as a fundamental sign of respect for workers' mental and physical health. As a result, European office buildings tend to be less efficient from a real estate investment viewpoint (i.e., with a lower ratio of net to gross leasable area, given that all high-rise buildings need about the same amount of core space for elevators, lobbies, fire escapes and restrooms).

For example, German building regulations for worker health and safety (similar to those of the Occupational Safety and Health Administration in the United States) require that a permanent workstation have direct access to fresh air and natural light; therefore, the maximum room depth is limited to about five metres (sixteen feet) from a window, unless higher ceilings are provided (for daylighting), in which case one might be seven or eight metres from a window.[4] This requirement makes European buildings longer and narrower than most typical American office buildings. Part of the reason is that the great building boom in the United States and Canada after World War II coincided with the advent of modern air conditioning, removing previous constraints on the use of glass and the need for operable windows in office buildings.

Europeans don't seem to be as sensitive as Americans to temperature excursions in the workspace. They would find somewhat comical Americans' insistence on wearing the same clothing in the office year-round and expecting the same 72°F to 75°F (22°C to 24°C) temperatures, with little variation. This expectation of year-round constant indoor air temperature is a great hindrance in adopting natural ventilation and using radiant space conditioning systems, which can't deliver the instant response of overhead-ducted, forced-air heating, ventilation and air-conditioning systems. In the United States, we're beginning to see some changes on this front, especially since 2004, when the American Society of Heating, Refrigerating and Air-Conditioning Engineers published its first adaptive comfort research and standards. However, one deterrent to the use of alternative comfort systems is that most office leases in the United States still specify narrow temperature ranges, giving designers far less latitude for using radiant heating and cooling.

Deciding when to open the windows to let natural ventilation into the building can be a major stumbling block to wider adoption of such systems … At the national telephone company's new office complex building in Oslo, Norway, … the group's manager made this decision … An American manager [would not] even want the responsibility for making that decision. Of course, American engineers are dismayed by the prospect of having to take user preferences for natural ventilation into account because it makes achieving constant interior temperatures more difficult, especially in hotter, more humid climates.

Politics

The European Union adopted its Energy Performance of Buildings Directive (EPBD) in 2002 and most individual countries achieved full implementation by 2010 … The goal is to reduce energy use in buildings to help meet the Kyoto Protocol targets for reductions in greenhouse gas (GHG) emissions. As one example, the German government plans to reduce GHG emissions 40 percent below 1990 levels by 2020 … By contrast, … former president George W. Bush pledged only that the United States would take until 2050 to reduce GHG emissions to 1990 levels. Going beyond just labelling buildings to actually implementing GHG reductions takes a comprehensive national approach that most European governments are still struggling to implement.

The most aggressive responder so far to the EPBD has been the United Kingdom, which has pledged that all new public (or social) housing, a much larger component of housing construction than in the United States, would be carbon-neutral by 2016, all new private housing by 2018 and all new commercial buildings by 2019.

In 2008, the United Kingdom implemented the directive's Energy Performance Certificates (EPCs) for all new commercial construction, which will publish the projected energy use of new buildings and give them a grade from A to G, with A being the best,

essentially a zero-net-carbon building, and G being the worst. Most new buildings in the United Kingdom are expected to get grades of D and E, which would represent the average energy use of the current building stock … The simple task of grading the buildings will lead to a dramatically increased demand from commercial building owners, developers and managers for low-energy building engineering services in the United Kingdom.[5] In turn, this should spur innovation and the adoption of new design approaches and new energy efficiency technologies. At this time, [there is] no such government mandate in the United States and Canada. One of the big issues in the United Kingdom is the cost of EPCs, which could cost a lot more than expected and take a lot longer to be issued.[6]

Other countries in Northern and Western Europe are expected to follow suit in the next three years, because the EPBD applies to all members of the European Union, so that much of the continent should become a hotbed for building technology innovation and low-energy design …

Economics

Energy prices historically have been much higher in Europe than in the United States, about twice as high … because European governments have taxed fuels more aggressively than those in the United States …

The psychology of saving energy is more deeply ingrained in Europe than in the United States because of a long history of higher fuel prices and fewer indigenous oil and gas resources. Of course, all countries were shocked at the fourfold increase in crude oil prices that began in 2004 and [has] continued … and energy conservation [has] become even more of a practical economic imperative … The message was clear: pay attention to energy costs, now and in the future. Nonetheless, Europeans generally consider the more casual approach to controlling energy use in buildings in North America both wasteful and impractical.

…

Economics drives most change in the advanced economies. Higher energy prices in the United States are going to drive [North Americans] more toward European approaches to building design and comfort engineering that place greater emphasis on achieving radically improved energy efficiency without adding initial costs to the building.

(2033 words)

Notes

1. Interview with John Echlin, August 2008.
2. Interview with Larry Malcic, August 2008.
3. Obviously, latitude alone doesn't explain climate. For example, proximity to the ocean and altitude are also important. In the British Isles and northwestern Europe, the warm Gulf Stream also plays a strong role in moderating annual temperature.
4. These are called Workplace Directives, or "Die Arbeitsstaattenrichtlinie," www.vdi.de, VD160000, accessed January 20, 2009. Behnisch Architekten and Transsolar Climate Engineering, *Ecology, Design, Synergy,* p. 60. Personal communication, Dr. Thomas Spiegelhalter, University of Southern California, September 4, 2008. "Die Arbeitsstaettenrichtlinie, VD1 6000, Blatt 2," www.vdi.de/401.0.html?&no_cache=1&tx_vdirili_pi2[showUID]=92588&L=0, accessed January 21, 2009.

5. In a May 2008 survey, only 20 percent of people polled said they would take no action to improve their EPC rating on a retrofit project. As many as 43 percent would try to increase their rating by two or more grades. *Building* (UK), 2008, May 2, p. 59.
6. "EPC costs balloon to ten times more than planned," *Building* (UK), 2008, May 2, p. 13.

Yudelson, Jerry. (2009). *Green building trend: Europe* (pp. xix–xxiii). Washington, DC: Island Press.

1. According to the author, which countries are leading innovators in green building design?

____

____

2. What is the main feature of the building the author uses as an example of innovative green building design?

____

____

3. What experiences make the people behind the quotations experts?

____

____

4. According to John Echlin, what are the factors that drive building in the US compared to Europe?

____

____

____

5. According to Larry Malcic, why do designers in Europe use sustainable principles more than non-European designers?

____

____

____

____

____

6. What are the driving forces in Europe that contribute to green building?

____

____

____

7. What are the climate characteristics in Europe that influence how buildings are designed and built? How are these different in North America?

____

____

____

____

8. What are the cultural characteristics in Europe that influence how buildings are designed and built?

9. What are the political conditions in Europe that influence how buildings are designed and built?

10. What are the economic conditions in Europe that influence how buildings are designed and built?

11. Do you believe that North Americans are as behind in green building design and energy reduction initiatives as this author implies? What evidence supports your answer?

Identifying Writer Perspective in a Text

Now that you have read the three texts in this chapter, you are in a good position to consider the differences in the writers' perspectives. It is important to notice a writer's perspective because it helps you understand why the information is presented in the way it is and if there is any bias.

Often a discussion of writer perspective is related to bias a writer might bring to the writing; the writer might want the reader to agree with his or her point of view. However, in this chapter, you will also see that writer perspective is related to the positioning of the writer as an expert or as an informed reader.

A. Answer the following questions to become aware of writer perspective in the readings in this chapter.

1. In Reading 1 and Reading 2, how do you know that the writers are not experts on the subject of green building?

2. In Reading 3, does the writer position himself as an expert or as an informed reader? ______

3. In Reading 3, the writer uses the pronoun *we* (and *us*) several times (see, for example, lines 3, 18, 97). Who does *we* refer to?

______

4. Why is this use of *we* (and *us*) unusual for a writer?

______

______

______

______

B. Your instructor will provide you with several short texts to read for this activity, or you can use readings from the Companion Website or bring in other texts to complete this task. Read the texts and consider these questions.

- Are the writers experts or informed readers, using the voices of other experts to give authority to the text?
- Is there evidence of writer bias in any of the texts? Is the writer trying to convince the reader of a specific viewpoint?
- Do any of the writers use the first person to associate themselves with a group of people?

C. Discuss the differences you find as a class.

Academic Survival Skill

Observing Text Features to Learn about Language

You can learn about your additional language by observing the features of texts closely, as you have done in this chapter. Through text observation, you can learn about grammar points, vocabulary selection, text organization and content development. Text observation is also something you can do on your own; you do not need your instructor to guide you.

It is best to start with two texts that are similar. They could be the same type of text (for example, excerpts from economics textbooks), or about the same topic (for example, an Internet article and an academic essay on global unemployment). Read the texts closely to look for common characteristics. These common characteristics will reveal written conventions in your additional language.

You might have questions of your own about how the language works, so look for evidence of those features. Alternatively, you can look specifically for the following features.

GRAMMAR POINTS: Use of specific verb tenses, punctuation, articles, word forms and noun, adjective or adverb clauses (full or reduced)

VOCABULARY SELECTION: Use of specific words, collocations, phrases and expressions; word frequency; words that appear to be discipline-specific; words that appear to have broader use outside a discipline

TEXT ORGANIZATION: Topic and concluding sentences in paragraphs; location of thesis statement; expressions used to draw the reader's attention to a new point; level of detail in introduction and conclusion sections; placement of main points

CONTENT DEVELOPMENT: Examples used to support points; how writers accomplish elaboration; presentation of divergent viewpoints; use of references; and use of paraphrases and summaries

A. To practise close observation of texts, use two texts from this chapter or two that you are reading for your academic work. Take notes on some of the common characteristics between the two texts. What have you learned about your additional language by taking note of these common features?

____

____

____

____

B. When you have finished, work with a small group to share your new understanding of how this language works.

FINAL ASSIGNMENT

Write an Extended Report

Write a report to explain the driving forces behind green building (or the lack of it) in the country or city in which you live or have lived. Use your description of the green building from the Warm-Up Assignment as the core of this longer report. Show how that building was the result of (or the exception to) the drivers of sustainable building in that country or city. Your goal for this report is to finish with a projection about the future of green building in the country or city you will write about.

Position yourself as an informed reader and let the experts' quotations give your writing authority. For this report, include references for the quotations. Move some of the background information about your expert voices from the text into the references for the quotations, using the quotations in Reading 3 as examples.

Your report should contain

- an introduction, with a definition of green building;
- a section on the driving forces in your country or city;
- an example of a sustainable building and its features;
- data on how much energy, water and CO_2 are saved (if available);
- a conclusion with your projections about the future of green building in your country or city.

Refer to the Models Chapter (page 202) to see an example of a report and to learn more about how to write one.

CRITICAL CONNECTIONS

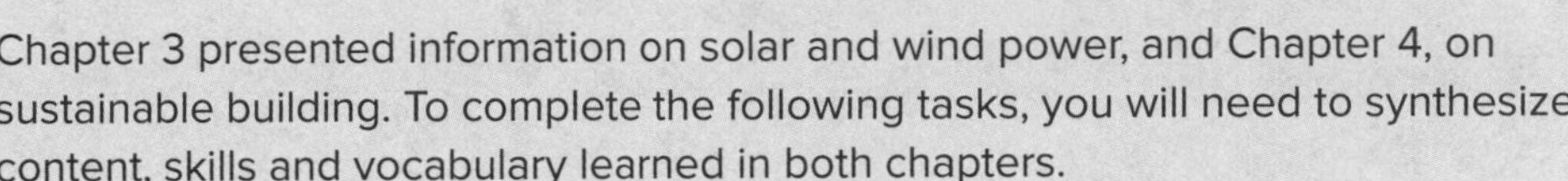

Chapter 3 presented information on solar and wind power, and Chapter 4, on sustainable building. To complete the following tasks, you will need to synthesize content, skills and vocabulary learned in both chapters.

1. Using the quotation from Chapter 3, Gearing Up, page 53, write a direct quotation as if you were writing about an interview that you had conducted with N. Petford. Before the direct quotation, use a sentence or two of indirect speech to provide context for the quotation. Use correct quotation format (see Chapter 4, Focus on Writing, page 86).
2. Write a paragraph to explain the relevance of wind and solar power to sustainable building design.
3. Skim the readings in Chapter 3 to determine each writer's perspective. Do the writers use *we* or *us* in the texts or include themselves as members of their audiences? Do the writers position themselves as experts or as informed readers? Do they use quotations to add authority to their writing?
4. Create a table in which you can summarize the information from Chapter 4, Reading 3 (page 90), about the forces that drive sustainable building in Europe and North America. Use the compare and contrast table layout that you used in Chapter 3, Focus on Reading (pages 60–61).
5. Based on the information in the table you generate for task 4, use your knowledge of the many ways to compare and contrast information to write four sentences that compare and/or contrast the European and the North American forces that drive sustainable design.
6. Create a discipline-specific list of vocabulary for the sustainable building topic of Chapter 4. Compare your list with other classmates' lists to ensure yours is as comprehensive as possible.

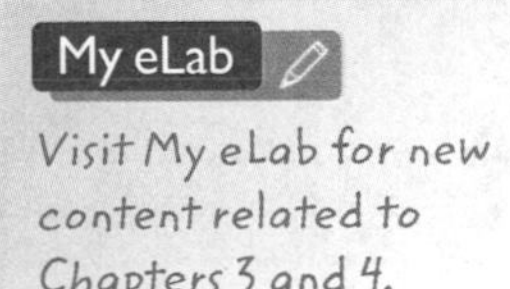

My eLab

Visit My eLab for new content related to Chapters 3 and 4.

CHAPTER 5

New Media: Advantages and Disadvantages

Organizations are constantly inventing electronic devices (cellphones), applications (Angry Birds), platforms (Facebook), and programs (Microsoft Windows) in an effort to facilitate communication and interaction. As all of these media were once new and are now *less* new, what does the term *new media* mean? Traditional media are technologies that provide information to the public: newspapers, television and radio. These media are one-way: information is transmitted by an organization and received by a person. However, new media allow people to interact: to share information, to communicate and to respond to each other. The advantages and attractiveness of interactive technology appear obvious; could there be any disadvantages?

In this chapter, you will

- learn vocabulary related to new media and their applications;
- use indicators to signal shifts in verb tense and voice;
- identify paraphrases and summaries in texts;
- learn techniques for paraphrasing and summarizing;
- write a paraphrase and a summary;
- write a persuasive essay integrating paraphrases and summaries.

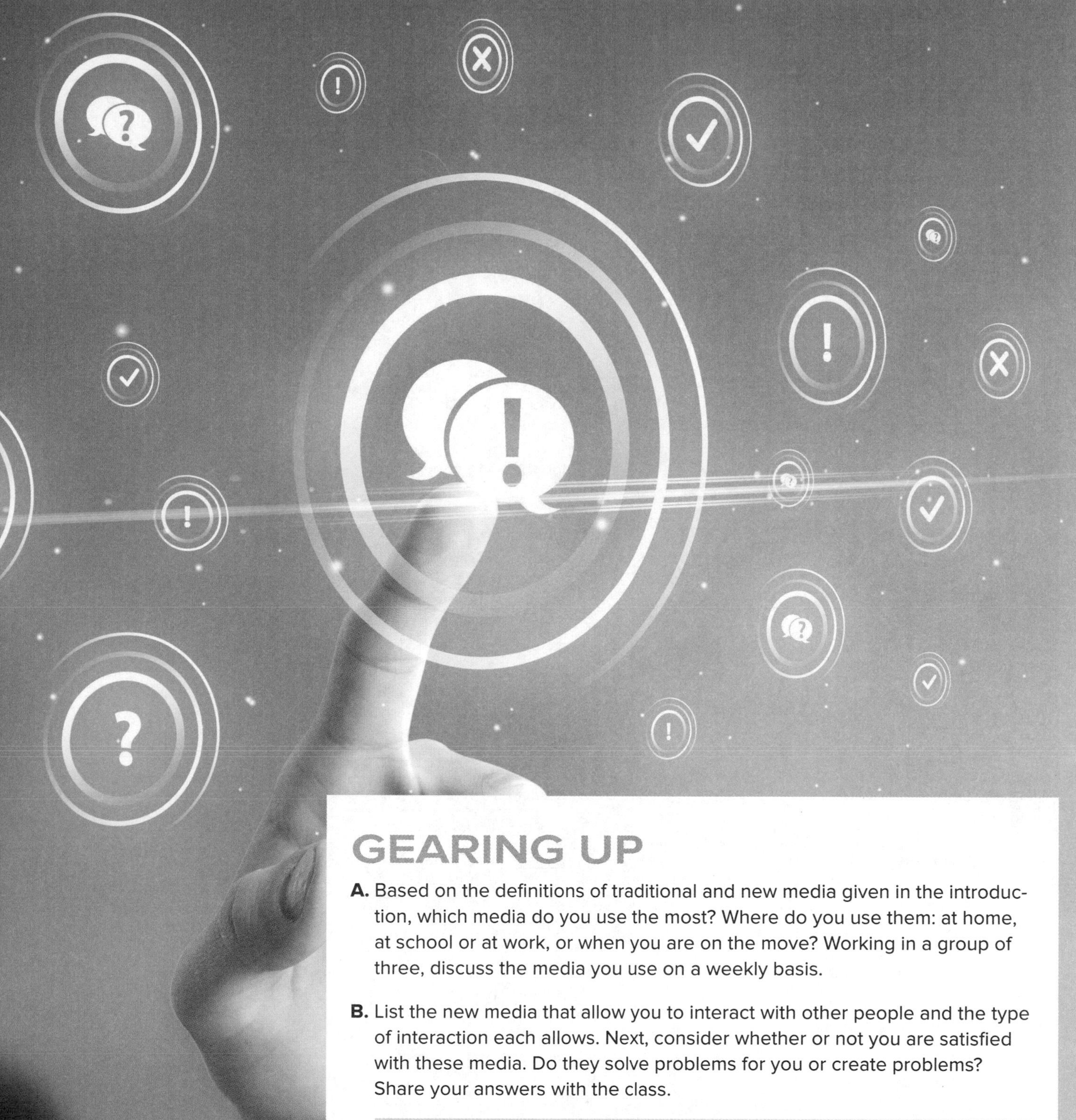

GEARING UP

A. Based on the definitions of traditional and new media given in the introduction, which media do you use the most? Where do you use them: at home, at school or at work, or when you are on the move? Working in a group of three, discuss the media you use on a weekly basis.

B. List the new media that allow you to interact with other people and the type of interaction each allows. Next, consider whether or not you are satisfied with these media. Do they solve problems for you or create problems? Share your answers with the class.

NEW MEDIA	PROBLEMS SOLVED	PROBLEMS CREATED

VOCABULARY BUILD

A. Below are key words and phrases from Reading 1 and Reading 2. Write definitions for words you already know. Look up each of the words you do not know, and write its definition. Where there is a phrase, write the definition of the underlined word. Then, answer the questions that follow.

WORD/PHRASE	DEFINITION
academy* (n.)	*academic organization*
apparently* (adv.)	
bonding* (adj.)	
commentary* (n.)	
concurrent* (adj.)	
converge (v.)	
cotton on to (v.)	
despite* (prep.)	
dimensions* (n.)	
overt discrimination* (n.)	
emergence* of (n.)	
ethnic* (adj.)	
evolve* (v.)	

WORD/PHRASE	DEFINITION
gender* (n.)	
implications (n.)	
incidentally* (adv.)	
Internet (n.)	
launch (v.)	
licensing* (adj.)	
media (n.)	
networks* (n.)	
participation* (n.)	
period* (n.) of time	
direct routes* (n.)	
sectors* (n.)	
versions* (n.)	

*Appears on the Academic Word List

1. Which noun is always capitalized and used with the definite article (*the*)? ____________
2. Which word looks singular, but is plural? (Hint: its singular form is *medium*.) ____________
3. Which word refers to either *male* or *female*? ____________
4. Which phrasal verb is an informal synonym of *realize*? ____________
5. Which word has the same meaning as the conjunction *although*? ____________

6. Write two nouns that have the root word *comment*. ______ ______

7. Which verb collocates with the following nouns: a boat, a product, an organization, an investigation or an attack? ______

B. Complete the following table by changing the form of each word to match the part of speech in the column heading.

NOUN	VERB	ADJECTIVE	ADVERB
academy		______	______
discrimination	______	______	
emergence	______	______	
______		ethnic	______
______	evolve	______	
participation	______	______	

READING 1 Something Has Happened to Communications

A. Skim the reading and, on a separate sheet of paper, take notes on the topic, length, text type and probable organization. Then, turn the title, the heading and the four subheadings into questions.

B. Read the text more closely and answer the questions you have generated. When you have finished, confirm your answers with a partner.

[These days,] we are in the midst of a communications upheaval more significant than the introduction of the printing press. The change began in rarefied academic circles in the 1960s, gathered pace with the emergence of the World Wide Web in the 1990s, but exploded into its most decisive phase in 2004 with the arrival of Web 2.0. The term was coined by Dale Dougherty of the US publishing company O'Reilly Media and it was first used for the highly influential Web 2.0 conference run by the company in 2004. In reality, Web 2.0 had begun much earlier, but with the beginning of a new millennium, it gathered pace. The Web has always been regarded as free but a new unregulated frontier is opening up in cyberspace. In the beginning, the "coders"—computer programmers—had ruled the environment. Later, the graphic designers arrived and made their mark on the space. Now the Web is finally opening up to anyone. Those with a spirit of adventure are staking claims to this virtual new territory.

Web 2.0 has a variety of definitions. It can be described simply as the version of the Web that is open to ordinary users and

where they can add their content. It refers to the sites and spaces on the Internet where users can put words, pictures, sounds and video. It is a very simple idea in theory. In practice, it signifies the transfer of control of the Internet, and ultimately the central platform for communication, from the few to the many. It is the democratization of the Internet. The names of some of these spaces, Facebook, YouTube, MySpace and *Wikipedia* are now familiar. There are many thousands of others.

Nothing fundamentally changed in 2004 from a technological point of view; all of the tools that were available to create Web 2.0 environments already existed. What changed was the way that people started to view the Internet. It was an organic change and it was driven as much by ordinary Internet users as it was by large organizations. In fact, a number of those ordinary Internet users created Web 2.0 environments that mushroomed into hugely valuable corporations and brands in a staggeringly short space of time. Bebo, the world's third-largest social networking website, was sold for £417 million to Internet company AOL, just three years after being set up by husband and wife team Michael and Xochi Birch.

...

How Communications Has Changed

Communications is undergoing a radical change. Every aspect of how we exchange information is feeling the impact of the technological revolution. Changes are taking place in the way we use the media channels that have been available to us for many years. Totally new communications channels are emerging ...

Newspapers and magazines

... The early Web versions of [newspaper and magazine] offline titles were essentially mirrors of the printed versions, but they started to create opportunities for extended PR [public relations] coverage as they rolled out revised websites that contained content that was unique to the Web. As they started to refresh content more frequently, something significant changed ... News organizations could release stories literally within minutes of receiving them.

[Currently,] major newspapers are in the business of reinventing themselves as brands. Their future role will be to disseminate news across a variety of platforms. When the *Guardian* relaunched itself in the smaller Berliner format in 2005, the editor, Alan Rusbridger, said at the time that the *Guardian* website was cannibalizing newspaper readership and that this was a factor in the fall of the paper's circulation. He also said something else that provided a fascinating insight into the future of national daily newspapers. The new format required the purchase of new printers at some considerable cost: £62 million, £12 million more than the paper had budgeted. The editor apparently said that he thought they would be the last printers that the paper bought. Given that the lifespan of these presses could be as little as twenty years, this suggests that for some national papers the future will not involve paper at all ...

Television

There are a number of significant changes happening to the way we watch television. One of these is viewer scheduling. Innovations like Sky+, BBC iPlayer and TV content on iTunes mean that we can watch favoured programs when it suits us and not just when they are broadcast. Incidentally, it also means that we can choose to skip TV advert[isement]s. The iPlayer and a number of similar platforms also mean that we are not just watching TV on the box in the corner of the living room but we are watching it on PCs, laptops and mobile devices, including iPods. Major manufacturers have cottoned on to this and have developed attractive-looking compact PCs that come with remote controls and are designed to operate through your TV. In 2008, Philips launched the EasyLife LX2000 computer with no monitor, designed to be attached to your TV like a DVD recorder and optimized for TV and video content viewing.

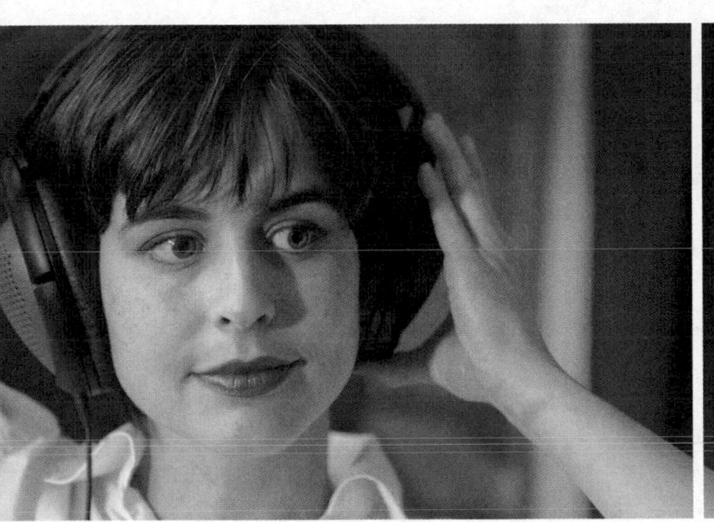

The natural conclusion is that content from broadcasters and from other sources, including those that incorporate user-generated content (UGC), will start to converge. Moving from BBC iPlayer to Sky to stored content on your PC or streaming content from the Internet will all be done in the same way that we used to channel hop. This means two things for the PR practitioner. The first is that there are more direct routes to market for TV or video. The second and related point is that the content needs to be genuinely engaging. In this new environment, content is king of kings and viewers will watch what they want and not just what they are fed.

There is another interesting issue that anyone involved in content production should consider. Big TV screens in the living room will become ubiquitous; the quality is improving with better high definition and the costs are falling. At the same time, TV is starting to appear on iPods and mobile phones. These two concurrent developments create a dilemma. Will something that works on a fifty-two-inch screen also work on a two-inch? Not always ...

Radio

Due to the greater simplicity of radio and the lower bandwidth requirements, radio has been available across a range of platforms for some time. Radio downloads that aren't ever broadcast in a traditional sense are becoming increasingly popular. We just don't call it radio; we refer to them as podcasts ... Podcasts are incredibly cheap and easy to produce and simple to make available. The key, however, is content once again ...

The Internet

Is the Internet a medium at all? I really don't think that it is—it is far richer and more complex than any of the traditional media channels. At one level it provides a platform that to varying degrees allows the traditional channels to migrate their content and reach different audiences. On another level it delivers a series of new media platforms and has created the forum through which the consumer and the brand can interact. For example, Facebook, as the leading social networking site, has characteristics all of its own. In fact, it doesn't even regard itself as a social networking or social media site; it describes itself as a social utility. It is also a perfect example of how platforms on the Internet mesh and mash up with each other. For example, YouTube provides a great deal of content for Facebook. Essentially, the way Facebook works is to draw content and applications from the widest possible range of sources ...

... I believe that the distinction between digital and offline will gradually disappear. The distinctions will become blurred, as we are starting to see with radio and television, and the number of platforms will grow. For example, the growth of hand-held mobile devices will create new opportunities as we integrate location and content. Knowing where our audience physically is at any one moment will have a dramatic influence on what we want to say to them.

The other important consideration is that traditional media will not go away. In that regard I am entirely persuaded by the view of Gary Carter, president of Creative Networks at FremantleMedia and chief creative officer, FremantleMedia New Platforms. In a keynote speech at the National Association of Television Program Executives conference in Las Vegas in January 2007, he argued the following:

> The simple historical fact is that mass communication technologies are never replaced by newer technologies. They co-exist, while continuing to evolve. We still have the newspaper, the telephone, the radio and the movies, despite the fact that each of these was at the time of introduction viewed as the beginning of the end for the other. (1451 words)

Although this reading comes from a book, the introduction of this quotation is typical of a magazine article. The speaker's name and position (and in this case the date) are stated before the quotation rather than in a more formal footnote.

Brown, R. (2009). *Public relations and the social Web: How to use social media and Web 2.0 in communications* (pp. 1–8). London, UK: Kogan Page.

C. Working as a class, discuss the answers to the following questions.

1. What is the purpose of the second paragraph, lines 17 to 24?

2. Choose the description that best represents the author's perspective. The author is ...
   a) an academic writer, writing in a neutral way to explain changes to communications
   b) a public relations expert, writing about challenges to public relations caused by communications innovations
   c) a newspaper publisher, writing persuasively that print newspapers must be retained

3. From the word box, select four words or phrases that represent the main ideas in Reading 1. Explain why you chose these words or phrases.

advertisements	converge	Facebook	public relations
coexistence	democratization of the Internet	interactive	small screen

____

____

____

Using Indicators That Signal Shifts in Verb Tense and Voice

The author of Reading 1 uses a variety of verb tenses and voice shifts. The topic of new media provides a rich context for this: the author writes about traditional media (past) and current media (present) and makes predictions about media in future. The author also shifts from active to passive voice.

An analysis of the first paragraph shows that, in almost all cases, indicators signal verb-tense and voice shifts within the sentence. In the examples that follow, verbs are in bold and indicators that signal the verb forms are underlined.

Signals event in the present → [These days,] we **are** in the midst of a communications upheaval more significant than the introduction of the printing press.

Signals past tense → The change **began** in rarefied academic circles in the 1960s, **gathered** pace with the emergence of the World Wide Web in the 1990s, but **exploded** into its most decisive phase in 2004 with the arrival of Web 2.0. ← *Signals past tense*

Adverb "first" is in mid-position; signals past tense → The term **was coined** by Dale Dougherty of the US publishing company O'Reilly Media, and it **was first used** for the highly influential Web 2.0 conference that **was run** by the company in 2004. ← *By-phrase signals passive voice* ← *Implied by-phrase ("by conference attendees") signals passive voice*

In reality, Web 2.0 **had begun** much earlier, but with the beginning of a new millennium, it **gathered** pace. ← *Signals time before an event in the past; verb shifts to past perfect*; *Signals past tense* → (the beginning of a new millennium)

Implied by-phrase signals passive voice; adverb "always" is in mid-position; no time indicator, but present perfect (passive) signals an action begun in the past and continued until the present time → The Web **has always been regarded** as free but a new unregulated frontier **is opening up** in cyberspace. ← *No time indictor, but present progressive shows an event is happening in the present*

In the beginning, the "coders"—computer programmers—**had ruled** the environment. ← *Signals event happened in the past; verb shifts to past perfect*

Signals past event → Later, the graphic designers **arrived** and **made** their mark on the space.

Signals present event; adverb "finally" is in mid-position → Now, the Web **is finally opening up** to anyone. Those with a spirit of adventure **are staking** claims to this virtual new territory. ← *Present progressive verb shows event is happening over an extended period in the present*

A. Complete the following sentences with key words from the analysis.

1. In most cases, there is an indicator that ______________________ the appropriate verb tense and voice.
2. The indicators can come before or ______________________ the verb in a sentence.
3. Passive voice *may* be indicated with a ______________________.
4. For academic writing, adverbs (such as *first*, *always* and *finally*) are often in ______________________ between the auxiliary and main verbs or between two auxiliaries.

B. Working with a partner, choose either lines 25 to 35 or lines 51 to 62 from the Reading 1 and analyze the verb-tense shifts. Underline the verbs and use arrows to point to the time indicators (if there are any). When you have finished, check your analysis with another pair of students who have worked on the same paragraph. Then, check your answers with your instructor.

C. On a separate sheet of paper, write a paragraph (of at least seven sentences) about media use among your friends in the last ten years and how it has changed. Use indicators to signal shifts in verb tense and voice. Write at least two sentences in the passive voice. When you have finished, exchange papers with a classmate and edit each other's paragraph. Revise as required. Submit your paragraph to your instructor. Write the best ones on the board, or post them on a shared website.

READING ❷

Blogs as Participatory Media and Social Software

In this textbook excerpt, the authors write about how Web 2.0 technologies, exemplified by blogs, can add to social capital. They also suggest that the advantages of new media may be undermined by disadvantages.

A. Read the text. Then, demonstrate your comprehension by answering the following questions. When you have finished, check your answers as a class.

1. What is the purpose of the first paragraph of the reading?

   ____

2. In lines 26 to 31, William Davies suggests that social software has a significant effect on our lives. What is that effect? Do you agree? Why or why not?

   ____

   ____

   ____

3. In the third paragraph (lines 49 to 59), three definitions of social capital are given. Which definition makes the most sense to you, and why?

   ____

   ____

   ____

4. What are the benefits of social capital?

   ____

   ____

   ____

5. E-mailing your parents is a personal example of bonding social capital. Give personal examples of the two other forms of social capital—bridging and linking—as defined by Aldridge et al.

   ____

   ____

   ____

Web logs, or blogs, are user-generated websites where entries are made either by individuals or by groups, in an informal journal style, and are displayed in reverse chronological order. Blogs are typically interactive and networked. They solicit and respond to the commentary of others on the material posted on the blog and they characteristically offer links to the blogs or website of others with related interests (what is known as blogroll), and—while mainly text-based—blogs can provide links to other media resources, such as video and photos (a video-based blog is called a vlog, while a photo-based blog is a photoblog). The term *blog* refers to both the online artifact created and to the act of maintaining such an online resource, or blogging. The social network of blogs and bloggers is referred to as the blogosphere and it is through this network that "the social networking of blogs and the potential for collaboration ... [provide] a decidedly human dimension to the publishing and publicizing of information" in ways that "represent for authors an opportunity to reach out and connect with an audience never before accessible to them, while maintaining control over their own personal expressive spaces" (Bruns and Jacobs 2006: 5). Blogs have been a vitally important component of social software and [William] Davies has argued that:

> The principle of social software is to break down the distinction between our online computer-mediated experiences and our offline face-to-face experiences. It is software that ... seeks to integrate the Internet further into our everyday lives, and our everyday lives further into the Internet. It is software that seeks to eradicate the gulf separating two such separate social networks. (2003: 7)

...

In placing the rise of blogs in Internet history, Clay Shirky argues that they are part of a "third age" of social software (Shirky 2003). The first age began with e-mail and, particularly, the "cc" tag line, which allowed one-to-one or one-to-few communications. The second age came with the rise of virtual communities, as discussed by Rheingold (1994). For Shirky, one of the key limitations of the technology and how it was used in this period (the mid to late 1990s) is that both the software and the modes of Web content development tended to be static, had limited interactivity, possessed a centralized mechanism of content control and operated on a largely "broadcast" model ... As a result, there was a limited sense of community and a lack of interactivity in the development of Web pages. By contrast, the "third age" of social software has evolved around the principles of Web 2.0, which place a particular emphasis on collaboration, community-building, simplification of software and access points for users, "light touch" regulation of site content and relative ease in producing, distributing, accessing and responding to the full range of forms of digital media content. In cases where such principles have been extended to collaborative publishing models, such as *Wikipedia*, this also includes collaborative editing (Bruns 2005).

Participatory Media, Social Software and Social Capital

One question that arises from the development of participatory media such as blogs and other forms of social software is whether their development contributes to the growth of social capital and, in particular, to new forms such as virtual social capital. In his well-known work on the significance of social capital, Putnam (1995: 665) defines social capital as "features of social life—networks, norms, and trust—that enable participants to act together more effectively to pursue shared interests ... Social capital, in short, refers to social connections and the attendant norms and trust." Woolcock (2001: 13) defines social capital as the "norms and networks that facilitate collective action" and Davies (2003: 11) defines it as the "value of social networks"; this is "a resource which we can invest time and money in, and which pays returns."

The promotion, nurturing and maintenance of social capital is seen as critical to overall economic performance, to the avoidance of adverse social consequences (crime, drug abuse, public health concerns) and to the emergence of new forms of social entrepreneurship that fill gaps between market-led solutions and government-driven reform programs (Davies 2003). In addressing such questions, Aldridge and colleagues (2002) distinguish between three main types of social capital:

1. bonding social capital, characterized by strong social bonds between individuals, for example members of a family, a local community or an ethnic community;

2. bridging social capital, characterized by weaker, less dense but more cross-cutting ties, for example with business associates, links across ethnic groups, links between families and communities; and,

3. linking social capital, characterized by connections between those with differing levels of power or social status, for example between political elites and the general public, policy-makers and local communities and individuals from different social classes.

Early commentaries on the relationship between the Internet and social capital identified a positive correlation between the decentralized and inclusive nature of the Internet and the revivification of civic engagement and a sense of community (Schuler 1996).

Putnam himself, however, does not fully embrace the idea that Internet users would be more civically engaged and he expresses concerns about unequal access to the new technology and "cyber-balkanisation" (2000: 177). There are related concerns about the adverse effects of Internet use on family life and on other offline activities (Nie and Erbring 2000) and the tendency toward group polarization and heightened political conflict among those with divergent points of view (Sunstein 2002). There was empirical work emerging during this period that showed the Internet acting, on balance, as a positive stimulus to community engagement and civic and political participation; however, there was also a need to recognize that the Internet was changing such forms of engagement and participation and that new ways of measuring engagement were needed for new media (Wellman et al. 2001). In a similar vein, Aldridge and colleagues (2002: 48–9) conclude that the Internet was promoting a transformation of forms of civic engagement, particularly among younger users, where sustained engagement with globally networked organizations was becoming more important than traditional, locally based forms of participation in community organizations (such as sporting teams, local churches or Rotary Clubs).

An important question that remains is whether social software and its facilitation and promotion of large-scale, public, online participation is changing the nature of engagement and participation and their relationship to social capital. Using the definitions of social capital provided, blogs are clearly a use of social software to develop new forms of social capital that are bridging and, to varying degrees, bonding and linking. The function of permalinks within blogs, which establish a permanent link to other blogs and the comments posted on them even as they change (and as the URL changes with them), is one of the many indicators of the desire of bloggers to maintain an ongoing sense of community, not only with their readers, but with the wider community of bloggers with whom they coexist. By a variety of indicators, it would seem that the rise of blogging and other forms of social software are having positive effects on the development and maintenance of social capital, even if they may also represent to their critics (e.g., Keen 2007) a new form of narcissism on a global scale.

...

Downsides of Networks, Social Media and Participatory Media Culture

It is important to conclude ... with some consideration of the potential downsides to the network form, both in terms of its internal logic and its wider socio-economic impacts. The first is that, at a purely technical level, networks frequently fail. Servers crash, infrastructure systems fail, and website access becomes overloaded and hence unavailable. There are also concerns ... [about the impact of large-scale events], which can range from a power blackout at a particular location because of an overloaded electricity grid, to an act of war or terrorism that decimates core communications infrastructure almost instantaneously, as happened in the Downtown Manhattan district of New York City in the immediate aftermath of 9/11.

Second, it is important to be conscious of the insider/outsider dimensions of networks. At a global level, Castells draws attention to the inclusion/exclusion dimensions of access, involvement and participation that arise in a networked global economy and are based on geographical location and the geopolitical significance of that location ... (see e.g., Castells 2000: 70–165). In relation to the creative industries, McRobbie (2005) argues that a form of "network sociality" in these sectors has generated a form of "PR meritocracy" whereby familiar patterns of social exclusion on the basis of gender, race, ethnicity, social location and other factors continue to occur, but they are based less upon overt discrimination than upon the question of who has the time and capacity for after-hours social networking. Gill's research (2002) on participation in project-based new media work and the very significant barriers confronting women and people with young children (again mostly women) is pertinent in this context.

A third, notable concern is that networks have historically been associated with corruption and crime. As we have noted, al-Queda and similar organizations, for example, use the innovative capabilities of networks and social media in ways that are massively damaging to populations worldwide both in terms of wider geopolitical implications and in how they affect populations at a very local level ... [Similarly, there are] family-based and ethnically structured ... criminal organizations such as the Sicilian mafia, the Colombian drug cartels, the Russian *mafiyas*, the Chinese Triads and the Japanese Yakuza.

In a different way, high levels of bonding social capital in particular have been associated with racial intolerance and conflict between communities. One example includes

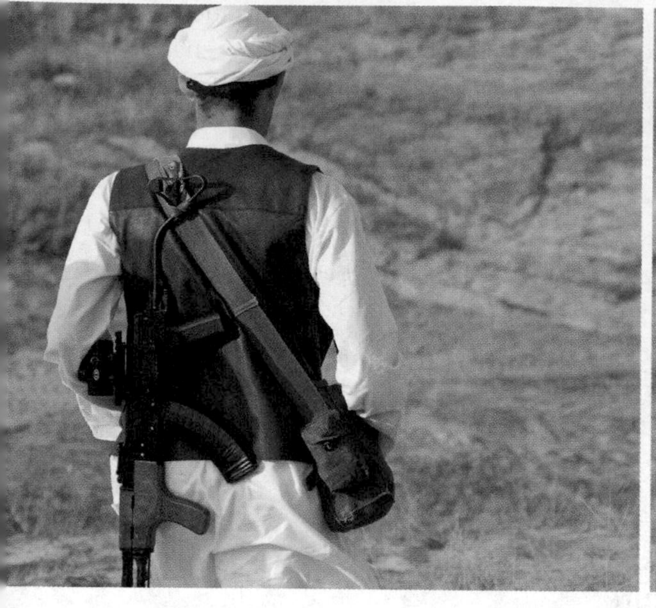

the Catholic/Protestant divide in Northern Ireland, where there is a great deal of bonding social capital within the sectarian communities, but what are missing are forms of social capital that bridge these community divides. Whether the rise of the Internet and social networking media provide new forms of virtual social capital that can effectively work across such divides remains to be seen.

Beyond these serious criticisms, participatory media is also vulnerable to the accusation that the "immaterial labour" (van Dijck 1999) of participants is being co-opted by owners of websites without any meaningful control over how it is being used. In part this is fostered by End-User Licensing Agreements (the notorious EULA) that assign blanket rights to the owner of the site. As well, user behaviour is meticulously tracked and, along with preferences and "likes," becomes data that can be sold to third parties for marketing purposes or other surveillance-related activities. (1755 words)

Bibliography

Aldridge, Stephen, David Halpern, and Sarah Fitzpatrick. 2002. Social capital: A discussion paper. Performance and Innovation Unit, London, UK, April.

Bruns, Axel. 2005. *Gatewatching: Collaborative online news production*. New York, NY: Peter Lang.

Bruns, Axel, and Joanne Jacobs. 2006. Introduction. In A. Bruns and J. Jacobs. Eds., *Uses of blogs*. New York, NY: Peter Lang, pp. 1–7.

Castells, Manuel. 2000. *End of millennium*, Vol. 3. of *The information age: Economy, society and culture*. Malden, MA: Blackwell.

Davies, William. 2003. You don't know me but ... Social capital and social software. London, UK: iSociety.

Gill, Rosalind. 2002. Cool, creative and egalitarian? Exploring gender in project-based new media work in Europe. *Information, Communication and Society 5*(1): 70–89.

Keen, Andrew. 2007. *The cult of the amateur: How today's Internet is killing our culture*. New York, NY: Doubleday.

McRobbie, Angela. 2005. Clubs to companies. In J. Hartley, Ed. *Creative industries*. Oxford, UK: Blackwell, pp. 375–93.

Nie, Norman, and Lutz Erbring. 2000. *Internet and society: A preliminary report*. Stanford, CA: Stanford Institute for the Quantitative Study of Society.

Putnam, Robert. 1995. Tuning in, tuning out: The strange disappearance of social capital in America. *Political Science and Politics 28*(4): 664–88.

Putnam, Robert. 2000. *Bowling alone: The collapse and revival of American community*. New York, NY: Simon & Schuster.

Rheingold, Howard. 1994. *The virtual community: Finding connection in a computerized world*. London, UK: Secker & Warburg.

Schuler, Douglas. 1996. *New community networks: Wired for change*. Reading, MA: Addison-Wesley.

Shirky, Clay. 2003. Social software and the politics of groups. Retrieved from http://shirky.com.writings/group_politics.html

Sunstein, Cass. 2002. The law of group polarization. *Journal of Political Philosophy 10*(2): 175–95.

van Dijck, J. 1999. *The network society: Social aspects of new media*. London, UK: Sage.

Wellman, Barry, Anabel Haase, James Witte, and Keith Hampton. 2001. Does the Internet increase, decrease or supplement social capital? Social networks, participation and community commitment. *American Behavioral Scientist 45*(3): 436–55.

Woolcock, Michael. 2001. The place of social capital in understanding social and economic outcomes. *ISUMA: Canadian Journal of Policy Research 2*(1): 11–17.

Flew, T., & Smith, R. (2008). *New media: An introduction* (Canadian ed., pp. 113–118). Toronto, ON: Oxford University Press.

B. According to the authors, there are both advantages and disadvantages to using social software. Each point given is attributed to the researcher(s) whose work the authors have paraphrased or summarized. In the table, list as many advantages and disadvantages as possible, citing the sources of the original ideas.

ADVANTAGES	DISADVANTAGES
The Internet seems to have a beneficial effect on community engagement and participation although current methods of measuring engagement must be updated to more effectively measure this characteristic (Wellman et al. 2001).	*Internet users are not necessarily more engaged in their communities. Not everyone has equal access to the new technologies (Putnam 2000).*

C. Based on the information in this table, do you think the impact of social software is mostly positive or negative? Why?

____

____

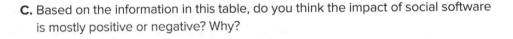

Identifying Paraphrases and Summaries

The authors of Reading 2, Flew and Smith, advanced their arguments about the positive and negative impacts of social software by integrating points made by other authors and researchers. Their views were not always integrated through direct quotations or indirect speech, (see in the Focus on Writing on page 86), but through paraphrasing and summarizing.

Through paraphrasing and summarizing, writers use their own words to present the ideas of others. For each paraphrase and summary, writers need to give an in-text citation, with a full reference at the end of the text. (See the Academic Survival Skill on page 38.)

What is the difference between paraphrasing and summarizing?

A paraphrase is approximately the same length as the original text. A summary is shorter than the original text. A formal summary is approximately one-third to one-quarter the length of the original text, but this is not an absolute rule. For both paraphrases and summaries, it is important for writers to use their own words, not the words of the original author.

Why paraphrase and summarize?

Writers paraphrase and summarize other authors for many reasons:

- to build their arguments for and against their thesis
- to give credit to the authors who wrote about these ideas first
- to avoid constant use of quotations
- to avoid plagiarism
- to show the reader they have extensive knowledge of this field
- to establish their writing as academic

In general, writers must paraphrase or summarize and provide a citation and reference for specific ideas and research outcomes.

A. Skim the citations in Reading 2 and complete the following.

1. Underline those that refer to direct quotations of the original authors' words.
2. Highlight those that are paraphrases and summaries of original authors.
3. Does anything about these citations surprise you?

   ____

   ____

4. When you look at a citation, can you tell if Flew and Smith have paraphrased or summarized the original authors' views? Why or why not?

   ____

   ____

B. To gain greater insight into Flew and Smith's paraphrases and summaries, look at two of the original texts they integrated into their writing. For each, find the corresponding citation in Reading 2 and identify whether Flew and Smith paraphrased or summarized the text.

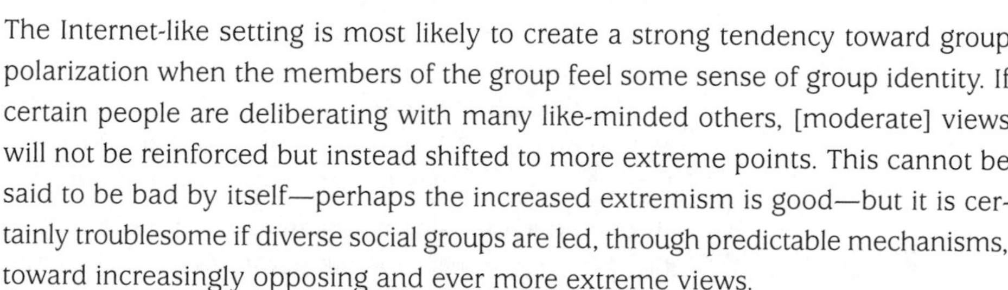

The Internet-like setting is most likely to create a strong tendency toward group polarization when the members of the group feel some sense of group identity. If certain people are deliberating with many like-minded others, [moderate] views will not be reinforced but instead shifted to more extreme points. This cannot be said to be bad by itself—perhaps the increased extremism is good—but it is certainly troublesome if diverse social groups are led, through predictable mechanisms, toward increasingly opposing and ever more extreme views.

Sunstein, C. (2002). The law of group polarization. *Journal of Political Philosophy 10*(2): 185–186.

Taken together, our results suggest that the Internet is increasing interpersonal connectivity and organizational involvement. However, this increased connectivity and involvement not only can expose people to more contact and more information, it can reduce commitment to community. Even before the advent of the Internet, there has been a move from all-encompassing, socially controlling communities to individualized, fragmented personal communities (Wellman 2001).

The security and social control of all-encompassing communities have given way to the opportunity and vulnerability of networked individualism. People now go through the day, week and month in a variety of narrowly defined relationships with changing sets of network members.

It is time for more differentiated analyses of the Internet, analyses that are embedded in everyday life offline as well as online. Although we have shown that the Internet affects social capital, the mechanisms are unclear. Knowing that people have been using the Internet for more than two years or that they are online for three hours per day does not provide a clear picture of the activities in which they are engaged.

Future analyses need to examine in more detail the effects of the Internet, focus on the types of activities performed online, and explore how these fit into the complexity of everyday life.

Wellman, B., Haase, A., Witte, J., & Hampton, K. (2001). Does the Internet increase, decrease or supplement social capital? Social networks, participation and community commitment. *American Behavioral Scientist 45*(3): 450–451.

C. The following two examples show how Flew and Smith integrated paraphrases and summaries into their writing. The notes illustrate the methods they used.

PARAPHRASE OR SUMMARY	NOTES ON INTEGRATION
In placing the rise of blogs in Internet history, Clay Shirky argues that they are part of a "third age" of social software (Shirky 2003).	• Author's name mentioned directly in the sentence • Use of verb *argues* • Use of quotation marks identifies the term coined by the author • Citation at end
In cases where such principles have been extended to collaborative publishing models, such as *Wikipedia*, this also includes collaborative editing (Bruns 2005).	• No use of verb to integrate summary • Author's name not mentioned directly in the sentence • Only the citation at the end attributes the information to the original author

1. Select one page of Reading 2 and review each citation to determine which paraphrases and summaries were integrated with a direct inclusion of the author's name and a corresponding verb, and which were not.

2. When Flew and Smith integrate a paraphrase or summary with a direct inclusion of the author's name, which verbs and phrases do they use?

   ____

   ____

   ____

3. Look closely at the Sunstein quotation above and then at Flew and Smith's integration of it in Reading 2. Identify the techniques Flew and Smith used to paraphrase Sunstein's text.

   ____

   ____

   ____

Academic
Survival Skill

Using Techniques to Paraphrase and Summarize

Although easy to say, transferring another author's words into your own words is harder to do. Fortunately, there are techniques that can help you paraphrase and summarize. We will examine these techniques by applying them to the following excerpt.

Two principal mechanisms underlie group polarization. The first points to social influences on behaviour and, in particular, to people's desire to maintain their reputation and their self-conception. The second emphasizes the limited "argument pools" within any group, and the directions in which those limited pools lead group members. An understanding of the two mechanisms provides many insights into deliberating bodies. If deliberation predictably pushes groups toward a more extreme point in the direction of their original tendency whatever it may be, do we have any reason to think that deliberation is producing improvements?

Sunstein, C. (2002). The law of group polarization. *Journal of Political Philosophy 10*(2), 176–177.

First, understand the meaning of the original. If you don't understand the meaning, it is impossible to paraphrase or summarize well. Sometimes it helps to cover up the original text and say (aloud) what you understand the text to mean. This moves you toward using your own words when writing.

Once you have a good understanding of the original text, there are several techniques you can use to arrive at your own wording, whether it be to paraphrase or to summarize.

Technical words, specific terms or very common words (like "the") do not require synonyms.

Paraphrasing

Using the first sentence of the excerpt as an example, here are some techniques you can use when paraphrasing.

USE SYNONYMS:	Two main reasons cause group polarization.	*A good start, but the sentence structure is too similar to the original.*
CHANGE WORD FORMS:	Two mechanical principles underlie the polarizing of group views.	*Good change in word forms, but "mechanical principles" sounds like it refers to machinery and "the polarizing of group views" does not show that "group polarization" is a term the author is using to name this phenomenon.*
CHANGE SENTENCE STRUCTURE:	There are two principal mechanisms that underlie group polarization.	*Good move to a new sentence structure, but the words are too similar to the original.*
MOVE FROM ACTIVE TO PASSIVE:	Group polarization is caused by two principal mechanisms.	*Good move to passive voice, but the words are still too similar to the original.*

These are all good techniques, but on their own, none is sufficient to create a good paraphrase. A combination of techniques yields the best results.

A. Which techniques were combined to create this paraphrase of the first sentence?

Group polarization is driven by two main effects.

____

____

We also have to remember to introduce the paraphrase to give credit to the author of the original.

Sunstein (2002) states that group polarization is driven by two main effects.

B. Paraphrasing one sentence at a time is a good way to analyze the different techniques, but it is more likely you will want to paraphrase several sentences at once. In the paraphrase that follows, which techniques have been used?

Sunstein (2002) suggests that group polarization is driven by two main effects. On the one hand, group members want to be liked by other participants and to feel good about themselves. On the other hand, if people form a group based on shared interests, it is unlikely the group will express divergent views.

____

____

Summarizing

While paraphrasing is useful, it is even more likely that you will want to summarize large amounts of information into small amounts that can be integrated into your writing. To write a summary, you first need to identify the main points.

A. In our example excerpt below, underline the main points.

Two principal mechanisms underlie group polarization. The first points to social influences on behaviour and, in particular, to people's desire to maintain their reputation and their self-conception. The second emphasizes the limited "argument pools" within any group, and the directions in which those limited pools lead group members. An understanding of the two mechanisms provides many insights into deliberating bodies. If deliberation predictably pushes groups toward a more extreme point in the direction of their original tendency whatever it may be, do we have any reason to think that deliberation is producing improvements?

B. When you have identified the main points, write a summary.

____

____

____

____

____

____

____

____

C. To practise paraphrasing and summarizing, work through the process presented in this section for lines 94 to 106 of Reading 2. Use a separate sheet of paper.

- Paraphrase the first sentence using the four paraphrasing techniques, and then combine the techniques into the "perfect" paraphrase.
- Paraphrase the first three sentences, combining techniques to write your best paraphrase.
- Summarize the full paragraph. Reduce it to approximately one-third of its current length.

In each case, include the author's name and the date of publication in an appropriate way.

WARM-UP ASSIGNMENT

Write a Paraphrase and a Summary

To cite a source written by multiple authors, use the first author's last name followed by the abbreviation "et al.," which means "and others." In the reference, include the full names of all the authors.

A. Read the following excerpt from Wellman et al. and, on a separate sheet of paper, paraphrase the first two sentences twice, using different techniques.

- In the first paraphrase, use synonyms, change word forms and change the sentence structure.
- In the second paraphrase, use synonyms and shift from passive to active voice (or the reverse) when possible.

For each paraphrase, cite the authors and the date of publication either at the beginning or at the end. When you have finished, compare your paraphrases with another classmate. Write your best paraphrase on the board.

When the Internet engages people primarily in asocial activities, then even more than television, its immersiveness can turn people away from community, organizational and political involvement and domestic life. By contrast, when people use the Internet to communicate and coordinate with friends, relatives and organizations—near and far—then it is a tool for building and maintaining social capital. Our research has shown that there are no single Internet effects. In this era of spatially dispersed community, the Internet fills needs for additional interpersonal contact that supplement in-person and telephone contact. At a time of declining organizational participation, the Internet provides tools for those already involved to increase their participation. Yet, at a time when networked individualism reduces group social cohesion, extensive involvement with the Internet apparently exposes participants to situations that weaken their sense of community online. This suggests that future examination of Internet use might identify what affects the quality as well as the quantity of online social interaction—for weak and strong ties.

Wellman, B., Haase, A., Witte, J., & Hampton, K. (2001). Does the Internet increase, decrease or supplement social capital? Social networks, participation and community commitment. *American Behavioral Scientist 45*(3): 450–451.

When you receive feedback from your instructor or your classmates on this Warm-Up Assignment, you will have some information that you can use to improve your writing on the Final Assignment.

B. Write a summary of the entire excerpt. Your summary should be approximately one-third of its original length. Include a citation within the text and the full reference at the end of the text. Then, identify the techniques you used.

VOCABULARY BUILD

A. Reading 3 contains a number of idiomatic words and expressions. Read the following sentences and then write the meaning of each of the underlined words and expressions.

IDIOMATIC WORD/EXPRESSION	MEANING
1 In 2007, Terry first began a blog about how she was doing her part to reduce plastic.	*doing her fair share of the work*
2 ... all requests for a meeting were denied, so they stepped it up a notch and decided to go public.	
3 She contacted every blogger she knew ... and tried to pitch the media.	
4 ... the company had to see it all in one place instead of people calling and writing in dribs and drabs.	
5 The Brita filter story also signals what happens when companies decide not to stonewall but to get into conversation with those who are trying to call for change.	

B. Replace the underlined informal phrasal verbs in the following sentences with a single, more academic, word.

1. Americans use and throw away 2.5 million plastic water bottles every single hour ... ________________

2. All that plastic not only ends up in garbage dumps ... but about 15 percent ends up in the oceans. ________________

3. But when Terry researched it further, she discovered that Brita, not the government, had actually <u>set up</u> the program in Europe. ____________

4. They <u>looked up</u> the names of the executive committee members ... ____________

5. Although they were disappointed to be <u>brushed off</u> with a form letter ... ____________

6. There are times when consumers have to <u>take on</u> companies about their social responsibility ... ____________

C. Identify the characteristics of academic writing that are missing in the sentences below.

1. ... it was a strong indicator that the company was obviously receiving tons of complaints.

 ____

 ____

2. She felt that if she got a bunch of filters, she could ...

 ____

 ____

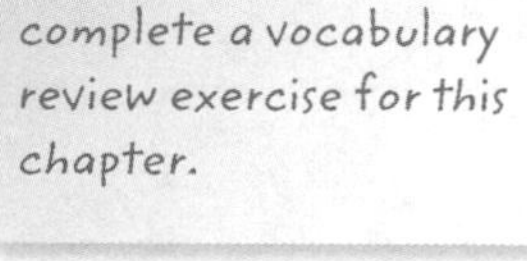

Visit My eLab to complete a vocabulary review exercise for this chapter.

D. Select the best synonym for the underlined words in the following sentences.

1. She chose instead to <u>rally</u> their customers to speak with one voice ...

 a) discourage b) regard c) encourage

2. The filters could only be recycled in Europe through a <u>facility</u> in Germany.

 a) specially constructed building b) large farm c) equipment

Consumer Activism and Corporate Responsibility: The Power of One

This reading is a short online text that explains how the efforts of a single person forced a large corporation to begin a recycling program for its products. Although the author, John Izzo, wrote this article to exemplify the concept of corporate responsibility, it is also a good example of how new media can be used to achieve social capital.

As you read, note the number and type of media (traditional and new) that Beth Terry used in her campaign to get a recycling facility in the United States for Brita water filters.

TRADITIONAL MEDIA: ____________

____

NEW MEDIA: ____________

____

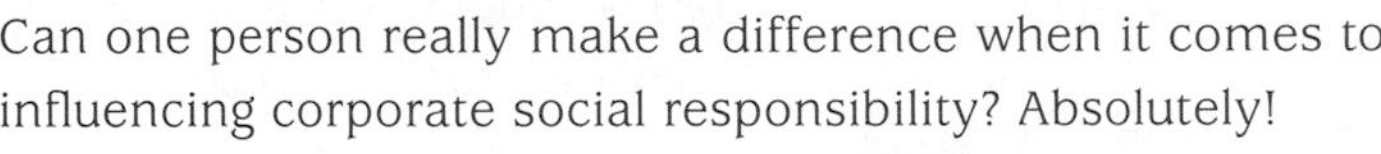

Can one person really make a difference when it comes to influencing corporate social responsibility? Absolutely!

Take the case of Beth Terry, an accountant in Northern California who challenged a major corporation to start a recycling program for one of their most popular products. Her story is an inspiring example of how one person with the right intentions can influence companies.

Plastic waste and pollution is a massive problem. Americans alone use and throw away 2.5 million plastic water bottles every single hour or almost two billion per month! All that plastic (from bottles, shopping bags, plastic straws, etc.) not only ends up in garbage dumps and fuels climate change but about 15 percent ends up in the oceans. The result is a permanent whirlpool of plastic garbage in the Pacific Ocean the size of Texas, and over one million sea birds and mammals die from ingesting this plastic every year.

Recycling Plastic Water Filter Cartridges

In 2007, Terry first began a blog about how she was doing her part to reduce plastic. She started using Brita water filters as an alternative to plastic water bottles but wasn't sure what parts of the filters were recyclable. She wrote to Clorox (Clorox had bought Brita's franchise in America in 2000) to inquire, and they told her they could only be recycled in Europe through a facility in Germany because North American community recycling systems were not set up to handle the filters. But when Terry researched it further, she discovered that Brita, not the government, had actually set up the program in Europe.

Dissatisfied with the answer, she began commenting on her blog. A few months later she went on Google analytics to view her blog stats and to her surprise she discovered that the most common search words to find her blog were "How to Recycle Brita Filters in North America."

Consumer Group Pressures Brita to Recycle Filters

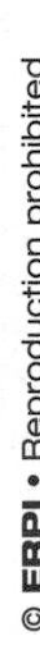

Terry realized that she was not alone in her concern about the issue so she started a campaign and created a Yahoo group. They looked up the names of the executive committee and wrote ten letters each to everyone on the board and they all received a form letter from them blaming the municipal recycling systems.

Although they were disappointed to be brushed off with a form letter, it was a strong indicator that the company was obviously receiving tons of complaints.

They requested meetings with the board but all requests for a meeting were denied so they stepped it up a notch and decided to go public. Terry created a website along with an online petition at www.takebackthefilter.org and set up a post office box asking people to send their used Brita filters.

She felt if she got a bunch of filters she could get media attention focusing on all the filters people were sending in. Terry had never done anything like this, but she took action anyway because it just felt "reasonable."

She contacted every blogger she knew, and despite her lack of experience, tried to pitch the media. She even made a Brita water filter costume and wore it! Her campaign began getting media attention including the *New York Times*.

Brita Responds to Consumer Pressure

A few days after the site went live, Terry got an e-mail from the brand manager at Brita saying, "We see what you're doing. Can we talk?"

He explained they had done focus groups asking if people would be willing to pay extra for a recyclable filter but they didn't get enough public support. But given the huge response Terry received, she *knew* there was support—but the company had to see it all in one place instead of people calling and writing in dribs and drabs.

During the campaign, people sent filters from all over the States and Canada. They didn't just write a letter to Clorox, they actually shipped the filters. They also sent Terry copies of the letters they got back from Brita and the Clorox CEO Don Knauss, who had started writing personal notes back saying they were working on the issue.

Later, when Terry met with the brand manager, he said, "You really didn't expect the CEO of Clorox to respond to you did you?" And Terry said, "Well, yes I did!"

Less than a year later, she got a call from the brand manager saying he wanted her to be the first to know they had developed a recycling program for the filters.

In November 2008, Clorox announced the recycling partnership with PRESERVE and Whole Foods. By January 2009, Terry had collected over 600 filters and delivered them to Whole Foods in Oakland. The brand manager from Brita was there and later the city of Oakland gave a commendation to her, Clorox and Whole Foods for their partnership.

Lessons for Consumer Activists

What is really fascinating about this story is that Terry says she never felt she was "fighting" Clorox but that she was trying to "help" the company. She wanted to make a deliberate attempt not to use language that made the company "the enemy." She chose instead to rally their customers to speak with one voice asking for change.

She picked a company like Brita that was already being environmentally friendly by making the filters as an alternative to using bottled water. Sometimes we can get more traction by helping good companies get better. You see Clorox was already crafting a brand image around being "green" so when Terry started the *Take Back the Filter* campaign, it made it easier to challenge the company to step up.

There are some important lessons in the Brita filter story.

There are times when consumers have to "take on" companies about their social responsibility, but this story illustrates that many times we can accomplish just as much by helping companies see the opportunity by doing good.

When Clorox CEO Don Knauss started sending personal letters saying "we are working on the issue," it moved the company into a different relationship with the activists.

The Brita filter story also signals what happens when companies decide not to stonewall but to get into conversation with those who are trying to call for change. (1032 words)

Izzo, J. (2012, May 14). Consumer activism and corporate responsibility: The power of one. *CSRwire Talkback. The Corporate Social Responsibility Newswire*. Retrieved from http://www.csrwire.com/blog/posts/405-consumer-activism-corporate-responsibility-the-power-of-one

FINAL ASSIGNMENT

Write a Persuasive Essay

Write a persuasive essay in which you agree or disagree with this statement.

> There are more disadvantages to new media than there are advantages.

In your essay, integrate at least four sources of information, writing paraphrases or summaries. Include

- the summary you wrote for your Warm-Up Assignment;
- a paraphrase or summary based on Reading 1, lines 116 to 131;
- a paraphrase or summary based on Reading 3, lines 68 to 92;
- a paraphrase or summary based on one (or more) current, reliable source(s) about the advantages and disadvantages of new media.

You may find and share your additional source(s) with another classmate, but summarize the source(s) and write the essay on your own.

Refer to the Models Chapter (page 204) to see an example of a persuasive essay and to learn more about how to write one.

CHAPTER 6

Online Collaborative Environments

An increasing number of people are participating in online collaborative environments. Together, they are able to exchange information, solve problems and enjoy the rewards of working collaboratively. This collective action would not be possible without new media. Researchers studying how people interact in these online environments are noticing that successful collective action depends on the skills of the online community leaders who host these virtual forums. The readings in this chapter will reveal the skills these leaders need to create successful collaborative environments.

In this chapter, you will

- learn vocabulary related to online collaborative environments;
- compare original and paraphrased text to learn more about paraphrasing and summarizing;
- identify and use metaphor and simile in texts;
- learn how to synthesize information;
- write a summary;
- write an essay in which you synthesize information from two different sources.

GEARING UP

Do you participate in Internet collaborative activities, working online with others to accomplish a common goal? If so, you may have participated in one of the forums listed below. To learn more about online collaborative forums, select two that are interesting, but unfamiliar to you, and find out 1) the goal of the forum, 2) what participants do to accomplish the goal and 3) how participants can get involved. Take notes on a separate sheet of paper so you can discuss what you have learned with the class.

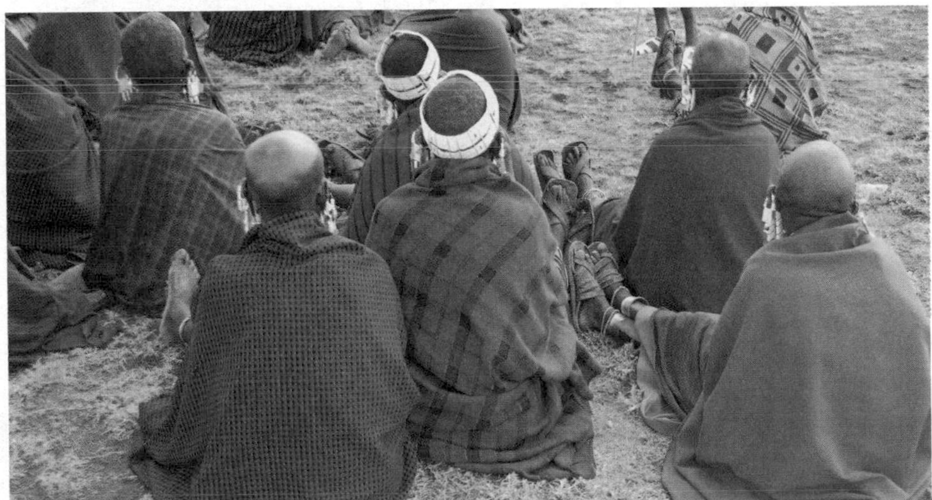

- CrisisWiki: Emergency services mapping game
- DonorsChoose.org: Fundraising for education projects
- EteRNA: RNA molecule mapping
- Folding@home: Biomedical protein-folding puzzles
- Galaxy Zoo: Galaxy classification
- Gene Wiki: Gene mapping
- Inuka.org: Microfinance for women in Africa
- Kickstarter.com: Fundraising for projects
- Kiva.org: Microfinance for the developing world
- Spot.us: Newspaper story identification
- txteagle: Outsourcing of microtasks (a workforce innovation)
- Ushahidi: Crowdsourcing crisis information

VOCABULARY BUILD

Match each of the key words and phrases from Reading 1 to its definition. When you have finished, check your answers as a class, and discuss strategies you will use to help you remember each definition.

Table A

WORD	DEFINITION
1 authority* (n.)	__6__ change
2 components* (n.)	_____ ask
3 differentiate* (v.)	_____ shared
4 enhancing* (v.)	_____ parts
5 explicitly* (adv.)	_____ rebellion
6 modify* (v.)	_____ never having happened before
7 mutual* (adj.)	_____ place used for a specific purpose
8 phenomenon* (n.)	_____ distinguish between
9 pose* (v.)	_____ power
10 revolution* (n.)	_____ improving
11 site* (n.)	_____ specifically
12 survivor* (n.)	_____ something worthy of study
13 unprecedented* (adj.)	_____ someone who continues to live despite threats to his or her life

*Appears on the Academic Word List

Table B

WORD/PHRASE	DEFINITION
1 amateur (n.)	_____ control the natural strength of something
2 augmented (adj.)	_____ find
3 harness (v.)	_____ having many sides
4 mobilize (v.)	_____ makes a great effort
5 multi-faceted (adj.)	_____ performed as well as
6 piecework (n.)	_____ people who are searching for something
7 rivalled (v.)	_____ someone who does something for pleasure, not for work

WORD/PHRASE	DEFINITION
8 seekers (n.)	________ increased or improved
9 sleuth out (v.)	________ help something move more easily
10 strives (v.)	________ employment that pays per number of items produced, not per number of hours worked

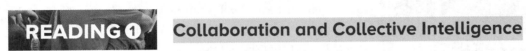

Collaboration and Collective Intelligence

This text was written by Howard Rheingold, one of the authors referenced in Chapter 5, Reading 2. In this reading, Rheingold defines online collaboration and provides some examples. Read the text and then answer the following questions.

1. What is collective action?

____

____

2. Which four terms does Rheingold define by paraphrasing Himmelman?

____

____

3. How do you know that these four terms form a continuum from simple to complex?

____

____

____

4. Give an example (not necessarily media-related) of each of the four terms.

____

____

____

____

5. What is the purpose of the last five paragraphs of this reading?

____

6. What is the definition of *crowdsourcing*, and why is the Eli Lilly example so unprecedented?

____

____

____

____

7. In which online collaborative forums (if any) would you consider participating?

____

____

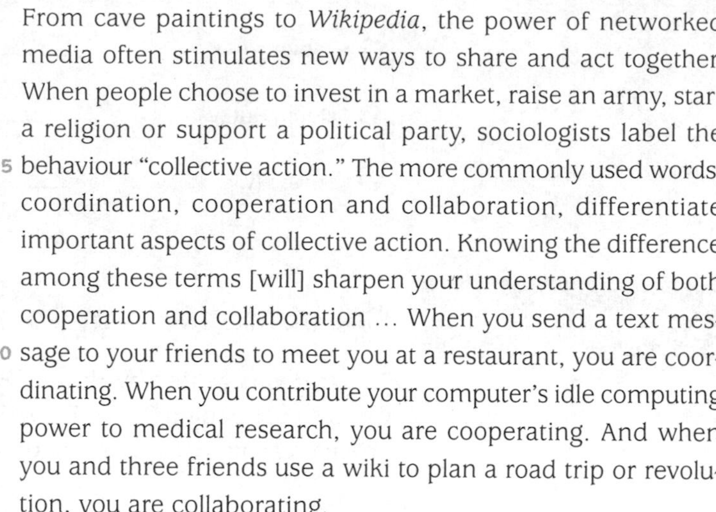

From cave paintings to *Wikipedia*, the power of networked media often stimulates new ways to share and act together. When people choose to invest in a market, raise an army, start a religion or support a political party, sociologists label the behaviour "collective action." The more commonly used words, coordination, cooperation and collaboration, differentiate important aspects of collective action. Knowing the difference among these terms [will] sharpen your understanding of both cooperation and collaboration ... When you send a text message to your friends to meet you at a restaurant, you are coordinating. When you contribute your computer's idle computing power to medical research, you are cooperating. And when you and three friends use a wiki to plan a road trip or revolution, you are collaborating.

... Arthur Himmelman detailed the differences between networking, coordination, cooperation and collaboration ... Here, paraphrased in my own words, is how Himmelman differentiates these four related components.

1. *Networking* is the simplest, with the least risk and commitment—such as handing out business cards, attending conferences, hanging out in a chat room or commenting on a blog.

2. *Coordination* means that all involved parties share information and agree to modify their activities for mutual benefit. Neighbours need to coordinate the time they flood rice paddies in order to control the population of vermin who eat the crop. If all the neighbours don't flood at the same time, then the vermin will simply move to the nearest dry ground and threaten the whole neighbourhood come harvest time.

3. *Cooperation*, as Himmelman defines it, is "exchanging information, altering activities and sharing resources for mutual benefit and to achieve a common purpose."[1] The amount of commitment and risk is higher than coordination (although cooperation often involves coordination) and the move from "mutual benefit" to "common purpose" requires moving from self-interest to agreement on what, exactly, all parties agree to hold as common goals. Sharing resources is a big step. Modifying activities may involve more systemic change by each party than simple coordination required. Himmelman emphasizes that groups can move from networking to coordination to cooperation by building trust, communication and explicitly seeking a common purpose ...

4. *Collaboration* is the most purposeful means of collective action. It uses networking, coordination and cooperation as building blocks, adding to "exchanging information, modifying activities, etc.," the requirements of "enhancing the capacity of another for mutual benefit and to achieve a common purpose by sharing risks, resources, responsibilities and rewards."[2] People collaborate because their coordination, sharing and attention to common goals creates something that none of the collaborating parties could have benefited from without collaboration. Collaborators develop and agree on common goals, share responsibility and work together to achieve those goals, and contribute resources to the effort.

...

Collective intelligence comes in many flavours. A tribe of television fans known as "spoilers" mobilize a kind of collective intelligence on a global scale in order to outwit the secretive producers of programs such as *Survivor* by figuring out who is going to win before the official announcement. Because the *Survivor* series is recorded months before it is broadcast, with the cast and crew sworn to secrecy, only a few people know who the final surviving winner is before the announcement. By talking to bartenders in hotels where the cast might have stayed, piecing together small pieces of information contributed by members of the online spoilers' community, and arguing vociferously online about what the evidence means, spoiler communities have rivalled intelligence services in their ability to collectively sleuth out the answers.

...

Tomas Malone, professor of management at the MIT Sloan School and founding director of the MIT Center for Collective Intelligence, not only strives to discover and apply knowledge about augmented collective intelligence to the challenges of business management but also to some of those "complex, urgent" problems that Engelbart and others foresaw such as climate change. One of the centre's projects is Climate CoLab, an online site that "seeks to harness the collective intelligence of thousands of people around the world to address global climate change. Inspired by systems like *Wikipedia* and Linux, the Climate CoLab is a global, online forum in which people can create, analyze and select detailed proposals for what to do about climate change."[3]

...

On January 28, 2007, Jim Gray, a sixty-three-year-old computer scientist and experienced sailor took his forty-foot cruiser out of San Francisco Bay on a mission to scatter his mother's ashes at sea. He never returned. No radio calls or emergency beacons signalled his disappearance. Gray had made significant discoveries in the field of distributed computation and had many friends in the computer science world—some of whom mobilized extraordinary resources to try to find their friend. Google and NASA provided recent satellite photographs of the forty thousand square miles where Gray had gone missing. Amazon engineers divided the photographs into a half-million fragments and used Amazon's Mechanical Turk engine to make these images available to twelve thousand online volunteers. This unprecedented mobilization of resources failed to find Gray, but illustrates just one aspect of the multi-faceted power of crowdsourcing: tackling massive problems by dividing them among online volunteers and aggregating their efforts.

Jeff Howe, writing in *Wired* magazine, gave the name *crowdsourcing* to the phenomenon of breaking problems or tasks into small pieces, and then making an open call for voluntary participation.[4] One of Howe's examples was Innocentive, the "solution market" that the pharmaceutical company Eli Lilly created in 2001 in order to take advantage of brainpower outside the company—a daring move to crowdsource ideas in a notoriously secretive industry.[5] Scientists with problems to solve ("seekers") can pose them in the marketplace. Others ("solvers"), not necessarily

in the same company or even an authority in the field where the problem arose, can sell their solutions to the seekers for ten to a hundred thousand dollars. Here's a typical story: a Swiss radiologist who was thinking about ways to look at bones in 3-D came up with a solution for a petroleum geologist seeking ways to analyze geologic structures in 3-D.[6]

The business world definitely started paying attention to crowdsourcing even closely held data when a failing mining company in Canada, Goldcorp, put all its geologic data—again, usually kept secret—online and offered prizes to anybody who could show where to find more gold. After paying out a half million dollars in prize money, Goldcorp mined an additional three billion dollars in gold from a previously underperforming mine.[7] Crowdsourced wealth is being created by amateur fashion designers as well as gold mine owners: one million online Threadless community members upload designs for T-shirts and vote on the best designs, and the weekly winners are manufactured and sold, sometimes bringing significant profits to the designers.[8] [Similarly,] Amazon's Mechanical Turk connects people willing to do small piecework tasks for small amounts of money—proofreading documents, classifying photographs or transcribing recordings—with people and enterprises looking for inexpensive labour.[9]

(1233 words)

Notes

1. Arthur T. Himmelman, "Collaboration for a Change: Definitions, Decision-Making Models, Roles, and Collaboration Process Guide," Himmelman Consulting, http://depts.washington.edu/ccph/pdf_files/4achange.pdf.
2. Ibid.
3. Available at http://climatecolab.org/web/guest.
4. Jeff Howe, "The Rise of Crowdsourcing," *Wired*, June 2006.
5. Available at http://www.innocentive.com.
6. "Innocentive: Crowdsourcing Ideas," *Finding Petroleum*, January 10, 2011, http://www.findingpetroleum.com/n/Innocentive_crowdsourcing_ideas/2bf5f9a7.aspx.
7. Don Tapscott, and Anthony Williams, "Innovation in the Age of Mass Collaboration," *Bloomberg Business Week*, February 1, 2007, http://www.businessweek.com/innovate/content/feb2007/id20070201_774736.htm.
8. Available at http://www.threadless.com.
9. "Mechanical Turk is a Marketplace for Work," http://www.mturk.com/mturk/welcome.

Rheingold, H. (2012). *Net smart: How to thrive online* (pp. 153–168). Cambridge, MA: MIT Press.

Comparing Original and Paraphrased Writing

As a developing academic writer, you are likely interested in how other writers paraphrase and summarize. In Reading 1, Rheingold paraphrases Himmelman's definitions of networking, coordinating, cooperating and collaborating.

In fact, if you compare Himmelman's four original definitions with Rheingold's paraphrased definitions, you will discover that Rheingold paraphrased the first sentence of Himmelman's definitions, and finished by providing his own examples to illustrate the definitions.

To learn more about paraphrasing and summarizing, compare each of Himmelman's original definitions with Rheingold's paraphrases and then answer the questions that follow.

HIMMELMAN'S ORIGINAL	RHEINGOLD'S PARAPHRASE
Networking is defined as exchanging information for mutual benefit. Networking is the most informal of the inter-organizational linkages and often reflects an initial level of trust, limited time availability and a reluctance to share turf.	*Networking* is the simplest, with the least risk and commitment—such as handing out business cards, attending conferences, hanging out in a chat room or commenting on a blog.

1. Why does Rheingold keep the word *networking* in his definition?

   ____

   ____

2. What examples does Rheingold give to define networking?

   ____

   ____

3. Which ideas from the original definition does Rheingold not include?

   ____

   ____

HIMMELMAN'S ORIGINAL	RHEINGOLD'S PARAPHRASE
Coordinating is defined as exchanging information and altering activities for mutual benefit and to achieve a common purpose. Coordinating requires more organizational involvement than networking and is a very crucial change strategy. Coordinated services are "user-friendly" and eliminate or reduce barriers for those seeking access to them. Compared to networking, coordinating involves more time, higher levels of trust yet little or no access to each other's turf.	*Coordination* means that all involved parties share information and agree to modify their activities for mutual benefit. Neighbours need to coordinate the time they flood rice paddies in order to control the population of vermin who eat the crop. If all the neighbours don't flood at the same time, then the vermin will simply move to the nearest dry ground and threaten the whole neighbourhood come harvest time.

4. Rheingold doesn't replace "mutual benefit" with a synonym. Can you think of one? ______________________________

5. Which synonyms does Rheingold use to replace "exchanging" and "altering"?

   ____

6. Which ideas in Himmelman's definition are not included in the paraphrase?

   ____

   ____

HIMMELMAN'S ORIGINAL	RHEINGOLD'S PARAPHRASE
Cooperating is defined as exchanging information, altering activities and sharing resources for mutual benefit and to achieve a common purpose. Cooperating requires greater organizational commitments than networking or coordinating and, in some cases, may involve written (perhaps, even legal) agreements. Shared resources can encompass a variety of human, financial and technical contributions, including knowledge, staffing, physical property, access to people, money and others. Cooperating can require a substantial amount of time, high levels of trust and significant access to each other's turf.	*Cooperation*, as Himmelman defines it, is "exchanging information, altering activities and sharing resources for mutual benefit and to achieve a common purpose."[1] The amount of commitment and risk is higher than coordination (although cooperation often involves coordination) and the move from "mutual benefit" to "common purpose" requires moving from self-interest to agreement on what, exactly, all parties agree to hold as common goals. Sharing resources is a big step. Modifying activities may involve more systemic change by each party than simple coordination required. Himmelman emphasizes that groups can move from networking to coordination to cooperation by building trust, communication and explicitly seeking a common purpose.

7. Why must Rheingold provide a citation for his first sentence?

____

8. Why did Rheingold decide not to replace "mutual benefit" and "common purpose" with synonyms?

____

9. Why does Rheingold not provide a citation for his mention of Himmelman in the last sentence?

____

HIMMELMAN'S ORIGINAL	RHEINGOLD'S PARAPHRASE
Collaborating is defined as exchanging information, altering activities, sharing resources, and enhancing the capacity of another for mutual benefit and to achieve a common purpose. The qualitative difference between collaborating and cooperating in this definition is the willingness of organizations (or individuals) to enhance each other's capacity for mutual benefit and a common purpose. In this definition, collaborating is a relationship in which each organization wants to help its partners become the best that they can be at what they do. This definition also assumes that when organizations collaborate they share risks, responsibilities and rewards, each of which contributes to enhancing each other's capacity to achieve a common purpose. Collaborating is usually characterized by substantial time commitments, very high levels of trust, and extensive areas of common turf. A summary definition of organizational collaboration is a process in which organizations exchange information, alter activities, share resources and enhance each other's capacity for mutual benefit and a common purpose by sharing risks, responsibilities and rewards.	*Collaboration* is the most purposeful means of collective action. It uses networking, coordination and cooperation as building blocks, adding to "exchanging information, modifying activities, etc.," the requirements of "enhancing the capacity of another for mutual benefit and to achieve a common purpose by sharing risks, resources, responsibilities and rewards." People collaborate because their coordination, sharing and attention to common goals creates something that none of the collaborating parties could have benefited from without collaboration. Collaborators develop and agree on common goals, share responsibility and work together to achieve those goals, and contribute resources to the effort.

10. For each quotation in Rheingold's paraphrase, underline the original part in Himmelman's definition. Do you notice slight differences between the texts? Discuss your observations with a partner.

WARM-UP ASSIGNMENT

Write a Summary

! When you receive feedback from your instructor or your classmates on this Warm-Up Assignment, you will have some information that you can use to improve your writing on the Final Assignment.

Before beginning this task, review the techniques writers use to paraphrase and summarize another author's work. (See the Academic Survival Skill in Chapter 5, page 116.) Then, summarize Himmelman's original definitions (from the Focus on Reading) in your own words. In order not to plagiarize Rheingold's paraphrases, be sure to include all of Himmelman's original ideas, and do not provide examples of the concepts to illustrate the definitions as Rheingold did.

You will need this summary for the Final Assignment.

VOCABULARY BUILD

A. Read the following sentences adapted from Reading 2. Use the context to define the words in bold.

WORDS IN CONTEXT	DEFINITION
1 The strongest predictor of whether someone will **assist*** you online is whether you've aided others.	assist (v.): *help*
2 I adopted this **attitude*** from the Wikipedians, some of whom write scholarly articles and some of whom clean up misplaced commas.	attitude (n.):
3 Communities don't just happen **automatically*** when you supply communication tools.	automatically (adv.):
4 Remember to be fair and **civil*** when challenged.	civil (adj.):
5 An online leader should add knowledge, offer help, be slow to anger, apologize when wrong, politely ask for **clarification*** and exercise patience.	clarification (n.):
6 An online leader encourages a shared **commitment*** to work together toward better communication and conversations.	commitment (n.):
7 Online leaders must acknowledge other people by name, assume benevolence and assert trust until **convinced*** otherwise.	convinced (v.):
8 A small number of simple, clear rules, sparsely **enforced,*** are important at first.	enforced (adj.):
9 **Eventually,*** natural hosts emerge in each community.	eventually (adv.):
10 An online community organizer is like a party **host**.	host (n.):
11 Online hosting establishes conditions for **ongoing*** collaboration that reward individual effort.	ongoing (adj.):
12 Good online discussions help people entertain themselves rather than being only **passive*** consumers of entertainment created by others.	passive (adj.):
13 A virtual host should point others to information that will be personally **relevant*** to them.	relevant (adj.):
14 You may build an online forum, and nobody will come, and if they come, they won't necessarily start a **self-sustaining*** conversation.	self-sustaining (adj.):

*Appears on the Academic Word List

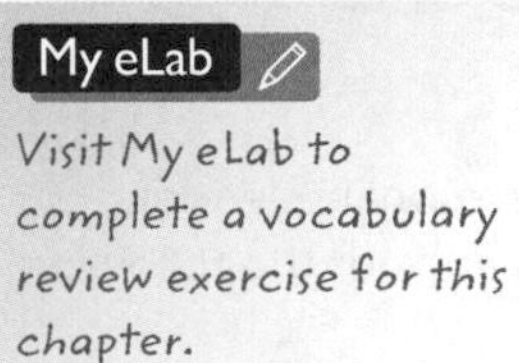
My eLab
Visit My eLab to complete a vocabulary review exercise for this chapter.

B. Based on your understanding of the sentences in task A, what do you think Reading 2 will be about?

____

____

C. There are a number of expressions in Reading 2 that make the writing more interesting. These are listed in the table on the next page. Read each expression and its explanation, and then connect each to a situation or event from your own experience. This is a good way to help you remember the expressions. Discuss your connections with the class.

EXPRESSION	EXPLANATION	CONNECTION TO MY EXPERIENCE
throw a great party	give or host an event	*When I graduate from school, I will throw a great party to celebrate.*
let their hair down	relax and have a good time after a period of hard work	
model the behaviour	demonstrate the behaviour that you want others to follow	
tempers flare	people get angry	
from the ground up	developed by the people or participants, not by the administration or government	
from the top down	developed by the administration or government, not by the people or participants	
scout and mentor [new hosts]	find and support new leaders	
bend over backward	make a great effort	
point out the pitfalls	show the problems with something	
One ounce of elegance and grace is worth ten pounds of argument. (An adaptation of the proverb "An ounce of prevention is worth a pound of cure.")	It is better to stop a problem before it happens than to deal with the consequences after it has happened.	

READING 2

Virtual Communities: Norms for Members and Advice for Hosts

In this excerpt, Rheingold provides guidelines for collaborative online leaders (hosts) and leadership development. Read the text and then answer the following questions.

1. What are the four norms of behaviour, which have evolved from the earliest days of the Internet, for people who want to participate in a collaborative online forum?

____

____

2. Why is it so easy to misunderstand someone's comments in an online forum?

3. What does Rheingold mean by the term "gift economies" (line 38)?

4. What are some of the most important pieces of advice that Rheingold gives to virtual community hosts?

5. Rheingold believes that any assertion of online authority won't work. Explain whether or not you agree with him.

6. In which other areas of life might the qualities of an ideal online community host (or leader) also be useful?

[What are] … the norms of behaviour that were propagated among the Internet pioneers in order to make life less stressful and more productive for everybody? The first norm was: *Pay attention before you join in.* Sample the stream of comments daily for a few days to get a sense of a blog community, chat room and discussion board …

Observe the way people interact in the community that interests you. If you have a question, ask someone quietly (that is, avoid broadcasting your question to the entire community if possible). Any community that rebuffs the informed question of a newcomer who has looked around and understands the local mores is not a community worth investing yourself in.

Without tone of voice, facial expression and body language, text-only online discussions strip a surprising amount of emotional context from the cues we use to surmise what other people really intend. It's easy to mistake mild sarcasm online as a personal attack, leading to what old-timers called *flame wars*, and that abound to this day in social media forums of all kinds. When I started my third or fourth virtual community, one of the first things I began asking all members to agree to was to *assume goodwill*. If it seems to you that someone else is directing a negative communication your way, I advised newcomers, assume that the lack of social cues is causing you to misinterpret: ask friendly questions to find out what the other party intended.

A third useful tool for aspiring virtual communitarians is to *jump in where you can add value*. I adopted this attitude from the Wikipedians, some of whom write scholarly articles and some of whom clean up misplaced commas …

Finally, *reciprocate* when someone does you a favour or shows a courtesy. If you are unknown to the community, reciprocate in advance. Pay it forward by answering questions or responding in other ways to the needs of community members. Show your willingness to help others ... There is hard evidence that the strongest predictor of whether someone will assist you online is whether you've aided others.

Do those four things—know the territory, assume goodwill, jump in wherever you can add value and reciprocate—and you'll succeed as a virtual community member.

Now that it's easy to start a mail group, publish a blog and create a chat room or wiki with a few keystrokes, knowing something about the art of hosting successful online communities is a skill that millions of people find useful ... [In my essay] titled "The Art of Hosting Good Conversations Online,"[1] [I state that] an online host wants to achieve a feeling of ownership by the group, whereby participants become evangelists; facilitate a spirit of group creativity, experimentation, exploration and goodwill; and encourage a shared commitment to work together toward better communication and conversations. Good online discussions help people make contact with other people, entertain themselves rather than being only passive consumers of entertainment created by others, create gift economies for knowledge sharing and establish conditions for ongoing collaboration that reward individual effort with a whole that is greater than the sum of its parts; they also make newcomers feel welcomed and contributors feel valued ...

A virtual community organizer is like a party host. You don't automatically throw a great party by hiring a room and buying some beer. Someone needs to invite an interesting mix of people, greet them at the door, make introductions, start conversations, avert [fights] and encourage people to let their hair down and entertain each other. Good hosts model the behaviour they want others to emulate: read carefully and post entertainingly, informatively and economically, acknowledge other people by name, assume benevolence, assert trust until convinced otherwise, add knowledge, offer help, be slow to anger, apologize when wrong, politely ask for clarification and exercise patience when tempers flare. They nurture the community memory, pointing newcomers to archives and explaining inside references, providing links to related conversations past and present and hunting down resources to add to the collective pool of knowledge—and teaching others to do the same.

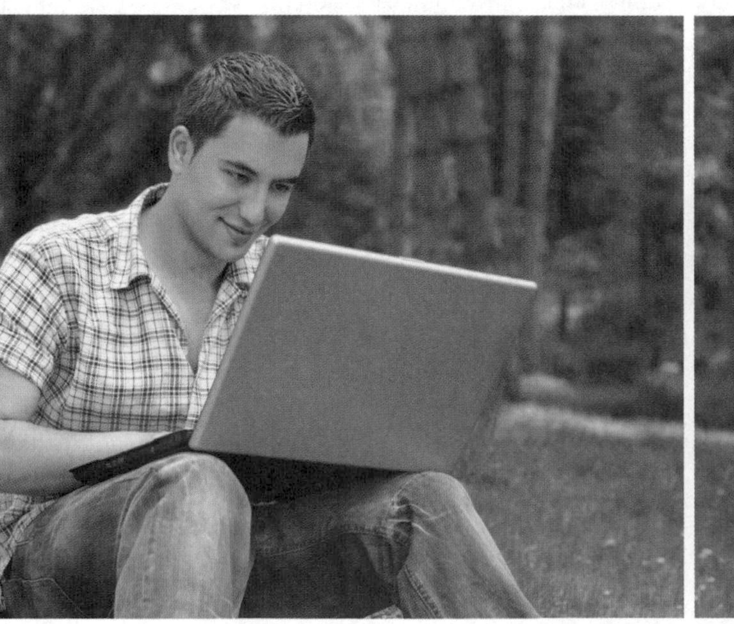

Communities don't just happen automatically when you supply communication tools; online communities grow under the right conditions. They are gardened. Online social systems will not cohere without careful intervention. Build one, and nobody will come, and if they come, they won't necessarily start a self-sustaining conversation. But the intervention has to be ground up, not top down. Positive effort is required to create the circumstances and tend the growth of a self-sustaining group.

A small number of simple, clear rules, sparsely enforced, with an explicit expectation that the community's own norms will emerge later, are important at first. Establish the rules at the outset and then move on. Those who don't like it will leave. The rest will make up their own minds after they get to know each other and the system. Making rules after launching or changing them from the top down is a recipe for a community-killing rules thrash. Provide a decision-making protocol at the beginning; don't negotiate it online or you will spiral into endless toxic metacommentary about how to decide to decide.

Eventually, natural hosts emerge in each community, and existing hosts should scout and mentor them. In regard to host behaviour, patience is rule numbers one through three. Deliberately add a time delay on your emotional responses before you make any public posting or send a private e-mail. In most cases, not saying anything is the best decision. The first art of the host is the knowledge of how and when not to act. Bend over backward to be fair and civil when challenged ... Have fun! Signal that it's OK to experiment as well as not take yourself and the whole enterprise too seriously. One ounce of elegance and grace is worth ten pounds of argument. You can charm or seduce discussions back on topic, and steer conflicts away from the brink of brawl, but you can't force them. Force backfires on authority online. You have to persuade and pull because pushing is an automatic loss for authority. People's first reactions are most important. Praise them by name. Be interested. Read their profiles and point them to information that you think will be personally relevant to them. Communicate privately via e-mail with both promising newcomers and troublemakers. Never disclose private e-mail in a public forum. Point out the pitfalls of the medium that cause people to misunderstand each other.

I've found the skills of participating in virtual communities along with creating my own virtual communities to prove valuable in finding friends, having fun, learning what I need to know, seeking support during a medical crisis, organizing business and political activities in the physical world, and finding and organizing collaborators for ventures lasting a week or decade, writing books and growing learning communities. These skills aren't going away, even if we now call it social media instead of virtual community. (1173 words)

Note

1. Howard Rheingold, "The Art of Hosting Good Conversations Online," 1998, http://rheingold.com/texts/artonlinehost.html.

Rheingold, H. (2012). *Net smart: How to thrive online* (pp. 163–167). Cambridge, MA: MIT Press.

Using Metaphor and Simile in Writing

A metaphor suggests one thing is equivalent to another (without using *like* or *as*); a simile is a comparison using *like* or *as*. In Reading 2, there are two excellent examples of the use of metaphor and simile, in which the author compares first an online leader and then an online community to other things.

A. Reread the first sentence of the paragraph beginning with line 42.

1. To which other activity does the author compare the work of a virtual community organizer (or an online leader)? Is this a metaphor or a simile?

2. Read the rest of the paragraph and underline other words that emphasize this comparison.

3. Reread lines 57 to 67 and identify the comparison made there. Is this a metaphor or a simile?

4. Which verb in the final sentence of that paragraph (lines 65 to 67) extends the comparison?

Using simile and metaphor in writing is one way to help readers understand concepts. Comparing an online leader to that of a party host helps readers better appreciate the skills required to do the job well. For example, "invite an interesting mix of people, greet them at the door, make introductions," are all key words or phrases that further the concept of online leader as party host. Using simile and metaphor also allows writers to select vocabulary that effectively illustrates what they want their readers to *see*. It is this feature that might interest you most as a writer.

To demonstrate this point, here is a list of other topics often illustrated through the use of simile and metaphor, with a series of words and phrases that can be used to support the comparison.

TOPIC	COMPARED TO A ...	WORDS/PHRASES THAT SUPPORT THE COMPARISON
ECONOMY	plant	The economy can *grow, wither, die, thrive* or *flourish*.
	car	The economy can *speed up, slow down, stall, run smoothly, break down, reverse, skid* and *crash*. The government can *lose control* of the economy.
MEDICINE	war	Medicine can *protect, defend* or *wage war* against disease. Medicine can *combat* illness. Illnesses *attack* the body. The body must *resist* disease.
STORM	angry person	A storm can *rage, hit, strike, lash* and *batter* a region.
ONLINE FORUM	physical space	You can *enter, visit, exit* or *look at* an online site. You can *meet* and *chat* with people online. Participants *form a community*.
COMPUTER VIRUS	disease	Your computer can be *attacked* by a bug or a virus, the virus can be *contagious* and *anti-virus* software can protect against it.

One way to find words and phrases that support your use of simile or metaphor is to look at collocations listed in the dictionary for your topic. Many of the verbs that collocate with a noun point to the type of comparison that may be appropriate.

B. Choose a topic from the table (or one of your own in consultation with your instructor) and, on a separate sheet of paper, write a paragraph of five or six sentences in which you use simile or metaphor to compare the topic to something else. You can use the comparison provided in the table or select another. Check the collocations in your dictionary to help you select appropriate words and phrases to support your comparison.

READING 3 Creative "Communities": How Technology Mediates Social Worlds

A. Skim the reading and, on a separate sheet of paper, take notes on the topic, length, text type and probable organization. Then, turn the seven headings from the text into questions.

B. Read the text more closely and answer the questions you have generated. When you have finished, confirm your answers with a partner.

Introducing Tom

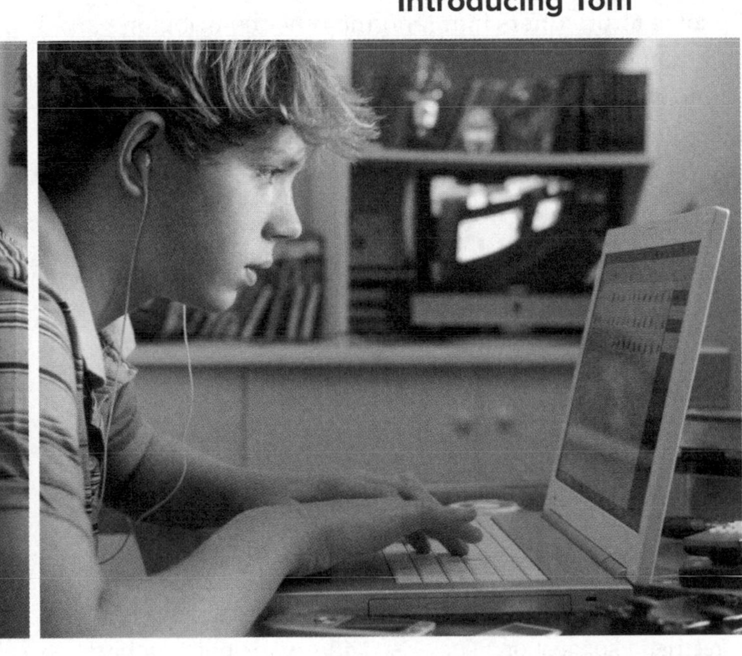

We first met Tom in 2001 when he walked through the doors of WAC [Weekend Arts College] Performing Arts and Media College, an informal education centre in London (www.wac.co.uk). The college runs a programme, on Sundays, offering performing arts and media production classes for young people aged fourteen to twenty-four. Tom (then only fourteen) had come along to sign up for Digital Design. It was clear from his admission interview that he was serious about developing himself as an artist and that he had an interest in the Internet as a potential platform on which he might publish his work. While his digital design skills were underdeveloped, what struck us at the time was Tom's ability to reference and name-drop other new media design companies and artists in the same way that aspiring filmmakers will comment on favourite directors. The positioning of himself as a young digital art student within the context of the "grown-up" new media industry, showed that even at fourteen Tom was thinking about how he might develop a career as a digital artist. At school, Tom's favourite and strongest subject was Art and Graphics, and after completing his GCSEs [General Certificate of Secondary Education] (now at sixteen years of age) he has been accepted into a full-time Graphic Design course at a well-known London art college. Besides graphic and multimedia design, Tom's interest in the creative industries (both as a producer and consumer) includes film, television, computer games, animation and music.

... In 2003 [Tom] found an online community, which would support and encourage his self-directed learning. However, this wasn't a website intended for e-learning or even digital artists, but instead was a forum on the message board for the official website of indie rock band Interpol. He discussed his interest and participation in this forum with us during a series of taped conversations in late 2003 ...

The Interpol Message Board

...

The forum that concerns us here is dedicated to the sharing of "Interpol artwork and photos." Within that forum users have hijacked the message board as a place to post original digital artwork for other Interpol fans to critique and share production tips ... Here users publish their self-produced alternative album covers, posters, desktop wallpaper and flyers.

It is clear that first and foremost, the message board as a whole offers a place in cyberspace for Interpol fans to socialize—exchanging thoughts about the band, jokes, musical tastes and recommendations—and in a sense the sharing of digital artwork within a dedicated forum grew out of this. According to Tom, this particular forum was developed because of pressure by fans, who began to post artwork, and requested that a dedicated forum for their work be set up. The site administrators obliged and the Interpol artwork and photos forum was born.

Finding an Audience

...

From talking to Tom and reading the exchanges, it is immediately apparent that the Interpol artwork and photos forum offers him (and the other contributors) an audience for their work. If nothing else, this sense of audience has provided Tom with increased confidence and motivation: "It's a good way to get your ego up and so you do more work," although at the same time he is adamant that he does not produce work "for" the forum but for himself. Posting to the forum is perceived as an afterthought ...

There exists a paradox here. On the one hand the audience is viewed as providing an ego boost "so you do more work," and yet work is not specifically produced for this audience. However, the audience that Tom has found (despite being made up of virtual identities), is acutely responsive and acts as a source of encouragement, criticism and even collaboration.

Practical Advice and Collaboration

Within the Interpol artwork and photos forum, messages ... [provide] practical advice. These are exchanges that directly offer specific suggestions about how to improve or develop a work in progress. This can be anything from how to make better use of the software used or detailed aesthetic suggestions such as "add text or put in a background image." Tom told us of one important instance (that is, important to him) where the forum moderator Chavo made several key suggestions resulting in the reworking of one of his creations ...

Tom had started with some raw source material, a picture of Interpol's lead singer: "It was a nice picture I found so I decided to trace[1] it ... so it looks like a comic or something ..." After Tom had published it on the forum, Chavo offered some suggestions as it "looked a bit odd":

> ... he told me to add some sort of background with buildings, which I did ... with a picture I'd done already where I'd traced a picture of the twin towers. So I just added that in the background ... and the work actually looked much better.

Sometimes practical suggestions lead to collaboration. Users request that they are sent an editable version of the work—in the native Photoshop file format (.psd) so that they can rework or remix it into something new ...

In [these cases], it is not just the distribution and communication function of the message board that supports creative collaboration but the digital authoring tools used by the members. Digital authoring software often allows users to save their creations in a file format that is open to further editing and changes ...

Learning Community Members and Leaders

...

Technically, Chavo is the Interpol artwork and photos forum moderator. Moderators are designated by members of a message board who have been given additional privileges by the message board administrator. Moderators are allowed to edit or delete posts within their allocated forum and are typically chosen because they are seen as active participants and are experienced or expert in the subject for which the forum is set up. Chavo's own Web presence suggests he is a professional graphic artist and he is obviously a dedicated fan of the band. Partly because he is such an active member of the forum and because his artwork is of professional standard, he has come to have an influence on the work and progress of forum members, and in particular Tom ...

Over time, Tom has come to trust the critique offered by Chavo, mainly we think, on account of the quality of Chavo's own artwork. Despite receiving praise from various members of the forum ("great work"), a recent creation that Tom posted did not receive approval. Chavo told him:

> Take it down and redo it. You have done much better and this isn't the quality we have come to expect from you. C'mon, you know you can do better. Rework and resubmit. (Post by Chavo, 22 October, 2003)

Here Chavo has clearly taken on the role of teacher or mentor. The final comment is perhaps most telling. To us, the words "rework and resubmit" echo an examiner's red pen! Yet, for Tom this is as far from formal education as it gets.

> It's completely different from college ... college is learning and stuff like that. This is just a board of people just doing whatever.

Tom's refusal to describe the learning that takes place within the forum as educational is of course consistent with his previous comments about how he does not create artwork for the forum. However, we would suggest that the forum is indeed a learning community—but that defining it as such is at odds with the forum's cultural meaning for participants.

...

Teaching and Learning—Technologies of Collaboration

...

Unlike live or real-time chat rooms, communication on a message board is asynchronous. This allows an idea or problem to be posted at the moment of discovery—and for it to be read and replied to by a wide range of participants because they don't have to be online at that moment in time. It could be minutes, days or months after the original post. Discussions are threaded and organized in such a way that allows latecomers to track back and see what has been said already—so that any insight or advice offered usually contributes something new to the solution creating a sense of an ongoing narrative.

Message boards set up to facilitate the exchange of practical knowledge tend not to discriminate between temporary and sustained collaboration. First-time or infrequent contributors are welcomed and supported in just the same way as regular users. It is not uncommon to hit a programming problem and, unable to solve it alone, to dive into a well-populated forum and ask for ideas and solutions from the wider development community. Often this will involve a number of exchanges—where a specific solution is not always given but is sufficient to point the user in the right direction or to kick start another round of creativity—only for that user to never frequent the board again. This kind of "no strings attached, just in time" creative collaboration is uniquely facilitated by the message board. However, as a tool, it does not limit users. Features such as the ability to create dedicated topic forums and send private messages to individual users, allow ad hoc collaborations to develop into sustained and more formal relationships. We will suggest below that this is common in the incubation of open projects, which go on to be supported by a community of developers.

As Turkle (1995) and others have argued, the identity of users in or on message boards is crucial to their success. Some message boards allow users to post anonymously, but most require that each user join the board after creating a user account, thereby creating an online identity whose sole purpose is to provide a voice for the contributions that they make ... An online identity can remain as anonymous as the user chooses. This, we suggest, removes many of the inhibitions associated with asking for help and from those perceived to be at a higher skill level. While this may make it easier to ask for assistance or to ask beginner questions, it would follow that it should be easier for users to criticize or put down other members of the community. However, in our experience this is rarely the case and, as Raymond (1999) argues, this kind of generous information exchange represents a "gift culture" which is based around the positive aspects of sharing practical knowledge quite dissimilar from any competitive or negative exchanges familiar to the assessed school environment.

The Interpol artwork and photos forum exhibits a strong sense of ownership by regular contributors. This is very much due to the way in which the forum was created (from the ground up) and the fact that the designated forum moderator Chavo was one of the original contributors who lobbied for it to be set up. Most message board software allows levels of control to be allocated to its users. Where this regulation is relaxed and allows for users to create new designated forums around particular topics, and where moderators use their powers for administrative purposes rather than to censor what has been posted, the best conditions for collaborative communities are created ...

Teaching and Learning—The Collaborative Model

...

Part of Tom's reluctance to identify the forum as in any way important to his development lay in his conceptualization of it as "fun" or "jokey," as a place to "have a laugh." We realized in discussion that this was an important classification for Tom ... Recently, considerable attention has been paid to how important a learner's concept of themselves is (as learners) as well as the complementary role that the activity of learning plays in identity construction ... (Davis et al., 2000; Gee, 2003) ...

It seems to us crucial that Tom felt confident to participate in this forum quite soon after he joined. He doesn't seem to have hung around waiting to get involved, but quickly introduced himself and his interests to the forum. Here the role of anonymity is crucial. Again and again, Tom emphasized how the forum didn't matter, that for all his work, for all the praise and feedback he received, it was fun and therefore not to be overvalued. We obviously didn't take this at face value, but what it shows us is how being able to put yourself in situations where you can take risks, where not so much hangs on each action or event and where trust in friendly camaraderie is almost part of the implicit contract you sign on joining up to such a forum (and we'd suggest that anyone in this community who broke such rules would have been excluded), is a rich and necessary creative environment.

Two other features of the social interaction fostered by the forum are important in this mix. First is the role of Chavo—the allegedly experienced, professional graphic artist—who seems to us to play a mentoring role for Tom in particular and possibly for the forum in general. Secondly, we were interested in the discourses of criticism, which seemed very important to us in specifically developing Tom's creative work. Chavo is important because he represents some sort of authority. We are sure he really is a professional artist, and his integrity is confirmed by his own website (hyperlinked to the forum). This gives him authority and authenticity and possibly gave Tom and the other younger members of the community a direction to which they could aspire. As we have already implied, the actual critical commentary used by Chavo and the other members of the group is also quite different from that used in education—even art schools ... The language used here was very practical and very direct. Phrases, like "use up the dead space," and "change fonts," etc., were used directly. Tom found this discourse helpful and clearly didn't find its brevity or directness off-putting. Again, the half anonymity of the remarks coupled with a sense of fun and consequent-less adventure (in the sense that it didn't matter and he could try out or experiment without worrying about formal feedback) is instructive. While

Tom's tutors at Art School, we are sure, would like to think they can create the same kind of trusting environment, Tom told us how much more worried he was by their comments on his work, whereas this medium allowed for a freer kind of exchange and development. The fact that this criticism was extremely practical and direct again seems to be more useful than the discourse of evaluation used in more formal educational settings. However, we would be cautious about this conclusion because it seems to us that the fact the forum is different and unlike Art School is important in itself. We aren't suggesting that Art School should become like the forum, more that a properly creative environment for young people like Tom requires exposure to both kinds of experiences, that the forum and the Art School together provide the right kinds of learning infrastructure.

(2608 words)

Note

1. Tracing refers to a technique in Photoshop whereby an original photo is digitally traced to create a new image which has a hand-drawn graphic quality and no longer resembles a photograph.

References

Davis, B., Sumara, D., & Luce-Kapler, R. (2000). *Engaging minds: Learning and teaching in a complex world*. Mahwah, NJ: Lawrence Erlbaum Associates.

Gee, J. (2003). *What video games have to teach us about literacy and learning*. New York, NY: Palgrave Macmillan.

Raymond, E. (1999). *The cathedral and the bazaar: Musings on Linux and Open Source by an accidental revolutionary*. Sebastopol, CA: O'Reilly.

Turkle, S. (1995). *Life on the screen: Identity in the age of the Internet*. New York, NY: Simon and Schuster.

O'Hear, S., & Sefton-Green, J. (2004). Creative "communities": How technology mediates social worlds. In D. Miell, & K. Littleton (Eds.), *Collaborative creativity: Contemporary perspectives* (pp. 113–125). London, UK: Free Association Books.

Academic Survival Skill

Synthesizing Information in Writing

One type of written task instructors may ask you to complete requires you to synthesize information from two sources. To do this, you need to apply knowledge learned from one source to information learned from another source (or sources). Here is an example of a task that would require synthesizing information from two sources.

> Using Rheingold's characteristics of an ideal virtual community leader, demonstrate whether Chavo is a good online collaborative forum leader.

In order to answer this question properly, you need to have good knowledge of content from both Readings 2 and 3. The solution to writing a good answer is to organize the information within your body paragraphs as demonstrated below.

A. In the following paragraph, underline information from Reading 2 and highlight information from Reading 3. When you have finished, compare your answers with those of a classmate.

> In his advice to virtual community leaders, Rheingold (2012) states that ideal hosts provide information that is relevant to the community's members. He suggests that in order for an online mentor to attract and retain active community members, the leader create a "gift economy" by freely sharing knowledge that is important to the online participant.

O'Hear and Sefton-Green (2004) write about Chavo, a professional graphic artist who acts as a leader to members of the Interpol message board. On this site, participants post graphic art they have created to honour the rock band Interpol. Chavo creates a gift economy by giving Tom (an online member) advice about the artwork Tom posted on the message board. In one case, Chavo suggested that Tom add an image to the background of a picture to enhance the artwork. When Tom did that, he felt the art was improved. This is one example of Chavo demonstrating the characteristics of an ideal virtual community leader as defined by Rheingold.

B. To further understand how this paragraph was constructed, work with a partner to answer the following questions.

		TRUE	FALSE
1	The purpose of the first two sentences is to clearly state a *single* characteristic of an online community leader as defined by Rheingold.	☐	☐
2	Which other verbs does the writer use as synonyms for "states that"?	__________ __________	
3	Which synonyms does the writer use to avoid repeating "leader" too often?	__________ __________	
4	Which synonym does the writer use to avoid repeating "community member"?	__________	
5	When writing about Chavo's activities, does the author write in general terms or does he give specific examples?	__________	
6	The concluding sentence clearly states the point of the paragraph: according to this characteristic, defined by Rheingold, Chavo is a good online collaborative leader.	☐	☐

C. The following paragraph shows an opposing viewpoint, but follows a similar structure. Again, underline information from Reading 2 and highlight information from Reading 3.

Another characteristic of an ideal online community leader, as defined by Rheingold, is the ability to lead without asserting authority. According to him, online "hosts" must be persuasive rather than assertive because if they are too authoritative, they risk losing the goodwill of the virtual participants. Chavo, in O'Hear and Sefton-Green (2004), does assert his authority on Interpol's message board. At one point, Tom posts an image to the site and Chavo tells Tom to remove the picture as it is not of high enough quality. He indicates that Tom should improve the work and repost the image. In this instance, Chavo definitely asserts his authority, and Tom respects him for it. This leader's insistence on exercising his authority is not a characteristic recommended by Rheingold.

Note the following elements the two paragraphs have in common.

- The topic sentences have different grammatical structures, so they do not seem repetitive.
- The writer uses synonyms of key words to avoid repetition.
- The information from one source is summarized first; the information from the second source follows.
- Concrete examples support the point of the paragraph.
- The concluding sentences are general; they shift the reader's attention from a specific example to a general statement about the point being discussed.

D. With your partner, select another of Rheingold's recommendations for successful virtual community leaders and write a paragraph indicating whether Chavo demonstrates that characteristic. When you have finished, show your work to another pair of students and ask them to underline information from Reading 2 and highlight information from Reading 3. They might also make useful suggestions about use of synonyms and specific examples. When you are satisfied with your paragraph, write it on the board, or post it to a class website or wiki.

FINAL ASSIGNMENT

Write an Explanatory Synthesis Essay

Write an essay that synthesizes your Warm-Up Assignment summary and information from Reading 3. Use the paragraph structure that you learned in the Academic Survival Skill in a response to the following.

> Using Himmelman's definitions, determine whether the interaction between Chavo and Tom could be considered networking, coordinating, cooperating or collaborating.

For this essay:

- Write an introduction (with a thesis statement), four body paragraphs (one for each definition) and a conclusion.
- Use your summarized definitions from the Warm-Up Assignment in the first half of each body paragraph; use information from Reading 3 in the second half of each body paragraph.
- Use concrete examples to support your points.
- Vary the grammatical structure of topic sentences so that they do not seem repetitive.
- Use synonyms for key words to avoid repetition.
- Write concluding sentences that are general to shift the reader's attention from specific examples to a general statement about the point being discussed.

Refer to the Models Chapter (page 208) to see an example of an essay that requires synthesis of multiple sources and to learn more about how to write one.

CRITICAL CONNECTIONS

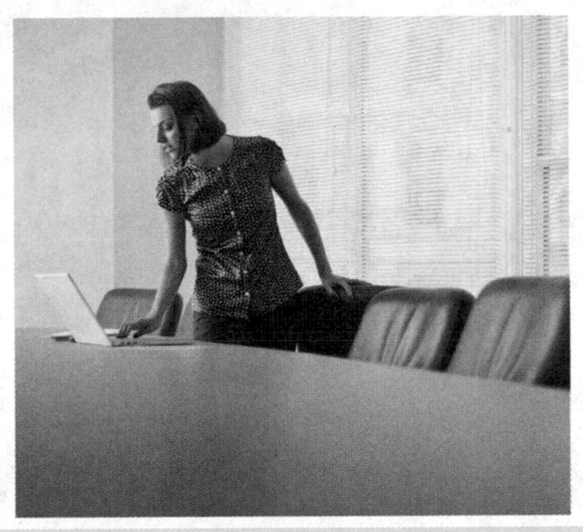

Chapter 5 presented information on new media, and Chapter 6, on online collaborative environments. To complete the following tasks, you will need to synthesize content, skills and vocabulary from both chapters.

1. At the end of the first paragraph of Reading 1 in Chapter 5 (page 103, lines 10 to 16), the author uses metaphor to compare the Internet to wild new land being settled. Read the paragraph and underline the words and phrases that support this metaphor.

2. Working with a partner, apply Himmelman's definitions of networking, coordination, cooperation and collaboration to each stage (described below) of Beth Terry's efforts to encourage Clorox to recycle Brita filters (Chapter 5, Reading 3, page 121). Share your answers with the class.

   a) Terry blogged about how she was trying to reduce her use of plastic bottles by using Brita filters instead. ________________

   b) She wrote to Clorox, and received a letter in response. ________________

   c) She commented on her blog about her dissatisfaction with Clorox's response. ________________

   d) She used Google analytics and found many people wanted to recycle Brita filters. ________________

   e) She created a Yahoo group and encouraged members to write letters to Clorox executives. ________________

   f) She set up a mailbox to receive Brita filters that others would mail to her. ________________

   g) She contacted other bloggers and got media attention, for example, from the *New York Times*. ________________

   h) A resolution was achieved, involving Clorox, Whole Foods and Terry. ________________

3. Paraphrase the first paragraph of Reading 1 in Chapter 6 (page 128, lines 1 to 14). Use the techniques you learned in the Academic Survival Skill (page 116). When you have finished, identify the techniques you used.

4. Now, summarize the same paragraph and compare your summary with that of a partner. Combine the best elements from each to draft an improved summary. Write the final version on the board, or post it to a class website.

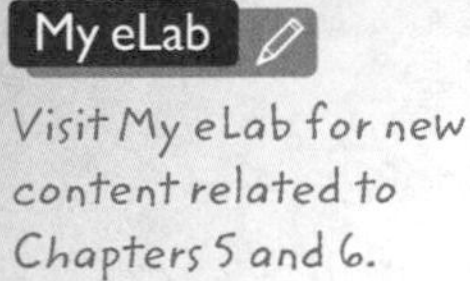

My eLab
Visit My eLab for new content related to Chapters 5 and 6.

CHAPTER 7

Performance-Enhancing Drugs

Every major sporting event brings news of athletes who have taken performance-enhancing drugs. Athletes from almost every country and every sport have been disgraced by medical tests that reveal their involvement with drugs. At the centre of the controversy are prominent sports figures like cyclist Lance Armstrong and baseball great Roger Clemens. With so many athletes testing positive for performance-enhancing drugs, perhaps it is time to legalize their use.

In this chapter, you will

- learn vocabulary related to the use of performance-enhancing drugs in sports;
- learn strategies to identify collocations;
- analyze text organization;
- express critical thoughts in writing;
- revise a text to add academic characteristics;
- write a persuasive essay.

GEARING UP

A. With your class, discuss what these elite athletes have in common. Can you add any names to this list?

- Lance Armstrong, American cyclist
- Jose Canseco and Roger Clemens, American baseball players
- Kunjarani Devi, Indian weightlifter
- Ben Johnson, Canadian sprinter
- Kostas Kenteris and Ekaterini Thanou, Greek sprinters
- Li Zhesi, Chinese swimmer

B. Many athletes take performance-enhancing drugs to improve their athletic performances, but could there be other reasons for the popularity of these drugs? Discuss the roles the following factors might play.

- desire for money or glory
- peer pressure
- drug availability
- desire to test limits
- low self-esteem
- desire to belong

C. Do you believe performance-enhancing drugs should be legalized in sport? Survey your class to find the majority opinion.

VOCABULARY BUILD

Below are some key words from Reading 1 and Reading 2. Working with a partner, choose the best meaning for each of the words in bold to complete the sentence. If you are not sure, locate the word in the reading and consider its meaning in context. When you have finished, compare answers as a class.

1. If someone has **abnormal*** (READING 1, LINE 17) levels of a hormone, they have ...
   a) very low levels b) very high levels c) either a or b
2. If something is **controversial**,* (READING 1, LINE 123) it is ...
   a) not universally agreed upon b) well known c) opposite to the truth
3. If you **deny*** (READING 1, LINE 125) something, you ...
   a) dislike it b) enjoy it very much c) say it is not true
4. If you **detect*** (READING 1, LINE 38) a problem, you ...
   a) discover it b) solve it c) challenge it
5. If an idea **distorts*** (READING 1, LINE 94) the truth, it ...
   a) misrepresents the truth b) supports the truth c) reflects the truth
6. If athletes are **doping**, (READING 1, LINE 34) they are ... [Choose two.]
   a) training hard b) using performance-enhancing drugs c) using non-chemical methods to enhance performance
7. If you **ensure*** (READING 1, LINE 154) something will happen, you ...
   a) are not sure it will happen b) hope it will happen c) make certain it will happen
8. When athletes are well **equipped*** (READING 1, LINE 111) to compete, they are ...
   a) prepared b) challenged c) approved
9. When something is **inherently*** (READING 2, LINE 4) risky, it is ...
   a) acceptably risky b) naturally risky c) unlikely to be risky
10. If someone is **lackadaisical**, (READING 1, LINE 83) he or she is ...
    a) challenged b) fascinated c) uninterested
11. If you have a **notion*** (READING 1, LINE 94) about something, you have ...
    a) a feeling b) a problem c) an idea
12. If you **obtain*** (READING 1, LINE 41) something, you ...
    a) get it b) hold it c) release it
13. Your **perspective*** (READING 1, LINE 166) on an issue is your ...
    a) discussion b) point of view c) concern
14. A **prohibition*** (READING 2, LINE 59) on something means it is ...
    a) available b) allowed c) forbidden
15. When there are **variants*** (READING 1, LINE 23) of something, there are ...
    a) changes b) different kinds c) problems

*Appears on the Academic Word List

Identifying and Learning Collocations through Reading

As you learned in Chapter 1, collocations are groups of two or more words that are often used together to express an idea. In the readings that follow, *blood doping* is a collocation that refers to the illegal practice of removing an athlete's blood long before a competition and injecting it back into the athlete just before a competition to increase the red blood cell count. This practice enhances athletic performance by improving the delivery of oxygen to the muscles.

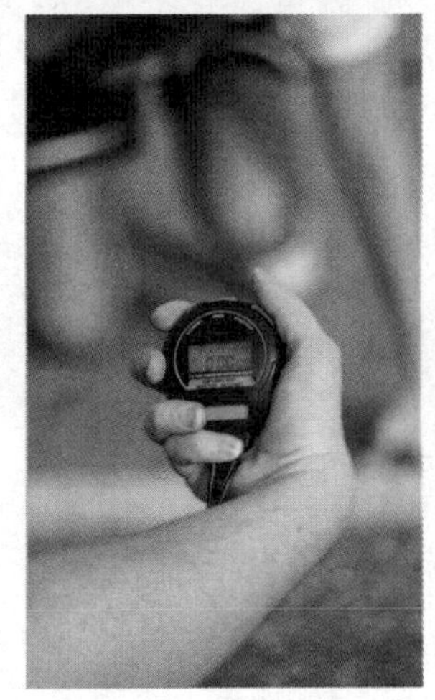

When you learn collocations, you can use them in your speaking and writing to improve your fluency and efficiency. However, some collocations are not immediately apparent. One technique for recognizing collocations is to look for *repeated* use of word combinations. If you have a reading in digital format, you can search for repeated use by using the search function of the program you are using to view the reading.

A. The collocations in this table can be found in multiple places in Reading 1. For each of the words, search Reading 1 to find the words that complete the collocation. Write the collocation and its meaning.

WORD	COLLOCATION	MEANING
ability LINES 101, 106, 116		
blood LINE 30 (+ 6 INSTANCES)		
contend LINES 109, 144		
level LINES 18, 48		
performance LINE 5 (+ 24 INSTANCES)		

Another way to identify collocations is to ask your instructor. Often, a collocation is a recognized way of expressing an idea, but it may be used only once in the text you are reading. In these cases, someone with more exposure to the language you are trying to learn may be able to help you identify them.

B. Follow the same steps as in task A to complete the table below and on the next page. Each collocation is presented once in Reading 1 but is a recognized combination of words. Locate the word by matching the line number. Write the collocation and its meaning.

WORD	COLLOCATION	MEANING
banned LINE 146		

WORD	COLLOCATION	MEANING
foreign LINE 64		
laced LINE 155		
lucrative LINE 74		
mimic LINE 13		
myriad LINE 77		
naturally LINE 39		
rampant LINE 82		
recovery LINE 21		
role LINE 2		
side LINE 24		
tacit LINE 81		

Performance-Enhancing Drugs in Modern Athletics

Use the approach to reading comprehension that you learned in Chapter 1 to help you understand this text.

A. Skim the reading and, on a separate sheet of paper, take notes on the topic, length, text type and probable organization. Then, turn the six headings into questions. (Two are already questions, but you will need to change the other four.)

B. Now, read the text more closely and answer the questions you have generated. When you have finished, confirm your answers with a partner.

Few people are more admired in today's society than successful athletes. Adolescents view them as role models, adults clamour for their autographs, and companies seek them out to endorse products. While most athletes become successful as a result of their talent and hard work, others take medical shortcuts. To the dismay of fans, the medical community and many athletes themselves, steroids and other performance-enhancing drugs have become a common element of modern sport.

What Are Performance-Enhancing Drugs?

Performance-enhancing drugs are substances or strategies used by athletes to improve their chances of winning competitions. The most common performance-enhancing drugs are anabolic steroids. *Anabolic* means muscle-building, while *androgenic* refers to masculine characteristics. First developed in the 1930s, these drugs were created to mimic the effects of the male hormones testosterone and androtestosterone, which regulate the development of muscles and secondary male sex characteristics. Synthetic steroids were initially developed to assist people suffering from abnormally low levels of testosterone or from diseases that attack muscles. However, as often happens with new drugs, other uses were quickly found for them.

Athletes use anabolic steroids to increase muscle development and to reduce recovery time from injury. Steroids can be taken orally, injected or applied topically as a cream. Different variants of the drugs are often used at the same time, a technique called stacking. Athletes stack steroids in an attempt to limit side effects while increasing the potency of the drugs. Steroid users typically take the drugs for a period of weeks or months, stop for a period of time, and then resume their use.

Another type of drug often abused by athletes is amphetamines. First developed in 1887, these drugs stimulate the body by spurring the release of the neural transmitters dopamine, serotonin and noradrenaline. Amphetamines, known colloquially by athletes as "greenies," increase heart rate and blood pressure and stimulate the pleasure centres of the brain. They are found in legal pharmaceuticals such as diet pills and Ritalin, but also exist as the street drugs methamphetamine and speed. Athletes take amphetamines to compete longer and improve their concentration.

HGH and Blood Doping

Some practices that boost performance do not involve drugs at all. Two primary examples are blood doping and the use of human growth hormone (HGH). Athletes who dope their blood or use HGH often do so because these methods not only improve their skills but are also more natural and nearly impossible to detect.

Human growth hormone (HGH) is a naturally occurring substance secreted by the pituitary gland. HGH promotes cell growth in the body and the development of muscle, cartilage and bone. Originally, the only way to obtain HGH was by extracting it from the pituitary glands of cadavers. Later, a synthetic version was developed. HGH is used to treat stunted growth in children and other growth-related diseases.

Athletes take HGH to increase muscle growth and to help tired muscles recover faster, making it possible for them to train longer and more frequently. Unlike other performance-enhancing drugs, HGH cannot be detected in urine; blood tests must be used to find the drug. Even with blood tests, however, it is often difficult to determine the difference between a naturally high level of HGH and one that has been artificially elevated.

The goal of blood doping is to increase the number of red blood cells in an athlete's body. Because red blood cells carry oxygen to the muscles, more red blood cells

means more oxygen, which is beneficial to performance in endurance events such as long-distance cycling races. Blood doping is the removal and storage of blood from an athlete well in advance of a competition. Doing so prompts the body to replace the missing blood, bringing the level of red blood cells back up to normal. Then, just before an event, the athlete is transfused with the stored blood, boosting the number of red blood cells well above normal.

Higher levels of red blood cells can also be achieved by using erythropoietin (EPO). First isolated in 1977, this substance occurs naturally in the kidneys and is responsible for regulating the production of red blood cells. The medical purpose of EPO is to treat anemia patients; however, athletes use EPO instead of transfusions to elevate their red blood cell count.

Blood doping is very difficult to detect. If an athlete uses the transfusion method, tests will not reveal anything unnatural because no foreign substances will be discovered; the blood is essentially that of the athlete. Tests to detect EPO were not developed until 2000. Even now, a test can find manufactured EPO only if the test is administered within eight days of the athlete using the drug. The most common way for athletes to be caught blood doping is for EPO or stored blood to be found in their possession.

...

Why Do Athletes Use Performance-Enhancing Drugs?

Athletes use performance-enhancing drugs for a number of reasons; the specific reason generally depends on the level at which the athlete performs. Professional athletes who take these substances hope if they hit more home runs or sack more quarterbacks, they will make more money and receive more lucrative endorsements. Olympic and top-tier amateur athletes want to succeed in order to gain corporate sponsorships. College athletes want to be drafted into the professional leagues, while the goal of high school athletes is college scholarships. The myriad of reasons for taking performance-enhancing drugs make their use a difficult problem to tackle because society cannot respond to or understand the needs of every athlete.

...

Changing Views toward Performance-Enhancing Drugs

Prior to the 1980s, the lack of testing, other than in the Olympic Games, gave tacit approval [for the use of] performance-enhancing drugs. The stories of rampant drug use in various professional sports leagues reveal a lackadaisical response that created a culture of acceptance and led to more and more athletes experimenting with drugs because they knew they could use whatever substances they wished without suffering any consequences. For example, Major League Baseball (in the US) did not ban steroids until 2003, and once it did so, the penalty for failing a drug test was only a ten-game suspension.

However, the indifference toward performance-enhancing drugs that marked the 1960s through the middle of the 1980s began to be replaced by greater concerns as people become more aware of the health effects of these substances ...

People also began to consider the use of performance-enhancing drugs to be cheating because athletes were using the drugs to enhance their abilities unnaturally. Such usage thus distorts the notion of a level playing field and misinterprets the importance of sports, many people argue. Former President George W. Bush has stated, "The use of performance-enhancing drugs … sends the wrong message … that there are shortcuts to accomplishment, and that performance is more important than character."[1] …

Claims That Performance-Enhancing Drugs Have Limited Effects

One of the counter-arguments to the idea that steroids cause a significant increase in athletic ability is that athletes still rely heavily on their natural ability; most people, no matter how hard they try, will never become professional or Olympic athletes. While performance-enhancing drugs can improve endurance and strength and speed up recovery, they cannot make a curve ball easier to hit or take seconds off a sprinter's 100-metre time …

Some people even argue that natural ability is as unfair an advantage as performance-enhancing drugs—perhaps even more so because while the drugs are available to anyone, athletes cannot change the genes with which they were born. In fact, many people contend that the use of performance-enhancing drugs is simply a way to level the playing field. They argue that it is genetics, not drugs, that makes a competition unfair; some people are simply better equipped to compete. One example is Finnish cross-country skier Eero Maentyranta, who won three gold medals in the 1964 Winter Olympics. Later tests revealed his blood naturally contained 40 to 50 percent more red blood cells than average. This gave him a significant advantage over his competitors because long-distance performance relies on delivery of oxygen to muscles, which is the job of red blood cells. His natural ability outmatched any benefit someone with an average level of red blood cells would receive from using drugs.

Similarly, one theory states that European distance runners lag behind their African counterparts because African runners, such as those from Kenya and Ethiopia, can resist fatigue longer and go farther on the same amount of oxygen. Studies also show that Kenyan runners tend to have slimmer legs than European runners, which means they do not need as much energy to run. Examination of this subject can be difficult, as it can lead to controversial conclusions on racial difference; however, physical evidence does suggest that body types are not universal—after all, no one would deny that the average man is too short to succeed in the National Basketball Association. As Julian Savulescu, Bennett Foddy and Megan Clayton argue, "Sport discriminates against the genetically unfit. Sport is the province of the genetic elite."[2]

At the same time, note people who disagree with that argument, performance-enhancing drugs can make a significant difference if taken by an elite athlete. If taking a steroid will enable a hitter to develop the arm strength needed to drive a baseball fifteen feet farther, that could be the difference between a fly ball and a home run. Using EPO might enable a world-class sprinter to shave enough time off his or her 100-metre dash to win an Olympic medal. Talent is essential for athletic success, but performance-enhancing drugs can provide a small but critical boost. At the topmost levels of sports, differences between athletic ability are minimal, save for a few exceptional athletes—the Michael Jordans and Wayne Gretzkys of the world.

Legalizing Performance-Enhancing Drugs

Some argue that the best way to level the playing field is by legalizing performance-enhancing drugs. Proponents of this view contend that legalization would eliminate any genetic advantages some athletes may possess. One writer even suggests that athletes who do not use steroids should be banned from competition. In the view of Sidney Gendin, "For all the money they have to lay out, fans are entitled to the best possible performances. Why, then, should they have to put up with the inferior performances of non-drug users?"[3]

Legalizing drugs would bring with it a host of new complications. First, each major sports organization would have to decide which performance-enhancing drugs its athletes would be permitted to use. The drugs would have to be strictly regulated to ensure that they were not laced with banned substances. Athletes would need to be recompensed if they developed health problems as a result of using steroids or other drugs. Society would also need to decide whether performance-enhancing drugs should be legalized at the high school or college level. In addition, as Charles E. Yesalis, an expert on the history of drugs in sports, states, "Legalization of steroids in sport might lessen hypocrisy, but it would place an extremely heavy burden on individual athletes who then would be forced either to take drugs known to be harmful or compete at a disadvantage."[4]

Whether using performance-enhancing drugs is a type of cheating or merely a way for athletes to create level playing fields is a matter of perspective. What is clear is that use of these drugs leads to considerable controversy and pointed debate. And as long as athletes come from different social and economic backgrounds and are of different shapes and sizes, athletic competitions can never take place between true equals.

(1989 words)

Notes

1. George W. Bush, State of the Union address, January 20, 2004.
2. Julian Savulescu, Bennett Foddy, and Megan Clayton, "Why We Should Allow Performance-Enhancing Drugs in Sport," *British Journal of Sports Medicine,* 2004, p. 667.
3. Sidney Gendin, "Let's Ban Those Who Don't Use Drugs," Fall 2000. http://meso-rx.com.
4. Charles E. Yesalis, and Virginia S. Cowart, *The Steroids Game*. Champaign, IL: Human Kinetics, 1998, p. 110.

Egendorf, L.K. (2007). *Performance-enhancing drugs* (pp. 8–23). San Diego, CA: ReferencePoint Press.

Analyzing Text Structure and Organization

Reading 2 is a short persuasive essay, taken from a textbook of short essays about issues in elite sports. In that textbook, each essay begins with an abstract as if it were a journal article.

A. Skim Reading 2 and identify the following features by line number.

- ABSTRACT — LINES ______
- INTRODUCTION — LINES ______
- THESIS AND THREE MAIN POINTS — LINES ______
- BODY PARAGRAPHS THAT SUPPORT EACH MAIN POINT — FIRST POINT: LINES ______ SECOND POINT: LINES ______ THIRD POINT: LINES ______
- CONCLUSION — LINES ______

B. This essay is missing some of the characteristics typical of an academic essay. Working with a partner, list the elements that are missing. As a class, discuss what you could do to make this essay more academic.

______

______

______

C. The topic sentences that introduce each main point of the essay, and the sentences that immediately follow, are carefully written. Find the similarities between the pairs of sentences that introduce the first and third main points and write them in the space that follows. Confirm your answers as a class.

SENTENCES THAT INTRODUCE THE FIRST MAIN POINT	SENTENCES THAT INTRODUCE THE THIRD MAIN POINT
The need for rules in sports cannot be dismissed. But the anchoring of today's anti-doping regulations in the notion of fair play is misguided, since other factors that affect performance—e.g., biological and environmental factors—are unchecked.	Acknowledging the importance of rules in sports, which might include the prohibition of doping, is, itself, not problematic. However, a problem arises when the application of these rules is beset with diminishing returns: escalating costs and questionable effectiveness.

______

______

______

______

D. The authors use a different technique to introduce their second point (lines 35 to 38). What technique do they use and why?

______

______

______

E. To summarize, what two techniques do these authors use to introduce the main points in their essay?

______

______

Some Performance-Enhancing Drugs Should Be Legalized

Read the text carefully. Then, indicate whether each of the following statements is true or false. When you have finished, compare your answers with those of a partner.

STATEMENTS	TRUE	FALSE
1 The authors support anti-doping regulations in sports.	☐	☑
2 The authors believe that "good genes" provide as unfair an advantage as performance-enhancing drugs.	☐	☐
3 Although taking performance-enhancing drugs may pose a risk to athletes' health, simply playing sports poses a risk, so taking drugs does not really increase the risk to their health.	☐	☐
4 Legalizing performance-enhancing drugs would allow doctors to study the effects of each drug to determine if it poses a risk. This is not possible while these drugs are illegal.	☐	☐
5 Doctors must consider their patients' best interests, and this includes giving athletes performance-enhancing drugs.	☐	☐
6 Doctors should be punished for giving athletes performance-enhancing drugs.	☐	☐
7 Doctors should only be punished if they give athletes performance-enhancing drugs that damage the athletes' health.	☐	☐
8 Sport organizations should invest more money in upholding anti-doping regulations.	☐	☐

While there is a definite need for rules in sport, prohibiting athletes from using performance-enhancing drugs is misguided. It does not make sense to ban the use of the drugs due to health issues because playing sports is inherently risky and dangerous. Instead, performance-enhancing drugs should be legalized and used under a doctor's supervision. There is little risk that permitting the use of these drugs would result in an increase in the rates of death and chronic illnesses among athletes. Furthermore, the costs associated with prohibiting the use of performance-enhancing drugs are escalating and the results are questionable.

The rules of sport define a level playing field on which athletes compete. Anti-doping policies exist, in theory, to encourage fair play. However, we believe they are unfounded, dangerous, and excessively costly.

The need for rules in sports cannot be dismissed. But the anchoring of today's anti-doping regulations in the notion of fair play is misguided, since other factors that affect performance—e.g., biological and environmental factors—are unchecked. Getting help from one's genes—by being blessed with a performance-enhancing genetic predisposition—is acceptable. Use of drugs is not. Yet both types of advantage are undeserved. Prevailing sports ethics is unconcerned with this contradiction.

...

Another ethical foundation for anti-doping concerns the athlete's health. Anti-doping control is judged necessary to prevent damage from doping. However, sport is dangerous even if no drugs are taken—playing soccer comes with high risks for knee and ankle problems, for instance, and boxing can lead to brain damage. To comprehensively assess any increase in risk afforded by the use of drugs or technology, every performance-enhancing method needs to be studied. Such work cannot be done while use of performance-enhancing drugs is illegal. We believe that ... the use of drugs should be permitted under medical supervision [so that it can be properly studied].

Legalization of the use of drugs in sport might even have some advantages. The boundary between the therapeutic and ergogenic—i.e., performance-enhancing—use of drugs is blurred at present and poses difficult questions for the controlling bodies of anti-doping practice and for sports doctors. The anti-doping rules often lead to complicated and costly administrative and medical follow-up to ascertain whether drugs taken by athletes are legitimate therapeutic agents or illicit.

If doping were allowed, would there be an increase in the rate of death and chronic illness among athletes? Would athletes have a shorter lifespan than the general population? Would there be more examples like the widespread use of performance-enhancing drugs in the former East German republic? We do not think so. Only a small proportion of the population engages in elite sports. Furthermore, legalization of doping, we believe, would encourage more sensible, informed use of drugs in amateur sport, leading to an overall decline in the rate of health problems associated with doping. Finally, by allowing medically supervised doping, the drugs used could be assessed for a clearer view of what is dangerous and what is not.

The role of the doctor is to preserve their patients' best interests with respect to present and future health. A sports doctor has to fulfill this role while maintaining the athlete's performance at as high a level as possible. As such, as long as the first condition is met, any intervention proven safe, pharmacological or otherwise, should be justified, irrespective of whether or not it is ergogenic. A doctor who tries to enhance the performance of their athlete should not be punished for the use of pharmacological aides, but should be held accountable for any ill effects. Rather than speculate on anti-doping test procedures, resources should be invested into protecting the integrity of doctors who make such judgments.

Acknowledging the importance of rules in sports, which might include the prohibition of doping, is, itself, not problematic. However, a problem arises when the application of these rules is beset with diminishing returns: escalating costs and questionable effectiveness. The ethical foundation of prohibiting the use of ergogenic substances in sports is weak. As the cost of anti-doping control rises year on year, ethical objections are raised that are, in our view, weightier than the ethical arguments advanced for anti-doping. In the competition between increasingly sophisticated doping—e.g., gene transfer—and anti-doping technology, there will never be a clear winner. Consequently, such a futile but expensive strategy is difficult to defend. (722 words)

Kayser, B., Mauron, A., & Miah, A. (2009). Some performance-enhancing drugs should be legalized. In T.L. Roleff (Ed.) *The Olympics* (pp. 76–78). Farmington Hills, MI: Greenhaven Press.

WARM-UP ASSIGNMENT

Revise an Essay to Add Academic Characteristics

Reading 2 demonstrates the organization of a short persuasive essay. It contains:

- an introduction
- a thesis, with three main points listed in parallel structure
- body paragraphs that support each main point
- a conclusion

Rewrite Reading 2 so that it contains the following characteristics, which are typical features of an academic essay:

- the third-person objective perspective
- a developed introduction
- a separate concluding paragraph
- academic references
- a Works Cited section

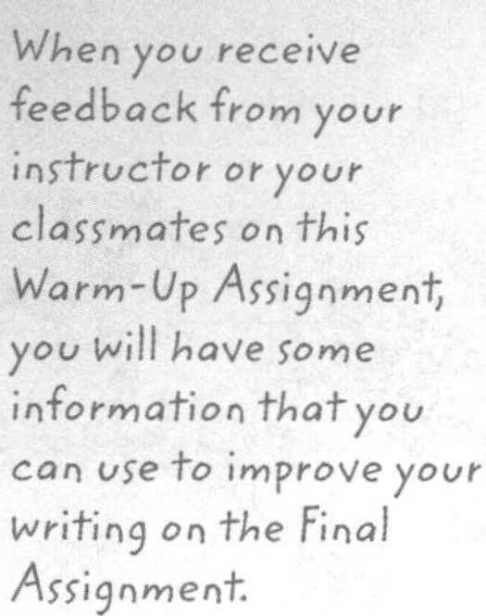

When you receive feedback from your instructor or your classmates on this Warm-Up Assignment, you will have some information that you can use to improve your writing on the Final Assignment.

Use the content from Reading 2, citing the authors of the reading. Also include at least one additional source to support each of the main points. There are many easily available sources online or in books in the library. You may work with other students to find the supplementary sources; however, you should write the revision of Reading 2 on your own.

VOCABULARY BUILD

Read the following sentences adapted from Reading 3. Write the definition of the words and phrases in bold in the second column. To learn the definition, use the sentence context, or consult your classmates or instructor, before using your dictionary. When you have finished, confirm your answers as a class.

WORDS/PHRASES IN CONTEXT	DEFINITION
1 Most substance use and **abuse** seems to be an expression of uncritical acceptance of the norms of the sport ethic.	abuse (n.): *misuse*
2 All of these questions can be **adequately*** answered only if we place athletes within the dynamic and increasingly complex networks of relationships associated with the use of illicit drugs in elite sport.	adequately (adv.):

WORDS/PHRASES IN CONTEXT	DEFINITION
❸ Marxist theory suggests that the use of drugs indicates the **alienation** of individuals—in this case athletes—in modern capitalist societies.	alienation (n.):
❹ The most highly organized programs of drug use in sport are unquestionably those that developed, not in the capitalist West, but in the former communist **regimes*** of the Soviet Union and, in particular, East Germany.	regimes (n.):
❺ **Deviants** do not **conform*** to widely accepted standards of behaviour; deviant behaviour, such as drug use, is "based on ignoring or rejecting norms."	deviants (n.):
	conform (v.):
❻ Elite-level athletes are simply new types of workers, and as sport becomes just another form of work, so it comes to represent **constraint*** rather than freedom, with the removal of all playful elements and creative spontaneity.	constraint (n.):
❼ Drug use by athletes does not involve a rejection of key sporting values; **on the contrary**,* it expresses not only an acceptance of, but an overconformity to, those key values.	on the contrary (adv. phrase):
❽ As they are pharmacologists, it is not surprising that these authors **couch their explanations largely in terms of** pharmacological developments.	couch (v.) their explanations (largely) in terms of:
❾ Human beings have lost touch with their true nature; the athlete is a controlled human being and is **exploited*** and alienated.	exploited (v.):
❿ Lüschen suggests the use of performance-enhancing drugs cannot be understood as the behaviour of an **isolated*** individual, for the use of drugs implies a network of relationships between users and suppliers.	isolated (adj.):
⓫ Researchers hypothesize that athletes most likely to take drugs include those who have **low self-esteem** or are so eager to be accepted as athletes that they will do whatever it takes to be acknowledged by their peers in sport.	low self-esteem (n.):
⓬ **Marxist** writers on sport such as Brohm (1978) and Rigauer (1981) have argued that under capitalism, elite-level athletes are simply new types of workers.	Marxist (adj.):

*Appears on the Academic Word List

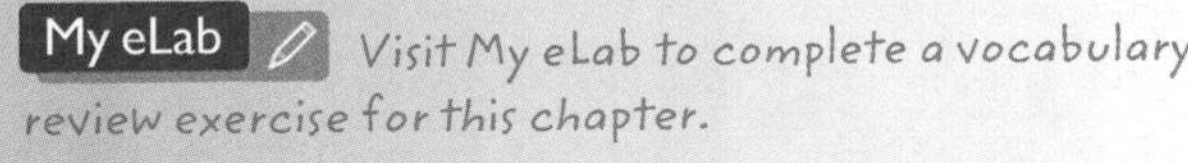

Visit My eLab to complete a vocabulary review exercise for this chapter.

READING 3 Theories of Drug Use in Elite Level Sport

Reading 3 is an excerpt from a chapter in a textbook. It presents four theories about why elite athletes take performance-enhancing drugs.

A. Read the introduction and answer the following questions. Check your answers with those of a classmate.

1. The authors cite Verroken, Lüschen, Donohoe and Johnson, and Donati to support their point. What is the point these researchers all make?

   ____

   ____

2. What are the three problems that must be addressed by any theory that attempts to explain why elite athletes take performance-enhancing drugs?

   ____

   ____

   ____

B. Now, read the entire text and, as you do, complete the following table. For each theory, summarize either the theory or the authors' evaluation of the theory. When you have finished, compare your answers as a class.

THEORY	EVALUATION OF THE THEORY
THE PHARMACOLOGICAL REVOLUTION During the last four decades, drugs have become "more potent, more selective and less toxic." As the quality of the drugs has improved, it has become safer for athletes to use the drugs. Amphetamines were used during World War II (which popularized their use) and synthetic hormones were developed (which made production easier).	
DRUG USE AS DEVIANT OVERCONFORMITY	This explains why athletes want to use performance-enhancing drugs, but it does not explain why more of them have wanted to do this over the last four decades.
MARXIST APPROACHES Athletes' use of performance-enhancing drugs is the outward sign of their increasing alienation from society and sports as the sporting world has become more commercialized. Marxist theorists contend that athletes are workers, and the importance placed on winning (and the financial rewards for winning) puts strain on their bodies. They react to this strain and alienation by taking illicit drugs.	
DIFFERENTIAL ASSOCIATION	This approach is mostly descriptive, so the researcher can't prove this in any objective way, but it opens up the issue to consideration from a wide range of perspectives.

In this reading, the authors use the Turabian citation style, which requires an in-text notation of author, date of publication and, when relevant, page number. For more information on citation style, see page 38.

Introduction

Although we cannot be sure of the precise level of drug use in modern sport, there are nevertheless grounds for suggesting that the illicit use of drugs by athletes has increased very markedly in the post-war period and more particularly since the 1960s. This is certainly the view of Michele Verroken, the former head of the Ethics and Anti-Doping Directorate of the UK Sports Council. Verroken (2005: 30) writes:

> Around the time of the Second World War, the development of amphetamine-like substances reached a peak ... Not surprisingly, in the 1940s and 1950s, amphetamines became the drug of choice for athletes, particularly in sports such as cycling, where the stimulant effects were perceived to be beneficial to enhancing sporting performance.

She suggests that the use of drugs in sport had become widespread by the 1960s. This view is echoed by Lüschen (2000: 463), who has similarly noted that "knowledge, information and supply of steroids changed quite drastically" from the 1960s.

In similar fashion, Donohoe and Johnson (1986: 2–4) have suggested that the "production of amphetamine-like stimulants in the thirties heralded a whole new era of doping in sport," and they go on to suggest that in recent times "a massive acceleration in the incidence of doping in the sport has occurred." This is also the view of the leading Italian athletics coach and prominent anti-drugs campaigner, Alessandro Donati, who has referred to what he describes as an "alarming increase in doping that has occurred in recent decades" (Donati, 2004: 45). But if there has been a significant increase in the use of performance-enhancing drugs in the last few decades then we need to ask why and how this process has taken place.

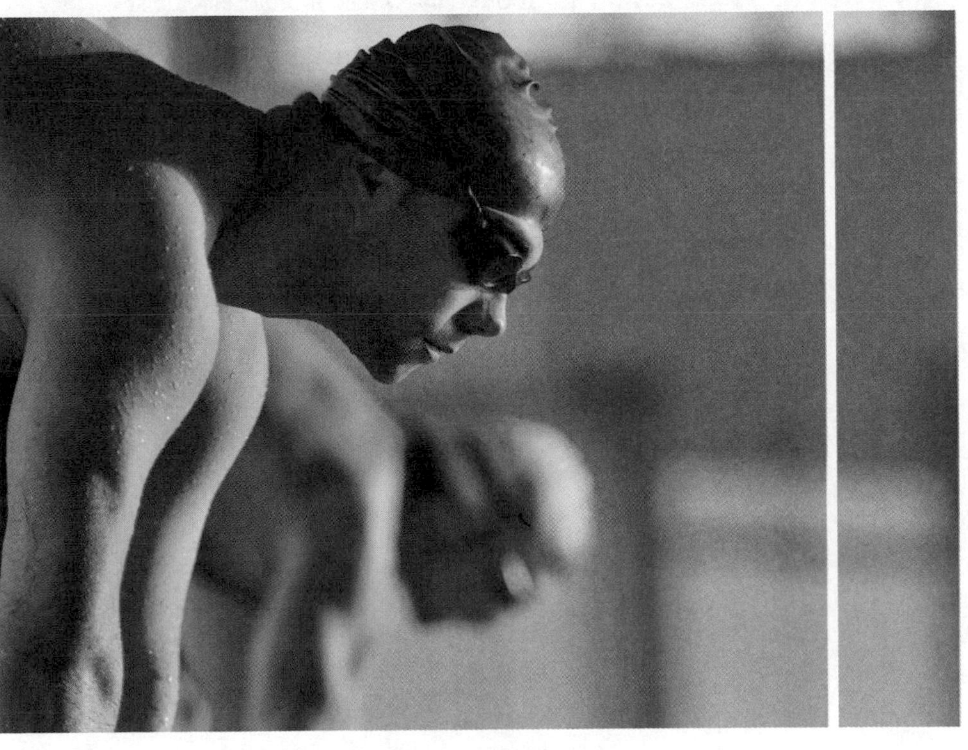

The central objective of this chapter is to examine and comment upon some of the major theories of drug use in elite level sport. In order to evaluate the major strengths and weaknesses of these approaches it will be useful to set out three problems which any approach to understanding drug use in elite sport must address. First, given the increasing use of performance-enhancing drugs in sport at the elite level, particularly since the 1960s, it is clearly not sufficient to ask why athletes take drugs; rather we need to ask why athletes have, over the past four decades, *increasingly* used drugs … Second, in order to help explain why athletes have increasingly used performance-enhancing drugs, we need a theory which can account for the growing demand for illegal drugs by athletes. The third, and final, question that needs addressing relates to the increasing supply of drugs to athletes. All of these questions, we suggest, can only be adequately answered if we place athletes within the dynamic and increasingly complex networks of relationships associated with the use of illicit drugs in elite sport.

…

Technological Explanations: The Pharmacological Revolution

In seeking to explain the increase in drug use in elite sport in the 1960s, Verroken points to "a more liberal approach to experimentation in drug taking" in society in general in the 1960s, but she adds that "of far greater significance" was the "pharmacological revolution" of this period, which resulted in the development of more potent, more selective and less toxic drugs (Verroken, 2005: 30). Like Verroken, Donohoe and Johnson (1986) similarly argue that the increase in the use of drugs in elite sport can be explained largely in terms of improvements in chemical technology.

It is perhaps not surprising that authors such as those cited above should couch their explanations largely in terms of pharmacological developments. Donohoe and Johnson are pharmacologists and their training will have made them keenly aware of such development. Verroken, in her analysis, relies very heavily on the writing of Mottram (1988; 2005), who is also a pharmacologist …

Coakley and Hughes (2007a) have correctly noted that there is evidence to indicate that athletes have for many centuries used a variety of substances in an attempt to improve their performances, and they suggest that

> Historical evidence shows an increase in the use of performance-enhancing drugs in the 1950s. This was due to two factors: (1) the development and official use of amphetamines in the military during World War II, and (2) advances in biology and medicine that led to laboratory isolation of human hormones and the development of synthetic hormones, especially hormones fostering physical growth and development.

…

They note that when Harold Connolly, the 1956 Olympic hammer-throw champion, testified before a United States Senate committee in 1973, he said that the majority of athletes "would do anything, and take anything, short of killing themselves to improve athletic performance." They suggest that, in making this statement, Connolly

> … was probably describing what many athletes through history would have done. The reason drug use has increased so much since the 1950s is not that sports or athletes have changed but that drugs believed and known to enhance physical performance have become so widely available (Coakley and Hughes, 2007a).

In considering explanations of this kind, it is of course important to recognize that in recent years more, and more effective, performance-enhancing drugs have been produced. It is also the case that any … analysis of increasing drug use amongst athletes would certainly have to take these pharmacological developments into account. However, to say that we should take such developments into account is very different from suggesting that the development of pharmacology should be given privileged status, and even further from the idea that it be given sole status, as an explanatory variable.

…

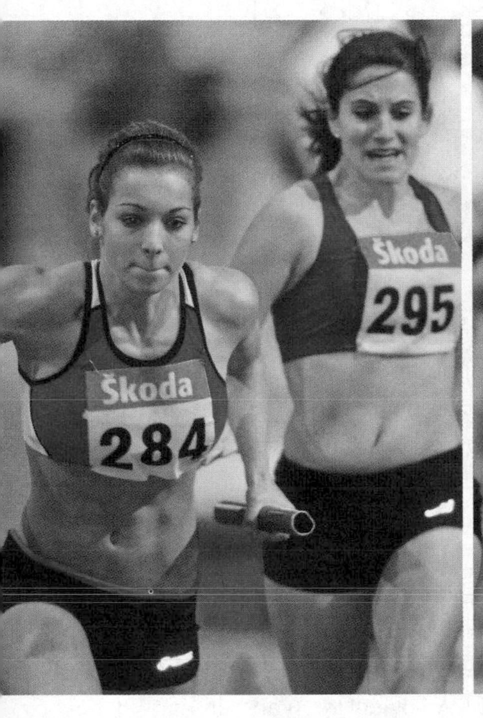

Drug Use as Deviant Overconformity

Coakley and Hughes offer what is, in effect, a two-pronged framework for understanding drug use in elite sport for, in addition to the drug availability hypothesis, they also suggest that drug use can be seen as a form of what they call "deviant overconformity." Coakley and Hughes note that explanations of deviance are often rooted in the idea of "underconformity," that is, deviants do not conform to widely accepted standards of behaviour; as they put it, this involves the idea that deviant behaviour, such as drug use, is "based on ignoring or rejecting norms" (Coakley and Hughes, 2007b: 159). However, they suggest that this is misleading, for drug use by athletes does not involve a rejection of key sporting values; on the contrary, it expresses not only an acceptance of, but an overconformity to, those key values, most notably the value attached to winning which may lead athletes to use performance-enhancing drugs in their pursuit of sporting success; in this sense, drug use can be seen as a form of deviant overconformity based on "uncritically accepting norms and being willing to follow them to extreme degrees" (Coakley and Hughes, 2007b: 159). In this regard, they suggest that research indicates that "drug and substance use by athletes generally is not the result of defective socialization or lack of moral character because many users and abusers are the most dedicated, committed and hard-working athletes in sports" (Coakley and Hughes, 2007b: 175–178); rather "most substance use and abuse seems to be an expression of uncritical acceptance of the norms of the sport ethic. Therefore, it is grounded in overconformity" (p. 178). Coakley and Hughes note that, of course, not all athletes are equally likely to overconform to the sport ethic and they hypothesize that those most likely to do so would include athletes who have low self-esteem or are so eager to be accepted as athletes that they will do whatever it takes to be acknowledged by their peers in sport and athletes who see achievement in sports as the only way to get ahead and gain respect.

There are some interesting and novel aspects to this approach, which certainly differs in important respects from other approaches to deviance. However, it may be argued that this approach … offers an explanation of why athletes may use drugs, but not why they have *increasingly* done so in recent years.

Marxist Approaches

In a useful review of work on drug use in sport, Lüschen (1993; 2000) identified several theoretical approaches to understanding the use of performance-enhancing drugs in sport. Amongst these he lists Marxist theory, which suggests that the use of drugs is indicative of the alienation of individuals—in this case athletes—in modern capitalist societies. Marxist sociologists could identify many structural clues that would illustrate "how human beings have lost touch with their true nature, how the athlete as a controlled human being is exploited and alienated, or how sport itself produces alienation" (Lüschen, 1993: 100) … As Coakley and Hughes (2007b: 156) have noted, within this perspective athletes are viewed as "victims of a profit-driven system." It is certainly the case that Marxist writers on sport such as Brohm (1978) and Rigauer (1981) have argued that under capitalism, elite level athletes are simply new types of workers and that, as sport becomes just another form of work, so it comes to represent constraint rather than freedom, with the removal of all playful elements and creative spontaneity; within such a framework, drug use may be seen as a form of alienation of sports workers. For example, Brohm (1978: 19) has suggested that even a world record holder in athletics may be seen as "a slave of the track," while drug use is seen as an aspect of alienation in sport, "stemming from the oppression of the body pushed to the limits of physical effort" (Brohm, 1978: 23).

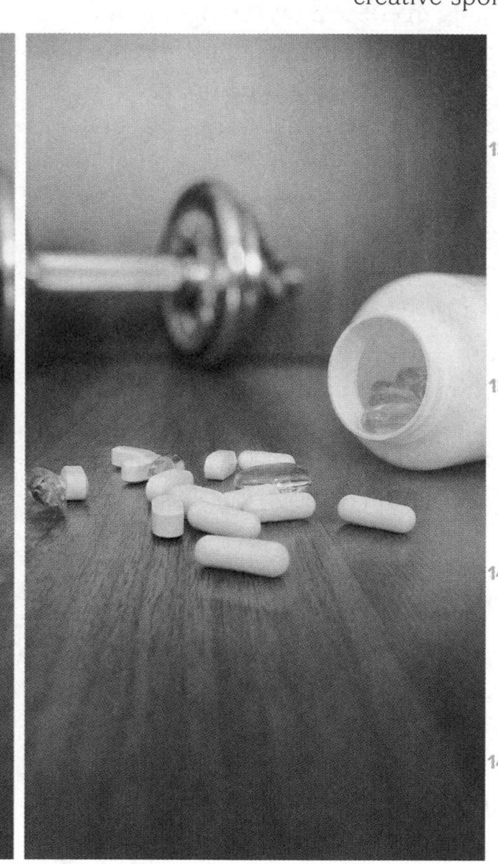

…

While the Marxist approach is not without value, particularly in its focus on changes in the relationship between sport and the wider society of which it is a part, this approach is not unproblematic. Here we draw attention to just two problems in this regard. First, although Marxists have made important contributions to the study of the relationship between the development of capitalism and the commercialization of sport … it is important to emphasize that the use of drugs in sport has not been confined to liberal Western capitalist societies; indeed, the most highly organized and systematic programs of drug use in sport are unquestionably those which developed, not in the capitalist West, but in the former communist regimes of the Soviet Union and, in particular, East Germany. Second, if capitalism and the associated commercialization of sport were indeed the key process in explaining the use of drugs in elite level sport, then we should expect that the earliest and most widespread use of drugs would be found in those sports which are the most highly commercialized. However, this is not what we find. One of the first sports in which the use of drugs, especially anabolic steroids, became widespread was weightlifting, but this is by no means one of the more highly commercialized sports and the financial rewards for success do not match those available in many other sports … In addition, as Coakley and Hughes (2007b: 156) correctly note, one of the key problems with a Marxist approach is that such an approach cannot easily explain why drug use occurs in "non-revenue-producing sports in which the athletes themselves may be in positions of power and control." Clearly, in order to explain drug use in sport, we need to do more than focus just on the links between capitalism, commercialization and sport.

…

Differential Association

The theory of differential association developed by Sutherland and Cressey (1974) is also seen by Lüschen as useful in that it suggests that the use of performance-enhancing drugs cannot be understood as the behaviour of an isolated individual, for the use of drugs implies not only a network of relationships between users and suppliers, but drug use itself is seen as a process involving learning from, and encouragement by, others such as peers and affiliates (Lüschen, 1993; 2000). Both these, he suggests, indicate how the use of illicit drugs "is performed as part of a deviant subculture, or by a group of persons that show features of secret societies" (Lüschen, 2000: 466). In this context, the theory of differential association seeks to explain the use of performance-enhancing drugs by exploring the particular subculture of drug-using athletes and suppliers of drugs; that is, the involvement of coaches, physicians and other members of the "doping network" (Lüschen, 2000). Lüschen notes that this approach is "mainly descriptive" but he recognizes that it nevertheless "suggests quite a number of research questions and interpretive suggestions" (p. 466). (2054 words)

Works Cited

Brohm, J-M. (1978). *Sport—A Prison of Measured Time.* London, UK: Ink Links.

Coakley, J., and Hughes, R. (2007a). "Deviance in Sports," in J. Coakley, *Sport in Society: Issues and Controversies*, 9th ed. Boston, MA: McGraw-Hill. Student edition, related readings: "Topic 1: A brief history of substance use and drug testing." Available at http://highered.mcgraw-hill.com/sites/0073047279/student_view0/chapter6/related_readings.thml

—·(2007b). "Deviance in Sports," in J. Coakley, *Sport in Society: Issues and Controversies*, 9th ed. Boston, MA: McGraw-Hill.

Donati, A. (2004). "The silent drama of the diffusion of doping among amateurs and professionals," in J. Hoberman, and V. Møller (Eds.), *Doping and Public Policy*. Odense, DK: University Press of Southern Denmark.

Donohoe, T., and Johnson, N. (1986). *Foul Play: Drug Abuse in Sports*. Oxford, UK: Blackwell.

Lüschen, G. (1993). "Doping in sport: The social structure of a deviant subculture," *Sport Science Review,* 2: 92–106.

—·(2000). "Doping in sport as deviant behaviour and its social control," in J. Coakley, and E. Dunning (Eds.), *Handbook of Sports Studies*. London, UK: Sage.

Mottram, D. (Ed.) (1988). *Drugs in Sport*. London, UK: E&FN Spon.

—·(2005). *Drugs in Sport*, 4th ed. London, UK: Routledge.

Rigauer, B. (1981). *Sport and Work*. New York, NY: Columbia University Press.

Sutherland, E., and Cressey, D. (1974). *Criminology.* Philadelphia, PA: Lippincott.

Verroken, M. (2005). "Drug use and abuse in sport," in D. Mottram (Ed.), *Drugs in Sport,* 4th ed. London, UK: Routledge.

Waddington, I., & Smith, A. (2009). *An introduction to drugs in sport: Addicted to winning?* (pp. 48–58). New York, NY: Routledge.

Academic Survival Skill

Expressing Critical Thoughts

In Reading 3, the authors presented possible theories about why increasing numbers of elite athletes take performance-enhancing drugs. The initial descriptions of the theories were factual; the authors supported each theory by providing citations to the researchers who believe in these theories. However, the authors also evaluated each theory; the evaluations were given at the end of each section.

What is an evaluation? An evaluation is the expression of an author's thoughts and opinions about the worth of the theory—its strengths and weaknesses and whether it is a useful explanation. An evaluation reveals a process of critical thinking and it can be positive or negative.

Being able to express critical thoughts is a characteristic of good academic writing.

A. The following table contains the evaluation sections of Reading 3. Look carefully at the way in which the authors move from a description of the theory to their evaluation of it. What organizational similarities do you see? Discuss your answers as a class. Then, answer the questions that follow.

THEORY	AUTHORS' EVALUATION OF THE THEORY
THE PHARMACOLOGICAL REVOLUTION	In considering explanations of this kind, it is of course important to recognize that in recent years more, and more effective, performance-enhancing drugs have been produced … However, to say that we should take such developments into account is very different from suggesting that the development of pharmacology should be given privileged status, and even further from the idea that it be given sole status, as an explanatory variable.
DRUG USE AS DEVIANT OVERCONFORMITY	There are some interesting and novel aspects to this approach, which certainly differs in important respects from other approaches to deviance. However, it may be argued that this approach … offers an explanation of why athletes may use drugs, but not why they have *increasingly* done so in recent years.
MARXIST APPROACHES	While the Marxist approach is not without value, particularly in its focus on changes in the relationship between sport and the wider society of which it is a part, this approach is not unproblematic. Here we draw attention to just two problems in this regard. First, although Marxists have made important contributions to the study of the relationship …
DIFFERENTIAL ASSOCIATION	Lüschen notes that this approach is "mainly descriptive" but he recognizes that it nevertheless "suggests quite a number of research questions and interpretive suggestions."

1. For the first three theories, what is the purpose of the first sentence of each evaluation section?

   ____

2. For the first two theories, underline the transition word that prepares the reader for the evaluation of the theory.

3. For the third theory, which words prepare the reader for the evaluation that follows?

   ____

4. For the fourth theory, the authors give credit to the original researcher for evaluating this theory. What weakness did the researcher identify?

   ____

5. With what interesting point did the researcher conclude?

   ____

   ____

B. Here are some examples of phrases that signal to the reader that an evaluation will follow. Underline the key transition words in each example. Identify which are adverbial conjunctions and which are subordinate conjunctions. (Refer to the Focus on Writing on page 65.) Can you and your class add to this list?

TRANSITIONS TO EVALUATION IN TWO SENTENCES	TRANSITIONS TO EVALUATION IN ONE SENTENCE
• This theory presents a useful explanation for ... However, it does not adequately explain why ... • The authors present a strong argument for ... Unfortunately, the theory does not explain why ...	• While the theory is a persuasive argument for ..., there are some weaknesses that must be considered. • Although/even though this theory attempts to explain ..., it is not successful at exposing the real reason for ... • Despite the ability of this theory to explain why ..., it does not cover all possibilities.

C. To develop the skill of expressing critical thinking in an academic way, and to prepare for the Final Assignment, return to Readings 1 and 2. On a separate sheet of paper, list the reasons for legalizing performance-enhancing drugs in sports from Reading 2. Then, add the argument from the last section of Reading 1 on page 156. As a class, review your list.

D. Working with one or two partners, write an evaluation of each of the reasons and the argument listed. Do you think each reason or the argument is a good one? Does it have any weaknesses? Does it seem logical or would its implementation cause other problems?

E. When you are satisfied with your evaluations, write sentences that will move the reader from each description to each evaluation. Write your best sentences on the board.

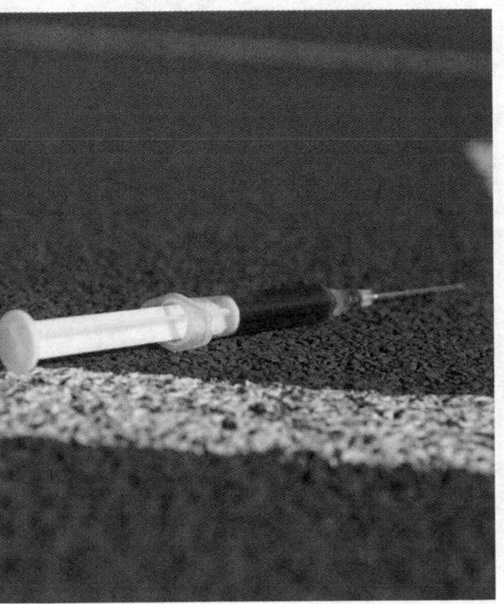

FINAL ASSIGNMENT

Write a Persuasive Essay

Write a persuasive essay in which you agree or disagree with this statement.

> Performance-enhancing drugs should be legalized.

- Base your essay on the reasons and arguments that you identified and support each reason or argument for or against this statement with a citation or two.
- Then, move from description to evaluation, using the organization patterns, sentence structures and vocabulary you have learned in this chapter.
- Include all the elements of an academic essay in your writing.

Refer to the Models Chapter (page 204) to see an example of a persuasive essay and to learn more about how to write one.

CHAPTER 8

Emerging Contaminants

Water scientists are discovering new (emerging) contaminants in rivers and lakes that may harm the natural environment. The sources of these contaminants are medicines for animals and people, and human personal care products (PCPs) such as deodorants and soaps. These contaminants, which are flushed down toilets and washed down drains, travel through our wastewater treatment plants and beyond into rivers and lakes where they cause physical changes to the fish population. What we don't know is the long-term effects these contaminants will have on the health of fish, other animals and even humans.

In this chapter, **you will**

- learn vocabulary related to emerging contaminants;
- analyze critical expression;
- discover the organization of a problem-solution text;
- combine different organizational patterns to suit your writing purpose;
- describe and evaluate a solution for a problem-solution text;
- write a complete problem-solution text.

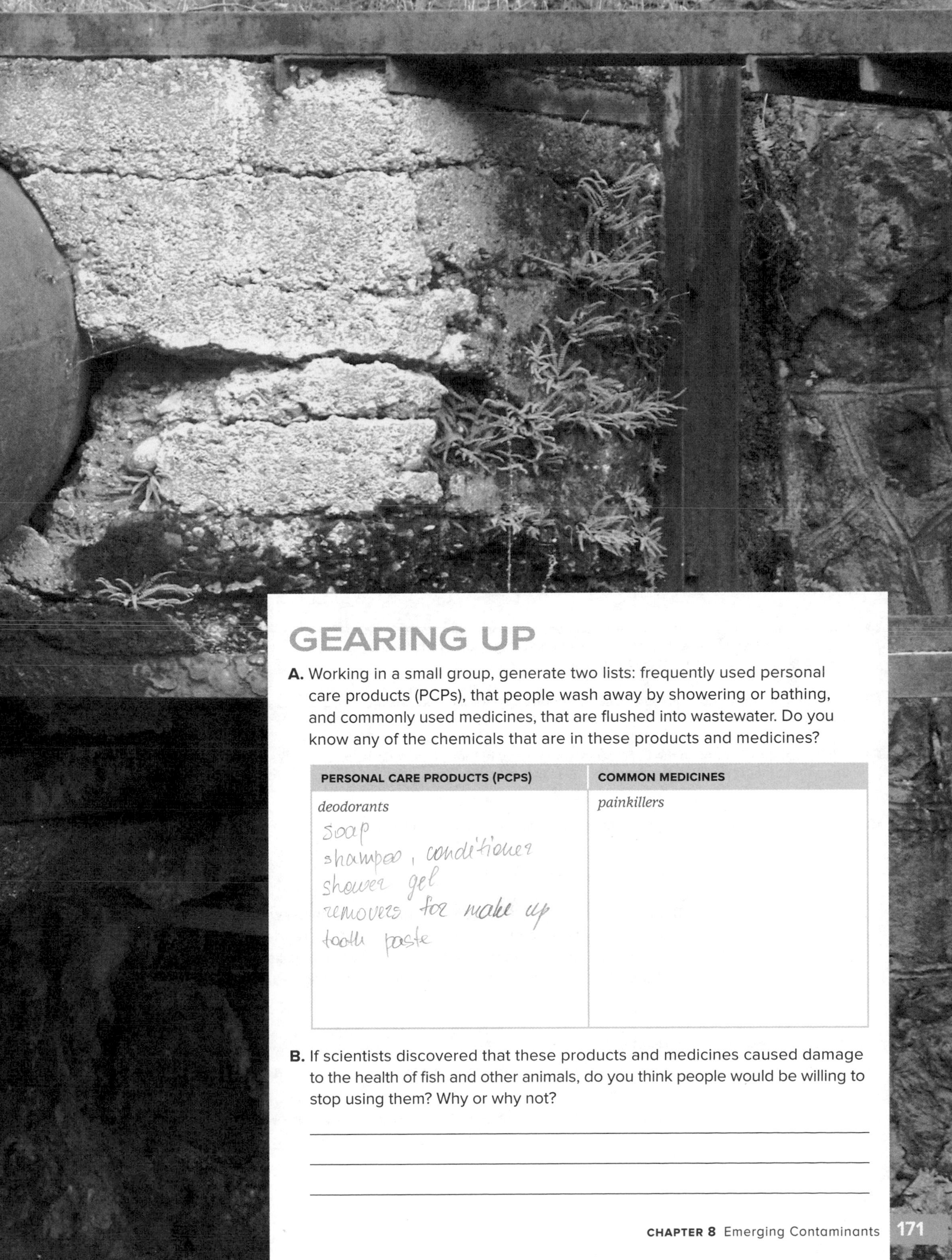

GEARING UP

A. Working in a small group, generate two lists: frequently used personal care products (PCPs), that people wash away by showering or bathing, and commonly used medicines, that are flushed into wastewater. Do you know any of the chemicals that are in these products and medicines?

PERSONAL CARE PRODUCTS (PCPS)	COMMON MEDICINES
deodorants soap shampoo, conditioner shower gel removers for make up tooth paste	*painkillers*

B. If scientists discovered that these products and medicines caused damage to the health of fish and other animals, do you think people would be willing to stop using them? Why or why not?

____

____

____

VOCABULARY BUILD

A. Read the following sentences adapted from Reading 1 and Reading 2. Using the context, choose the best definition for each of the words in bold. When you have finished, confirm your answers as a class.

WORDS IN CONTEXT	DEFINITION
1 A growing number of pharmaceutical **compounds*** (n.) are showing up in America's drinking water.	____ process that changes a complex compound to a simpler form
2 Reverse osmosis water filtration uses large amounts of electricity and produces a highly **concentrated*** (adj.) wastewater stream.	____ carefully checking a situation to see how it changes over time
3 If we are able to identify certain compounds that seem to be the **culprits** (n.) in potential human health risks, technology could be developed to remove those compounds rather than take out all impurities.	____ improve a situation or make its effects less harmful
4 You may be successful at removing the original contaminant, but through **degradation** (n.), you may be worse off than when you started.	____ substances containing atoms of two or more elements
5 Some fish in close proximity to wastewater discharge points **exhibit*** (v.) multiple sexual abnormalities.	____ at regularly occurring intervals
6 We just don't know what the **exposure*** (adj.) risk is to many of these compounds.	____ controlled with rules usually established by government
7 First we need to figure out whether we need to **mitigate** (v.), and if we do, then we'll address those larger issues of how to do it.	____ display
8 "These contaminants are active at very low concentrations in the water," says Jeff Armstrong, senior scientist in the ocean-**monitoring*** (adj.) group for the Orange County, California Sanitation District.	____ reasons for a problem or difficulty
9 The filters get dirty and must be washed **periodically*** (adv.); otherwise, the water can become infected with *Cryptosporidium*.	____ start or set in motion
10 Due to insufficient data on the occurrence and toxicity of these compounds, it appears that they will not be **regulated*** (v.) any time soon.	____ stronger because most of the water has been removed from it
11 These contaminants **trigger*** (v.) abnormal reproductive responses in fish and possibly in humans.	____ contact (with danger)

*Appears on the Academic Word List

B. In Readings 1 and 2, there are a number of technical words and phrases related to wastewater treatment. Working with a partner, read the words and phrases (all are nouns or noun phrases) and their definitions, listed in Table A. Then, in Table B, categorize each according to its meaning.

Table A

TECHNICAL WORD/PHRASE	DEFINITION
chlorine	chemical often used in swimming pools to disinfect, clean and purify water
effluent	clean water that leaves a wastewater treatment facility; wastewater effluent is cleaner than the water that enters the plant

TECHNICAL WORD/PHRASE	DEFINITION
endocrine-disrupting compounds*	chemical compounds that change or modify (or disrupt) hormone levels in the body
endocrine disruptors	synonym for endocrine-disrupting compounds
estrogenic compounds	medical compounds that contain estrogen, the hormone that regulates female characteristics
granular activated carbon filters	filters made of specially treated carbon used to remove impurities from wastewater by passing dirty water through them
hormones	chemicals produced naturally by the body to regulate growth and development; people with growth problems may take synthetic (artificial) hormones
influent	dirty water entering a wastewater treatment facility through underground pipes (sewers)
microconstituents	chemicals found in very small quantities in water
outfall	place where wastewater effluent is released (discharged) into a body of water; fish that swim near the wastewater outfall may be affected by the compounds in the water
ozonation	process used to purify wastewater by dissolving ozone gas in the water, changing organic material in the water to carbon dioxide and inactivating bacteria
pathogen	germ, bacterium or virus that causes disease
reverse* osmosis filtration	high-energy method used to clean wastewater by forcing dirty water through a membrane to remove impurities
trace organic compounds	very small amounts of naturally occurring substances
wastewater treatment facilities*	buildings and equipment used to clean dirty water, sometimes referred to as WWTFs
wastewater treatment plants	buildings and equipment used to clean dirty water (synonym for WWTFs)

*Appears on the Academic Word List

Table B

WORDS/PHRASES THAT DESCRIBE POSSIBLE CONTAMINANTS	WORDS/PHRASES THAT COLLOCATE WITH WASTEWATER	WORDS/PHRASES THAT DESCRIBE WATER TREATMENT METHODS
endocrine disruptors – effluent – hormones – endocrine disruptors – microconstituents – pathogen – trace organic compounds	*wastewater effluent* – wastewater tr. plants – outfall – wastewater tr. facilities – influent	*chlorine* – granular activated carbon filters – reverse osmosis filtration – ozonation

C. Based on your understanding of the chapter so far, explain to a classmate your understanding of the *problem* of emerging contaminants, and give possible *solutions* to the problem.

READING 1

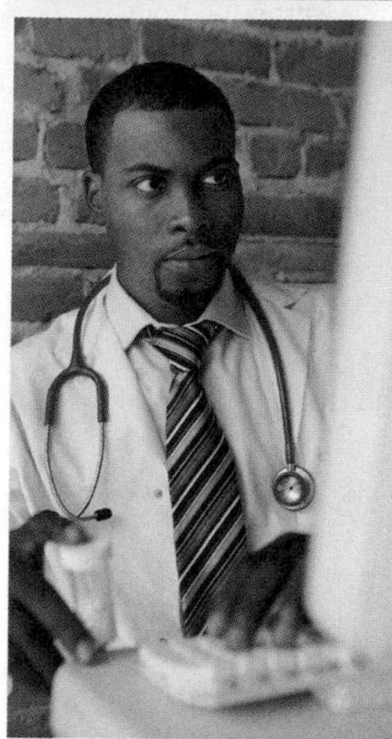

Pharmaceuticals May Be Poisoning America's Drinking Water

This article is an excerpt from a magazine, republished in *Pollution*, part of a textbook series called *Opposing Viewpoints*. The author of this article presents one view of emerging contaminants in the water supply.

A. The article begins with an abstract. Read the abstract and write short answers to the following questions. When you have finished, confirm your answers with a classmate.

1. What type of compounds does the author write about, and in which country's waters are they found?

 ____

2. What term does the author use to describe these compounds?

 ____

3. What is the problem with current wastewater treatment facilities?

 ____

4. What happens to the fish that live near the wastewater treatment plant's discharge area?

 ____

5. Why is fish health important?

 ____

 ____

6. What does the author hope for in the future?

 ____

 ____

7. In the abstract, what verbs are used as synonyms for *states*?

 ____

B. Using the approach to reading comprehension that you learned in Chapter 1, skim the reading and, on a separate sheet of paper, take notes on the topic, length, text type and probable organization. Then, turn the title and the five headings into questions.

C. Read the text more closely and answer the six questions you generated. When you have finished, confirm your answers with a classmate.

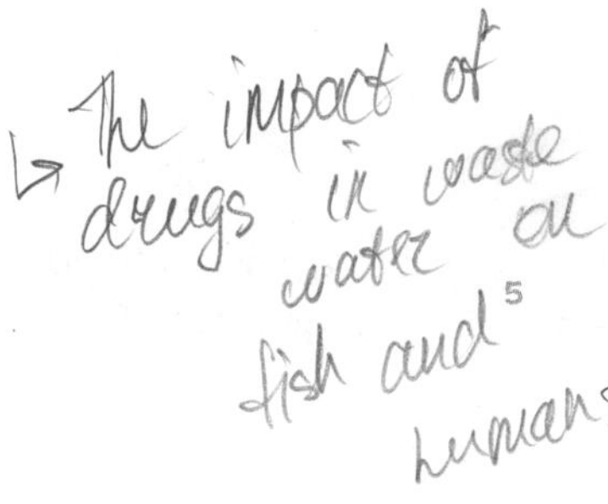

↳ The impact of drugs in waste water on fish and humans.

A growing number of pharmaceutical compounds are showing up in America's drinking water, claims Patricia Frank in the following essay. More Americans than ever are being treated with prescription drugs that often end up in wastewater facilities that are not designed to filter out these compounds of emerging concern (CECs), she maintains. As a result, Frank asserts, fish found close to watershed and wastewater discharge areas show reproductive abnormalities, which is raising concerns about

the impact of CECs on human health. Growing public concern may pressure wastewater treatment facilities to find ways to safely remove CECs from America's drinking water, she contends.

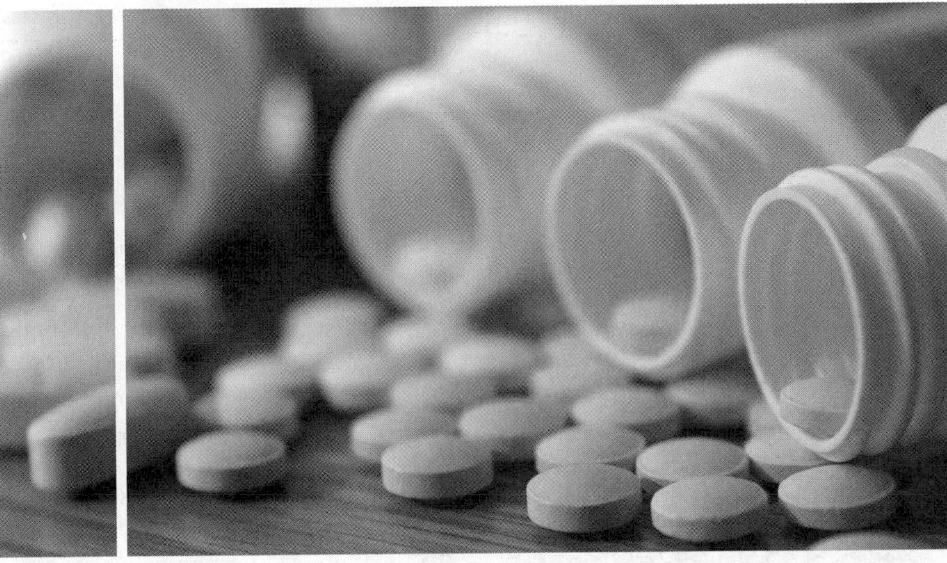

Hidden among the well-known problems faced by water professionals—aging infrastructure, dwindling supply—is another emerging issue: rising amounts of pharmaceutical compounds in surface water and drinking water. And, considering the increasing numbers of people being treated with drugs at earlier ages and an aging population taking multiple medications for a variety of health conditions, more of those compounds likely will find their way into the nation's wastewater facilities.

Early signs of the problem were discovered by the US Geological Survey (USGS) research in 1999. Of the sixty pharmaceuticals the agency was testing for, it found thirty of them in 139 streams in thirty states. In addition, 80 percent of the streams had one or more contaminants, 54 percent had five or more, and 13 percent showed twenty or more.

"We can measure over 150 compounds in water alone," says Dana Kolpin, a research hydrologist and member of the USGS study team. "Now, the big question is what kind of environmental consequences [do they pose] to terrestrial and aquatic ecosystems and, maybe in the long term, even human health. We just don't know what the exposure risk is to many of these compounds."

Determining the Effects

Scientists from the ... USGS, other government agencies and universities are attempting to determine the potential effects of chronic exposure to pharmaceutical mixtures—otherwise known as Compounds of Emerging Concern (CECs)—such as endocrine disruption and the development of antibiotic resistance, in the aquatic environment, soil, plants, animals and humans.

Though the amounts being measured often are in parts per million or parts per billion, many of the compounds are designed to have effects at low levels. "These CECs are active at very low concentrations in the water and in the sediments," says Jeff Armstrong, senior scientist in the ocean-monitoring group for the Orange County, California Sanitation District. "It's not so much the death of the animals [that is a concern], it is reproductive effects or effects on other areas of the endocrine system, the ability to fight off infection or other aspects of reproduction."

Endocrine disruptors are chemicals that mimic or block hormones or trigger abnormal reproductive responses in fish and possibly in humans. Nevertheless, our ability to measure the compounds is ahead of our knowledge of their long-term effects.

Increasing Sexual Abnormalities

However, some fish in close proximity to wastewater discharge points exhibit multiple sexual abnormalities, such as male fish with deformed testes or low to no sperm counts, for example. Some fish are classified as "intersex" with sex characteristics of both genders. Kolpin says a large proportion of the male fish have either female egg protein or female characteristics.

Following a high number of fish deaths in the Potomac River basin and the Shenandoah watershed between 2003 and 2005, the USGS and scientists from Virginia and West Virginia analyzed samples of thirty smallmouth bass from six sites. A microscopic examination of the fish testes discovered 42 percent of the male bass had developed eggs. A second USGS study found an even higher number of intersex fish—79 percent. "[In the Potomac, we found] a big portion of the male fish having either female egg yolk protein or female characteristics," Kolpin says. Douglas Chambers, the study's lead scientist, says that all water samples contained detectable levels of at least one known endocrine-disrupting compound.

Pacific Ocean flatfish found in sediment near Orange County, California's Huntington Beach effluent discharge point, exhibited similar effects. "We're finding that male fish are producing [endocrine-disrupting compounds] in concentrations that normal males should not," Armstrong says. "That means they're being exposed to some kind of estrogenic compound. We're finding the fish near our outfall and [the estrogenic compound] seems to be in higher concentrations [there, which indicates] that something's coming out in the treated wastewater that might be causing this."

"It's really not certain what's going on, but [there is no doubt] that there is evidence of endocrine-type biomarkers in fish downstream from wastewater outfall," says Shane Snyder, research and development project manager for the Southern Nevada Water Authority in Las Vegas. "The degree of magnitude of the effect seems like it's going to be related to the treatment type, the degree of mixing and the mobility of the fish."

The Sources and Treatment of CECs

The contaminants may originate from hospitals and medical facilities, vet clinics, pharmaceutical manufacturers and people using prescription and over-the-counter medications and personal care products. "[Medical facilities] can be a big source of ... pharmaceuticals, X-ray and MRI contrast agents and chemotherapy drugs," Kolpin says. "Maybe they need to have separate wastewater treatment so they're not just put in with residential waste."

Designed to remove conventional pollutants, such as suspended solids and easily biodegradable organic materials, most conventional wastewater treatment plants do not remove CECs. The concentration of the compounds that remain in wastewater treatment plant effluent depends on the type of treatment, the specific compounds as well as the concentration in the influent entering the plant.

Techniques for removing compounds from drinking water included advanced oxidation, membrane filtration and filtration with granular activated carbon, and nano-filtration combined with reverse osmosis, which eliminates all the drugs. Each technology serves a function, but each can produce an unwelcome side effect.

Conventional ozone renders certain CECs inactive, but its use comes with a price, Snyder warns. "Ozone creates regulated by-products—regulated on cancer endpoints. [It's] great [that] you're putting in ozone, but what about all the cancer-causing by-products they form?"

Chlorine, the most commonly used wastewater disinfectant ..., is the least effective in removing the CECs. Kolpin's concern is the creation of chlorination by-products. The [Environmental Protection Agency] already has set drinking water standards of 100 parts per billion for one group of by-products, called trihalomethanes, because of their potential to cause cancer. "You may be removing the parent compound [of CECs] by creating these chlorinated degradation products, [and you] may be worse off than when you started," he says. "Certainly chlorination has the advantages of removing pathogens, but we are not certain that it's the best route to remove CECs. It needs to be researched."

Reverse osmosis (RO) offers the most promise as the technology can remove CECs to the point where they are no longer detectable. However, it uses large amounts of electricity and produces a highly concentrated wastewater stream. "[RO] creates a stream of concentrated waste; what do you do with the concentrated waste stream that you've generated?" Snyder says.

Techniques that combine ozone and granular activated carbon (GAC) are effective for removing industrial and agricultural pollutants, and also improve the water's taste and odour. The filters get dirty and must be washed periodically; otherwise, the water can become infected with *Cryptosporidium* and *Giardia*.

The Challenge of Identifying CECs

Before water utilities can choose an effective technology, though, the harmful CECs have to be identified. "First we need to figure out whether we need to mitigate, and if we do, then we'll address those larger issues of how to do it," Armstrong says.

Still, common wastewater treatments can be useful in removing CECs. "The tertiary treatment, like reverse osmosis (RO) or micro- or nano-filtration, removes pretty much 100 percent of [CECs]," Armstrong says. "There's a lot in the literature that [says] ozonation renders these [compounds] biologically inactive. The problem is doing that on a large scale. [We process] 255 million gallons of wastewater a day. There's no way we can remove all CECs from that much wastewater, so we have to look to other ways to figure out what kind of mitigation strategy's going to work for us."

CECs will not be regulated in the near future, at least. "Due to insufficient data ..., it appears that pharmaceuticals will not be regulated any time soon," says Snyder ...

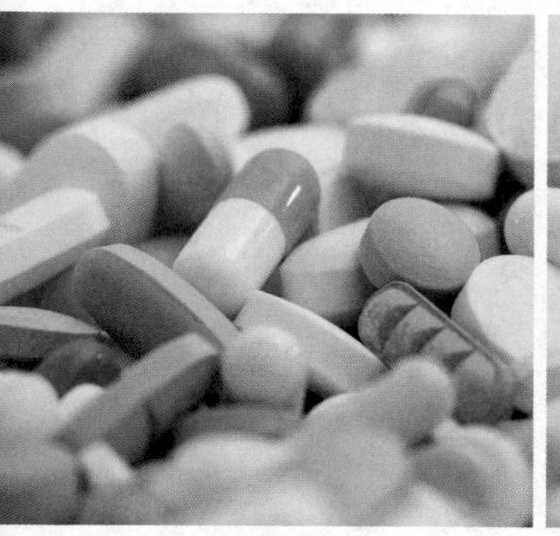

Meanwhile, the Las Vegas [Valley] Water District has added ozone to its expanded wastewater treatment facility. Ozone was chosen for its disinfection power ... "Ozone is extremely effective for destroying estrogenicity, and that's where our concern lies for the fish," Snyder says.

The Use of Take-Back Programs

Because 50 to 90 percent of ingested drugs are excreted, state and local governments are attempting to involve the public through drug take-back programs to stem the flow at one of its source points. "We'll deal with that in the treatment plants as best we can, but keeping the extraneous pharmaceuticals out of the environment is where the majority of the action seems to be at the municipal level today," Armstrong says.

...

The public also seems ready to address the issue. In May 2006, the San Francisco Bay Area Pollution Prevention Group collected 3,634 pounds of pharmaceutical waste from 1,500 residents, and South Portland, Maine, recently sponsored a one-day event and collected 55,000 pills. The state's legislators currently are exploring instituting turn-in, mail-back and other disposal programs.

Making it convenient for the public to participate in drug take-back programs appears to be helping. San Mateo County, California, featured repainted and donated postal service mailboxes, which made their program as easy to access as mailing a letter. Their pilot program in four locations collected nearly 590 pounds of unwanted drugs in just four months, at a cost of $924, plus the costs of the police to collect the drugs.

Despite the best efforts to control the drugs that enter the wastewater stream, water utilities still can expect challenges to meet growing needs and the delivery of safe drinking water to their customers, including removing CECs. "I'm hoping if we are able to identify certain compounds that seem to be the culprits in potential human health risks, that technology could be developed to mitigate those, rather than take out everything," Snyder says. "People have the perception that utilities like ours pull from some giant coffer of money and we can do whatever we want to get down to the last nanogram [of contaminant], but the public will pay." (1756 words)

Frank, P. (2011). Pharmaceuticals may be poisoning America's drinking water. In L.I. Gerdes (Ed.), *Pollution* (pp. 78–85). Farmington Hills, MI: Greenhaven Press.

D. Discuss with the class how worried we should be about CECs in the water supply.

READING 2

Naming the Substances We Detect

Reading 2, a persuasive essay, was published in a magazine written for water engineers and scientists. Read the essay and answer the following questions.

1. In the first paragraph, underline the thesis of the essay and then paraphrase it.

2. Which two risks from synthetic organics (emerging contaminants) are given in the second paragraph?

3. Why are humans not likely to respond to endocrine-disrupting compounds in the same way as fish? (Give two reasons.)

4. Why is the public so worried about emerging contaminants?

5. What are the problems with using reverse osmosis to eliminate contaminants?

6. According to the authors, what is the critical question?

7. What statement is inappropriate to make at this time?

8. In both the introduction and the conclusion of this essay, the authors state that the water industry is searching for a single term that will describe all the compounds now found in water. Why is this simplification a problem?

There is a movement in the water and wastewater industry to find a name to use when discussing the large number of substances that are found in water at trace concentrations. Several terms have been proposed and used in technical and media communications, including the terms microconstituents, trace organics and endocrine-disrupting compounds. However, these names are not well understood by either the public or the media, resulting in confusion regarding the implications for human health. A major challenge surrounding the topic is communicating the significance of trace concentrations, and how these compounds should be addressed from a regulatory standpoint. The water and wastewater industry needs to change its vocabulary and develop a clear method of communicating about these trace substances in a way that fosters public trust and understanding.

Many synthetic organic chemicals have found their way into the environment. They include pharmaceuticals, detergents, insecticides, pesticides, cosmetics, fragrances, plasticizers and many more—there is scarcely any part of our modern lives where we do not come into contact with them. Society chooses to use them for many good reasons, including the fact that they can extend our lifespan and improve our quality of life. Synthetic organics have been the subject of many attention-grabbing press accounts due to the fact that they tend to bioaccumulate (show up in increasing quantities the higher up an animal is in the food chain) and because they may be linked to sexual abnormalities in fish.

People are understandably concerned when they read that these substances are detected in drinking water. Media has taken the descriptive scientific name of endocrine-disrupting compounds out of context while cartoons have humanized the sex-change effects observed in fish, leading some to believe similar reproductive problems are inevitable in humans. This fails to reflect the fact that humans do not spend 100 percent of their lifetimes immersed in water, as do fish. Of course it is important to understand the influences on aquatic life, but it confuses the real findings to draw inappropriate inferences for human health. The other critical thing that is often overlooked in media reports is the fact the concentrations being detected are exceedingly small. As Southern Nevada Water Authority (SNWA) researcher Dr. Shane Snyder recently noted, "The highest concentration of any pharmaceutical compound in US drinking water is approximately 5,000,000 times lower than the therapeutic dose." Imagine drinking a glass of water that had one five-millionth of an ibuprofen tablet dissolved in it. Is it reasonable to think that this could have a measurable effect on your body? You would need to drink five million glasses of water in order to consume the equivalent of a single tablet (and that might not even be enough to take care of your headache).

Unfortunately, we are not given the tools in our education or media communication to differentiate between our considerable exposure to these substances during our everyday activities and our minimal exposure to them in water, nor to understand what effects, if any, they might really have. When the media runs an alarming headline calling these everyday substances contaminants, compounds of emerging concern or, worse, unknowable unknowns, those of us who are not scientifically trained to understand those terms grow fearful. Our gut reaction is to demand the complete removal of these trace substances.

Highly advanced wastewater treatment processes like reverse osmosis can reduce concentrations to below current detection limits, effectively meeting the common definition of removal. However, current detection limits may soon be obsolete, as detection technology grows more and more advanced, allowing detection of smaller and smaller concentrations. "Zero" and "completely removed" will always remain elusive, but we can expect the concentration of the compounds to be "reduced" so they do not pose a threat to human health.

Although water treated by reverse osmosis meets the current definition of pure (non-detectable concentrations), this advanced wastewater treatment requires a large capital investment and a large amount of electricity to operate. The ecological impacts of this cannot be ignored in light of the current global realization of the negative effects of rampant energy consumption. Treatment technologies need to be thoughtfully considered and selected to provide the right level of treatment for the intended use.

Regulation of these substances should only follow, not precede, a very thoughtful, thorough and scientific examination of the risks and environmental and public health impacts of such choices.

The critical question is not whether we can find things in water or what one word we should call them, but, rather, do they exist in concentrations that cause harm? Continued research is needed to assist decision-making about future management of these substances. It is inappropriate to equate detection of such materials with unacceptable risk to humans or the aquatic environment.

The water and wastewater industry is actively engaged in the discussion about the threat of harm, potential regulation and the best way to effectively communicate with the public in a way that builds trust and reduces fear. The industry has just begun to realize there is public and media confusion regarding substance detection, the impact of the small concentrations of synthetic organic compounds and their implications for human health. This confusion underscores the need for the water industry professionals and scientists to communicate clearly with each other and with the public.

In summary, within the water industry, there has been an extraordinary focus on naming the substances we are detecting. The industry is looking for just the right word or phrase to group together a broad and disparate group of substances that are by-products of everyday modern life so that we can talk about them neatly, succinctly and, above all, scientifically. Unfortunately, such a grouping and generalized characterization of these substances tends to frustrate rather than advance public understanding, as it implies there is a scientifically valid commonality of risk from the materials at trace concentrations. This well-intentioned simplification suggests that a host of potentially harmful substances are being detected in our nation's waters. What we need is an honest presentation of scientific findings about detection and risk in familiar terms, without confusing the issue with a catch-all umbrella phrase, especially one with ominous overtones that leads us to believe there is something new and evil lurking in our waters.

Scientists and water professionals have a responsibility to help people understand risks and to pay attention to the impact their words have on a community that has poor understanding of water science. (1067 words)

Callaway, E., Macpherson, L., & Simpson, J. (2010). Talking substance about detection ... or naming the substances we detect? *Influents, 5,* 30–31. Retrieved from http://www.weao.org/assets/docs/INFLUENTS/archive/influents_2010_1_spring.pdf

Analyzing Critical Expression

In Chapter 7, you learned how writers express criticism of established theories by using specific words and expressions that are appropriate in an academic context (see the Academic Survival Skill on page 167). In Reading 2 of this chapter, the authors are critical of the media and of public scientific education.

A. Use the line numbers in the first column of the following table to identify the words and phrases from Reading 2 that express criticism. Write these in the second column. In the third column, identify the target of the authors' criticism. The first one has been done for you.

READING 2	WORDS/PHRASES THAT EXPRESS CRITICISM	TARGET OF AUTHORS' CRITICISM
LINES 6–9	*However, these names are not well understood by either the public or the media, resulting in confusion ...*	*uninformed public and media*
LINES 21–22		
LINES 26–29		
LINES 32–33		
LINES 42–43		
LINE 79		

READING 2	WORDS/PHRASES THAT EXPRESS CRITICISM	TARGET OF AUTHORS' CRITICISM
LINES 94–96		
LINES 97–98		
LINES 103–105		

B. Compare the criticisms expressed in Chapter 7, Reading 3, page 163, with those expressed in Chapter 8, Reading 2, and discuss with your class which criticisms are more direct and strongly worded.

C. The authors of Reading 2 are critical of media coverage of emerging contaminants. To practise expressing critical thoughts, read the media headlines in the first column and, in the second column, use the words and phrases from the table in task A to write sentences critical of each headline. The first one has been done for you.

MEDIA HEADLINE	CRITICAL SENTENCES
Weed killer linked to gender-bending in animals (*Globe and Mail*, December 1, 2011)	*This attention-grabbing headline implies that male and female characteristics of animals are being changed (bent) by exposure to weed killer. The reporter is taking the results of this study out of context, leading some to believe that the weed killer should be banned.*
Researchers blame fish mutations on local sewage plants (*Waterloo Record*, October 9, 2012)	
US Drinking Water and Watersheds Widely Contaminated by Hormone Disrupting Pesticide Atrazine (*Natural Resources Defense Council*, August 24, 2009)	
Cocaine, Spices, Hormones Found in Drinking Water (*National Geographic News*, February 26, 2010)	
Mineral water in plastic bottles contaminated with hormones (*Local: Germany's News in English*, March 13, 2009)	
Atrazine in Water Tied to Hormonal Irregularities (*Scientific American*, November 28, 2011)	

Discovering the Organization of a Problem-Solution Text

Readings 1 and 2 are examples of problem-solution texts. A typical problem-solution text has four parts. This pattern of organization is common in academic and technical texts.

A. The first three components of a typical problem-solution text are given in the first column of the following table. The first paragraph of Reading 2 (page 180) contains these three parts. As this paragraph is the introduction to the reading, each part is presented as a summary statement. Read the paragraph and identify the line numbers that represent each component and write them in the second column. When you have finished, discuss your answers as a class.

COMPONENTS OF A PROBLEM-SOLUTION TEXT	EXAMPLES FROM READING 2
Description of the current situation	LINES ______________
Statement of the problem (Note the use of a transition word as the authors move from the situation to the problem part of the text.)	LINES ______________
Description of a possible solution	LINES ______________

B. Working with a partner, now consider a larger section of the text and identify all four components. As this section of the reading is part of the body of the text, each component is developed more fully than the summary statements you identified in task A. Read lines 16–64, and as you did in task A, identify the line numbers that represent each component and write them in the second column.

COMPONENTS OF A PROBLEM-SOLUTION TEXT	EXAMPLES FROM READING 2
Description of the current situation	LINES ______________
Statement of the problem	LINES ______________
Description of a possible solution	LINES ______________
Evaluation of the solution (Note the use of a transition word as the authors move from solution description to evaluation of the solution.)	LINES ______________

C. Take a closer look at the move from solution to evaluation of the solution, by rereading lines 92–122 of Reading 1 (page 177). Here you will see repeated movement from solution to evaluation. Again, identify the line numbers that represent each component and write them in the second column.

COMPONENTS OF A PROBLEM-SOLUTION TEXT	EXAMPLES FROM READING 1
Description of possible solutions (several)	LINES ______________
Description of a possible solution (ozonation)	LINES ______________

COMPONENTS OF A PROBLEM-SOLUTION TEXT	EXAMPLES FROM READING 1
Evaluation of the solution	LINES ______
Description of a possible solution (chlorine)	LINES ______
Evaluation of the solution	LINES ______
Description of a possible solution (reverse osmosis)	LINES ______
Evaluation of the solution	LINES ______
Description of a possible solution (ozonation and granular activated carbon filters)	LINES ______
Evaluation of the solution	LINES ______

In this excerpt from Reading 1, the move from solution to evaluation is not marked by a transition word or phrase (except in the case of the reverse osmosis solution), but the text might have been improved if some form of transition had been used.

The four parts of problem-solution texts are not always placed in order from description of the situation to evaluation of the solution. While the description of the situation and problem typically come first as a form of introduction, the remaining parts of the text can vary in order, as you saw in Reading 1 and in Reading 2.

WARM-UP ASSIGNMENT

Describe and Evaluate a Solution for a Problem-Solution Text

For this Warm-Up Assignment, you will write the last two parts of a problem-solution text: the description of a solution and your evaluation of it. Start by selecting one of the solutions to the problem of emerging contaminants that were mentioned in Readings 1 and 2:

- chlorine
- granular activated carbon filtration
- ozonation
- reverse osmosis (RO) filtration

When you receive feedback from your instructor or your classmates on this Warm-Up Assignment, you will have some information that you can use to improve your writing on the Final Assignment.

Find and document reliable sources of information about your chosen solution. Paraphrase and summarize (providing accurate references in the citation style required in your discipline). Write a description of at least two paragraphs. Then, use a transition to signal your move to the evaluation of the solution,

and write another complete paragraph. As your evaluation is likely to be critical of the solution, use words and phrases learned earlier to express criticism in an appropriate academic manner. This Warm-Up Assignment text will be integrated into your Final Assignment for this chapter.

Refer to the Models Chapter (page 211) to see an example of a problem-solution text and to learn more about how to write one.

VOCABULARY BUILD

Working with a partner, read the following sentences and write a definition for each of the words and phrases in bold. As you work, read the sentences aloud. Check a dictionary for pronunciation assistance if needed. When you have finished, review your definitions as a class.

WORDS/PHRASES IN CONTEXT	DEFINITION
❶ Some compounds are regulated once they reach a trigger concentration, or an **accumulated*** amount per year.	accumulated (adj.): *gradually increased*
❷ Further research must be done to understand the **attenuation** and degradation processes of these compounds.	attenuation (n.):
❸ Emerging contaminants threaten the feminization of fish and other **biota** in the environment.	biota (n.):
❹ Research and regulation are made more difficult by the current **compartmentalized** approach to removing emerging compounds from water. For example, chemists analyze water samples, but engineers build water treatment technology, and governments regulate allowable concentrations.	compartmentalized (adj.):
❺ Manufacturers should be made responsible for the **cradle-to-grave** lifespan of any compound used in a medicine they produce.	cradle-to-grave (adj.):
❻ Some chemicals have **deleterious effects** on fish and wildlife that should be mitigated through various wastewater treatment processes.	deleterious effects (n.):
❼ There are many unknowns about the life cycle of emerging compounds, from when they are **ingested**, to when they are **discharged** from the wastewater treatment facility.	ingested (v.):
	discharged (v.):
❽ There is a **salient** gap in our knowledge of the impacts emerging compounds have on fish and the environment.	salient (adj.):
❾ **Ultimately**,* the manufacturer who uses the compound should be responsible for the fate of that compound in the environment.	ultimately (adv.):
❿ All new drug products must **undergo*** an environmental assessment to determine if they will have deleterious effects on the environment.	undergo (v.):

*Appears on the Academic Word List

My eLab Visit My eLab to complete a vocabulary review exercise for this chapter.

READING 3

Environmental Fate of Microconstituents and Removal during Wastewater Treatment: What Do We Know, What Do We Still Need to Find Out?

Reading 3 is an academic paper that summarizes the research on the effects of emerging contaminants (microconstituents) in the water.

A. Read the text and answer the following questions.

1. What terms do the authors of this reading use to refer to emerging contaminants?

   ____

   ____

2. What is the problem with using these compounds (EDCs and PPCPs)?

   ____

   ____

3. As wastewater treatment facilities (WWTFs) are not successful at removing emerging compounds from the wastewater, what must be done now?

   ____

   ____

4. What procedure is common across the US, the EU and Canada before a new product or drug can be sold to the public?

   ____

   ____

   ____

5. What is the weakness of the Canadian models that predict the fate of these compounds in the environment?

   ____

   ____

   ____

6. The authors advocate for collaborative efforts in the future to solve the complex problem of emerging contaminants in water. What example do they give of the current compartmentalized approach to research in this field?

   ____

   ____

   ____

7. What would be the benefit of making manufacturers responsible for the cradle-to-grave life of the contaminant?

   ____

   ____

   ____

8. What solutions do the authors propose?

9. What is the problem with using advanced oxidization and RO processes to reduce the presence of these compounds in the water supply?

10. What do the authors suggest is the best way to address this issue?

Introduction

In recent years, the occurrence of endocrine-disrupting compounds (EDCs) and pharmaceutical and personal care products (PPCPs) in surface and ground water has received significant attention. Treated wastewater effluents from wastewater treatment facilities (WWTFs) are important routes for these compounds to enter the environment. Although the concentrations of EDCs and PPCPs are very low in wastewater effluents, these point sources have been extensively studied in recent years, since these compounds have been shown to have deleterious effects on aquatic life. The most frequently cited impact of EDCs and PPCPs is the feminization of fish and other biota due to the presence of estrogens (Danish Environmental Protection Agency, 2002 and other sources) … A few regulatory agencies have begun the process of monitoring for selected EDCs and PPCPs (California, 2007); however, there are currently no mandatory regulatory requirements to meet EDC or PPCP effluent standards.

The use of EDCs and PPCPs over the last thirty years has exploded. They are essential to modern society: they have helped eradicate and/or control several diseases, improved quality of life and increased our lifespans. Markets for new and current PPCPs continue to grow in both the developed and developing world (Robinson et al., 2007). One can say with a large degree of certainty that the use of PPCPs will only increase in the years to come. EDCs and PPCPs have been shown to negatively impact reproductive potential and behavioural responses of animals. While some of these effects are reversible, other anatomical, physiological and genetic alterations are permanent (Larsen, 2009). Although to date, no data have been published on adverse effects on humans, even extremely low concentrations of these compounds potentially affect surface waters and, in turn, our drinking water sources.

Engineered systems such as wastewater treatment plants provide a direct route for EDCs and PPCPs to enter the aquatic and subsurface environments that serve as sources for drinking water (Heberer, 2002). While there are clearly benefits associated with controlled use of PPCPs, an increasing body of evidence suggests that EDCs and PPCPs are not fully removed or fully transformed in conventional wastewater treatment processes (Heberer, 2002; Ternes et al., 2004; Stephenson and Oppenheimer, 2007). Therefore, it is essential to study and understand the fate of these chemicals as they move through the engineered systems and subsurface and aquatic environments.

...

A Historical Perspective of the Regulatory Framework

A look at regulatory process provides some background into the research on ... new PPCPs. The policies in select regions are outlined below.

United States

Prior to being released for public consumption in the United States, new drug products undergo an environmental assessment in accordance with the *National Environmental Policy Act* of 1969. As part of this process, the FDA [Food and Drug Administration] requires an environmental assessment (final rule in *21 CFR Part 25, 1997*) for new products entering the market. The trigger level for the environmental assessment is set at a concentration ≥1 μg/L in the effluents of sewage treatment facilities, expected annual use of ≥44,000 kg, or extraordinary circumstances. At levels below 1 μg/L, manufacturers can request an exemption from performing the environmental assessment (Meyerhoff and Perkins, 2007).

European Union (EU)

The European Union Council Directive 2001/83/EC requires an environmental risk assessment for drugs meant for human consumption. The trigger is a concentration ≥0.01 μg/L in surface waters, expected individual use ≥2 mg/day, or potential for reproductive effects at levels <0.01 μg/L. In addition, specific EU member countries are developing water quality standards for specific constituents. For example, the German Environmental Protection Agency has proposed a limit of 0.03 ng/L maximum annual average concentration for 17α-Ethinylestradiol (Moltmann et al., 2007).

Canada

The New Substances Notification Regulations of the Canadian Environmental Protection Act, 1999, requires environmental assessments. Product use amounts >1000 kg/year or accumulated use >50,000 kg trigger a requirement to provide environmental data under current *New Substance Notification Guidelines*.

In order to determine the risk in the environmental assessment, the producer must submit results from a model that predicts the concentration of the proposed PPCP in the WWTF effluent or in the receiving surface water (Cunningham, 2007) ...

While these models provide an indication of PPCP concentration in the environment and potential behaviour under specific conditions, they do not account for conditions when there are mixtures of these PPCPs in the environment. The models also do not account for daughter products formed through the biodegradation of the parent PPCPs in the WWTF.

...

So, Where Do We Go from Here?

Significant strides have been made in research related to the fate, attenuation and impacts of EDCs and PPCPs in engineered and natural environmental systems in recent years. It has become abundantly clear that this is a complex problem, and it is not likely that there exists a single "magic bullet" that could reduce or eliminate the discharge of EDCs and PPCPs into the environment. Therefore, it is imperative that the various stakeholders work collaboratively on a number of fronts to achieve a potentially optimal solution.

The current compartmentalized regulatory approach has a tendency to not look comprehensively at the effects that EDCs and PPCPs could have in the environment. Health and pharmaceutical regulatory bodies remain focused on the important work of ensuring the safety of new compounds for patient (human and veterinary) consumption, but not long-term environmental impacts. The environmental protection agencies are taking steps toward evaluating the fate and potential ecotoxicological risks associated with these new compounds in the environment. However, there remains a salient gap in our understanding of the life cycle of an EDC/PPCP between the point of ingestion and the point of discharge from a WWTF.

To address this compartmentalization problem, some have advocated for an approach much like the US-EPA's [Environmental Protection Agency] *Comprehensive Environmental Response, Compensation, and Liability Act* of 1980 (CERCLA), where potential responsible parties are responsible for the cradle-to-grave life of the microconstituent. The benefit of such a program would be that the end users (in this case, the WWTF and, ultimately, that specific community's tax base) are not stuck with the price tag for "remediating" the raw water and reducing the risk of impact on the environment.

... The regulatory community should work more closely with the pharmaceutical and chemical industries and the local community on multi-pronged approaches. These may range from simple solutions such as community-level pharmaceutical take-back programs to more elaborate green-chemistry replacements for chemicals where possible. Doctors could write prescriptions with smaller supplies of medication, thus reducing the overall waste. Similar considerations should be taken with veterinary medicines, particularly considering the intensive use of such medicines at the numerous concentrated animal feeding operations (CAFOs) worldwide.

Evidence from numerous studies indicates that it is possible to reduce the discharge of EDCs/PPCPs for WWTFs using advanced treatment technologies such as advanced-oxidation processes and reverse osmosis. Indeed, today's "gold standard" for treatment is based on a multi-barrier approach utilizing some of these technologies. While the use of these technologies undoubtedly improves EDC and PPCP removal, it comes at a significant increase in energy use and great capital expense … Undoubtedly, there is a need to address the environmental consequences of these discharges on biota in our receiving streams. Before jumping headlong into upgrading WWTFs with state-of-the-art technologies to remove minute amounts of microconstituents, we should consider our complete environmental stewardship, socio-economic and collective financial responsibilities.

It is also clear that we must continue making advances in research on the fate and transport of EDCs/PPCPs in natural and engineered environmental systems. The available analytical tools allow evaluation of the formation and fate of parent and daughter compounds. Clearly, this work will be extremely beneficial, not only to better understand the attenuation and degradation processes within the treatment plant "fence line," but also as input to risk assessment models and ecotoxicology studies.

(1294 words)

References

California Department of Public Health. (2007). Groundwater Recharge Reuse. Draft Regulation. C.D.O.P.H.D.W. Program.

Cunningham, V.L., Modeling Methods for Environmental Exposure Assessment. WERF Symposium on Compounds of Emerging Concern. Providence, RI. 2007.

Danish Environmental Protection Agency. (2002). Feminisation of fish: The effect of estrogenic compounds and their fate in sewage treatment plants and nature.

Heberer, T. (2002). "Occurrence, fate, and removal of pharmaceutical residues in the aquatic environment: a review of recent research data." *Toxicology Letters 131*(1–2): 5–17.

Larsen, M.C. Statement of Dr. Matthew C. Larsen, Associate Director for Water, USGS, Department of the Interior, Before the Committee on Natural Resources Subcommittee on Insular Affairs, Oceans, and Wildlife, June 9, 2009. Retrieved from (www.usgs.gov/congressional/hearings/docs/larsen_09june09.doc)

Meyerhoff, R.D., and Perkins, A.N. Evaluating the Effects of Pharmaceutical Products on Aquatic Organisms. WERF Symposium on Compounds of Emerging Concern. Providence, RI. 2007.

Moltmann, J.F., Liebig, M., Knacker, T., Martin, S., Scheurer, M., and Ternes, T. Relevance of Endocrine-Disrupting Substances and Pharmaceuticals in Surface Waters. Federal Environmental Agency of Germany, Report No. UBA-FB205 24 205, March, 2007.

Robinson, I., Junqua, G., van Coillie, R., and Thomas, O. (2007). "Trends in the detection of pharmaceutical products, and their impact and mitigation in water and wastewater in North America." *Analytical and Bioanalytical Chemistry 387*(4): 1143–1151.

Stephenson, R., and Oppenhiemer, J. (2007). Fate of Pharmaceuticals and Personal Care Products Through Municipal Wastewater Treatment Processes, WERF.

Ternes, T.A., Janex-Habibi, M-L., Knacker, T., Kreuzinger, N., and Siegrist, H. (2004). Assessment of Technologies for the Removal of Pharmaceuticals and Personal Care Products in Sewage and Drinking Water Facilities to Improve the Indirect Potable Water Reuse: Detailed Report related to the overall project duration, January 1st, 2001–June 30th, 2004, EU, Poseidon Project.

Sathyamoorthy, S., & Reid, A. (2010). Environmental fate of microconstituents and removal during wastewater treatment: What do we know, what do we still need to find out? *Influents, 5,* 38–41. Retrieved from http://www.weao.org/assets/docs/INFLUENTS/archive/influents_2010_1_spring.pdf

B. Reading 3 is another good example of a problem-solution text. Working with a partner, reread the text and mark the moves from a) description of the situation to b) statement of the problem to c) description of a solution to d) evaluation of the solution. Label these moves in the margin of the text, and underline any transition expressions used. Compare your decisions with those of another pair of students.

Academic Survival Skill

Combining Different Organizational Patterns to Suit Your Writing Purpose

As your English writing and reading skills improve, you will notice that the texts you read, and the ones you write, are increasingly complex; they are no longer organized according to a single pattern. Instead, you may recognize different patterns of organization within longer texts. In the readings of this chapter, you may have recognized the following patterns:

- definition in Reading 1
- compare and contrast in Reading 3 (While this is not a conventional compare and contrast pattern as the authors do not compare and contrast directly, the placement of the three regions' regulatory frameworks one after the other invites a comparison from the reader.)
- process text in the description of the solution in your Warm-Up Assignment (as you describe how the solution works)
- persuasive text in the conclusions of all three chapter readings

The writers of these texts followed different patterns to suit the purpose of their writing, and you should also do this when you write. Knowledge of the conventional patterns of organization is the foundation on which you can base your reading and writing of increasingly complex texts.

Although Reading 1 in Chapter 7 is an expository text (written to provide explanation), it also contains components of a problem-solution text. Skim the reading (pages 152 to 156) and identify the four components of a typical problem-solution text: situation, problem, solution and evaluation. Note the importance of definition in this text. When you have finished, discuss your answers as a class.

FINAL ASSIGNMENT

Write a Problem-Solution Text

Write a problem-solution text that includes all four components: situation, problem, solution and evaluation. Paraphrase and summarize the readings in this chapter, with appropriate citations and references, to complete the first two components (situation and problem). Integrate the solution and evaluation from your Warm-Up Assignment into the text. Write another solution and evaluation section in order to compare and contrast the two solutions. Finally, write a conclusion for your problem-solution text.

In your text, you should include
- a definition (in your situation component);
- process descriptions (as part of your solution components);
- a compare and contrast text (also in your solution components);
- expressions of critical thought (in your evaluation components);
- a persuasive text (in your conclusion).

Refer to the Models Chapter (page 211) to see an example of a problem-solution text and to learn more about how to write one.

CRITICAL CONNECTIONS

Chapter 7 presented information on performance-enhancing drugs, and Chapter 8, on the effects of emerging contaminants (including performance-enhancing drugs) on ecosystems. To complete the following tasks, you will need to synthesize content, skills and vocabulary from both chapters.

1. Read the following headlines about athletes who have taken performance-enhancing drugs. Write sentences that criticize the headlines, using academically appropriate ways to express your critical thoughts.

MEDIA HEADLINE	CRITICAL SENTENCES
Disgraced cyclist Tyler Hamilton wins prize for drugs book (*Independent*, November 27, 2012)	*While books like Hamilton's give readers an insight into the lives of athletes who take performance-enhancing drugs, it is not appropriate to give a prize to an author who has clearly taken these banned substances himself.*
Nike performs about-turn by ending contract with Lance Armstrong (*Times*, October 17, 2012)	
Armstrong 'had drugs courier' (*Sunday Times*, September 2, 2012)	
Congress to Propose Stiffer Rules on Drugs (*New York Times*, April 29, 2011)	
More NFL players testing positive for amphetamines, many blaming Adderall (*Globe and Mail*, November 28, 2012)	

Visit My eLab for new content related to Chapters 7 and 8.

2. Write a persuasive paragraph to convince the management of a wastewater treatment facility to implement reverse osmosis to remove pharmaceutical contaminants from the wastewater.

3. Write a problem-solution paragraph that explains the problem of athletes taking performance-enhancing drugs and then suggests a solution.

MODELS CHAPTER

This chapter provides models of the writing assignments that you may be required to write as you progress through this textbook. All of the assignments are about standardized testing, allowing you to see how the same information can be arranged to meet the demands of different writing assignments.

Before each model assignment, you will find

- instructions that highlight the key characteristics of the writing assignment;
- the outline that the writer used to prepare for the writing assignment.

MODEL 1 How to Write an Extended Definition

Definitions, and extended definitions, are common in academic writing. To write a definition, start with a sentence that includes the term you want to define. Then, use one of the following strategies to define the term or use several strategies to extend the definition.

- Provide an equation (if the term can be represented mathematically).
- Write a description.
- Make reference to the root word of the term.
- Describe the evolution of the term.
- Explain what the term is, and is not.
- Describe the process represented by the term.

MODEL 2 How to Describe a Data Set

Show data in table, graph or chart form. When describing data in academic writing, follow these guidelines.

- Start with a sentence that points the reader to the data; for example, Table 1 shows/demonstrates/indicates/illustrates/provides/reveals/summarizes/presents ...
- Continue with sentences that describe the data, drawing attention to the most important trends. Do not simply repeat what the data show; add information in order to "add value" to the data.
- Finish by telling the reader the significance of the data.

Example of an Extended Definition Including a Data Set

What is PISA and what do the results show?

WRITER'S PLAN	
DEFINITION	• PISA: Programme for International Student Assessment • conducted by the Organization for Economic Co-operation and Development (OECD) • tests 15-year-olds in OECD and partner countries: 74 countries in 2009 • reading, math and science tests
DATA SET	• figures show average student scores for top 20 countries in reading, math and science for 2009 • reading scores used to select top 20 countries; math and science scores superimposed on reading scores; math/science scores show more variability • China (Shanghai) had the highest scores in all three subjects; China reached this milestone by creating an inclusive educational system of high quality • in general, math scores keep pace with science scores for each country • reading scores remain below math/science scores, suggesting that math/science tests assess similar skills while reading tests assess distinct skills • size of country and politics do not seem to matter • speculation that poverty has a depressing effect on scores

PISA Results for 2009

The Programme for International Student Assessment (PISA) is a standardized test program that assesses the math, science and reading skills of fifteen-year-old students in many countries. The program is run by the Organization for Economic Co-operation and Development (OECD), and countries that participate in PISA are affiliated with that organization. The purpose of the multi-country comparison is to enhance the quality of education and educational policies in member countries.

The initial offering of PISA was completed in 2000, and the tests are now offered every three years. Each year that the tests are administered, one of the three fields of knowledge (math, science or reading) is emphasized, although the tests cover all three subjects. In 2009, the emphasis was on reading skills. Over 470,000 students from seventy-four countries completed the tests. The PISA results have inspired many research studies that attempt to explain the variation in scores.

Figure 1 shows the average student scores for the top twenty countries in reading, math and science for 2009. The reading scores were used to select the top twenty countries while math and science scores were superimposed on the reading scores; consequently, the math and science scores show more variability than the reading scores. Reading scores remain mostly below the math and science scores, suggesting that the math and science sections of the test assess similar skills while the reading section tests distinct skills.

In 2009, students in Shanghai, China, scored the highest in all three subjects. China reached this milestone by creating an inclusive educational system of high quality. In general, math scores keep pace with science scores for each country. It appears that the size of the country has no bearing on test score, and that politics and religion have little impact. However, there is speculation that poverty has a depressing effect on scores (Strauss, 2010).

Figure 1: Average reading, math and science scores for the top 20 countries participating in PISA, 2009

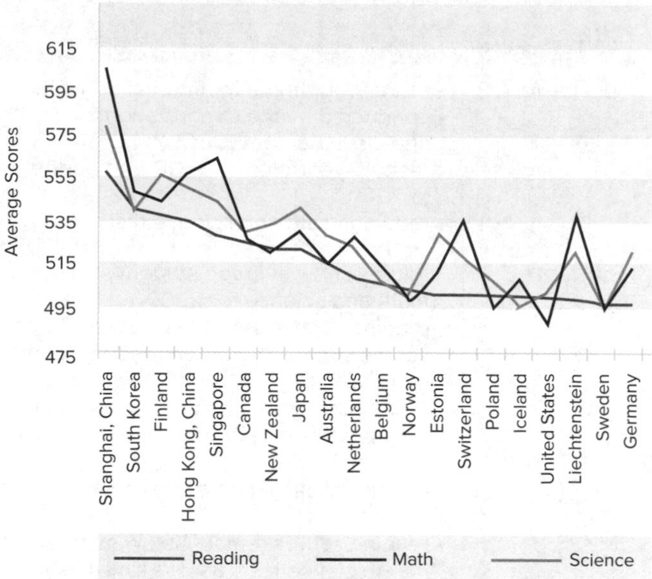

Source: Statistics Canada, 2010.

References

Statistics Canada. (2010). Measuring up: Canadian results of the OECD PISA study. The performance of Canada's youth in reading, mathematics and science. 2009, First results for Canadians aged 15. (81-590-XPE no. 4). Ottawa, ON: Statistics Canada.

Strauss, V. (2010, December 9). How poverty affected U.S. PISA scores. *Washington Post.* Retrieved from http://voices.washingtonpost.com/answer-sheet/research/how-poverty-affected-us-pisa-s.html

MODEL 3 How to Write a Process Essay

Process essays are written to explain *how* something is done. Therefore, a process essay often explains the steps in a process. The following guidelines will help you write an effective process essay.

- Like all essays, a process essay must have three general sections: an introduction, a body and a conclusion.
- The introduction announces the topic of the essay. Although there are many good ways to start an essay, the introduction usually begins with a general statement about why the topic is important. The introduction might also start with a definition.
- The introduction finishes with a *thesis statement*. A thesis statement is a sentence that includes the topic of the essay and the opinion that the essay will present. It may or may not include the main steps of the process that you are writing about.
- The body of the essay will contain a number of paragraphs. For a short process essay, usually each paragraph describes one step in the process.
- Each body paragraph should start with a topic sentence that clearly indicates the topic of the paragraph. If your thesis listed the main steps of the process, you can repeat the key words (or synonyms of the key words) from the thesis.
- Each body paragraph should finish with a sentence that makes the point of the paragraph clear.
- The conclusion summarizes the main steps in the process. It often finishes with a sentence that restates (but does not repeat) the thesis.

Example Process Essay

How is a standardized test developed?

WRITER'S PLAN	
INTRODUCTION	• definition of a standardized test: description + distinct from a classroom test
BODY	• six steps in development – state the purpose of the test – write test specifications – write test items – evaluate the test items – determine scoring procedures – validate the test and develop new versions
CONCLUSION	• standardized test development a continuous process

Developing a Standardized Test

Almost all language students, even very young students, are familiar with tests. The majority of language tests students take are developed by their teachers and are known as *classroom tests*. However, there is another type of test that students are taking with increasing frequency: standardized tests. Zwaagstra (2011) states that standardized tests are distinct from classroom tests because they are developed by expert test developers, written by students at a set time in their learning and scored by trained raters in a single location. In theory, when two students from very different schools write a standardized test, they should receive the same score if they have similar knowledge and skills. Standardized tests allow students, teachers, parents and administrators to compare student proficiency. Brown and Abeywickrama (2010) divide the process of creating a standardized test into six steps.

The first step in developing a standardized language test is to state the purpose of the test. Carr (2011) explains test purpose as determining the decisions that can be made based on the test results. For example, will the test measure language proficiency for the workplace or for academic study (or something else)? Will students with high scores be hired for a job, admitted into a university or placed in a high-level program? Test developers express the purpose of the test when they decide what it will be used to measure.

As the development and administration of a standardized test requires the cooperation of many people, the second step of development is writing test specifications. Test "specs," as they may be referred to, define all elements of the test, such as the skills to be assessed, method of assessment, number of test items, delivery method, length, scoring and method to return scores. In short, the specifications establish key information that must be shared for the test development process to be a success.

Once the test specs have been written and shared, developers begin to write items. At this stage, test questions are developed according to the specifications. Questions can range from multiple-choice, fill-in-the-blank or matching items to more open-ended tasks that require students to read and listen to texts and speak or write in response. Essentially, the test itself is written during this step.

Although the test is written, it is not yet ready for use; evaluating the items is the fourth step in the development of a standardized test. Hughes (2003) points out that language test items must be tested on native speakers as well as on non-native speakers to identify any problems. For example, if native speakers have trouble answering a question, then it should not be used to test non-native speakers. Test items that produce unexpected responses should also be eliminated at this stage. The evaluation stage is key to ensure the questions are as good as they can be.

Determining scoring procedures is the next step in the development process. For closed questions, this can be relatively simple; a correct answer and the number of marks allocated to the item are determined. For items that require interaction or extensive response, scoring can involve the development of a rubric. Any open-ended questions require rater training to ensure that all raters score consistently. It is also important that the number of marks per question reflects the amount of time students have spent studying for that question. At the end of this stage, all scoring issues must be solved.

Finally, developers must prove the validity of the test. While the meaning of validity has changed over time, Carr (2011) states that for a test to be valid, developers must prove in a variety of ways that it is useful. To do this, developers show that questions represent tasks students would perform in real-life contexts; that the test scores reflect a student's likelihood of success; that scoring procedures are reliable; that the test is free of cultural bias; that test language is authentic; and that test feedback has a positive impact on learning and teaching. If a test meets all of these criteria, then developers can say that it is valid.

Clearly, the development of a standardized test is a lengthy process requiring the collaboration of many people. It is also true that standardized tests are rarely ever finished. The continual need to develop new versions that are equivalent in difficulty to the original test ensures ongoing efforts. Standardized test development is a challenging process that never ends.

References

Brown, D., & Abeywickrama, P. (2010). *Language assessment: Principles and classroom practices* (2nd ed.). White Plains, NY: Pearson Longman.

Carr, N. (2011). *Designing and analyzing language tests*. Oxford, UK: Oxford University Press.

Hughes, A. (2003). *Testing for language teachers* (2nd ed.). Cambridge, UK: Cambridge University Press.

Zwaagstra, M. (2011, October). Standardized testing is a good thing. *Frontier Centre for Public Policy: Policy Series* 119. Retrieved from http://www.fcpp.org/files/1/PS119StandardizedTesting.pdf

MODEL 4 How to Write a Compare and Contrast Essay

Compare and contrast essays are written to show the similarities and differences between two items. When you compare items, you show the similarities; when you contrast items, you show the differences. The following guidelines will help you write effective compare and contrast essays.

- Decide what points of comparison or contrast you wish to explain to your reader.
- Decide which pattern of organization fits your information best. There are two standard ways to organize a compare and contrast essay: block style organization and

point-by-point style organization. Generally, block style organization is best for less technical information while point-by-point style organization is best for more technical information. As advanced language learners, your content is likely to be technical or more complex, so a point-by-point style of organization is demonstrated here.

- Like other kinds of essays, a compare and contrast essay has three general sections: an introduction, a body and a conclusion.
- The introduction announces the topic of the essay. Although there are many good ways to start an essay, the introduction usually begins with a general statement about why the topic is important. The introduction might also start with a definition.
- The introduction finishes with a *thesis statement*. A thesis statement is a sentence that includes the topic of the essay and the opinion that the essay will present. It may or may not include the main points of comparison or contrast.
- The body of the essay will contain a number of paragraphs. For a short compare and contrast essay, usually each paragraph explains one point of comparison or contrast.
- Each body paragraph should start with a topic sentence that clearly indicates the topic of the paragraph. You can do this by repeating key words (or synonyms of the key words) from the thesis.
- Each body paragraph should finish with a sentence that makes the point of the paragraph clear.
- The conclusion summarizes the points of comparison and/or contrast. It often finishes with a sentence that restates (but does not repeat) the thesis.

Example of a Point-By-Point Style Compare and Contrast Essay

Explain the differences and similarities between classroom and standardized language tests.

WRITER'S PLAN		
INTRODUCTION	• classroom tests versus standardized tests • different based on purpose, development and impact	
BODY	CHARACTERISTICS FOR COMPARISON AND CONTRAST	
	CLASSROOM TESTS	STANDARDIZED TESTS
– PURPOSE	• criterion-referenced	• criterion- or norm-referenced
– DEVELOPMENT	• simple, quick • usually involve only one teacher	• complex, time-consuming • six-step process that is never finished
– IMPACT	• generally low-stakes • extensive feedback, often formative • less stressful • test preparation individualistic	• usually high-stakes • minimal feedback • more stressful • test preparation often systemic
CONCLUSION	• classroom and standardized language tests different in purpose, development and impact • a need for both types of tests	

Classroom versus Standardized Language Tests

Almost all language students, even very young students, are familiar with tests. The majority of language tests students take are developed by their teachers and are known as *classroom tests*. In most cases, these tests are developed by a single instructor and vary from teacher to teacher. However, there is another type of test that students are taking with increasing frequency: standardized tests. Zwaagstra (2011) states that standardized tests are distinct from classroom tests because they are developed by expert test developers, written by students at a set time in their learning and scored by trained raters in a single location. Classroom and standardized tests may have similar purposes, but they differ in their development methods and their impact.

Classroom and standardized tests may share a common purpose; they may both be criterion-referenced tests. A criterion-referenced test is designed to measure the extent to which students achieve the criteria established in the test objectives. The test scores show how successful students were in achieving the objectives. While learners can compare their scores, the purpose of the test is to compare each learner's performance to the test objectives (Brown and Abeywickrama, 2010).

A norm-referenced test has a different purpose. Norm-referenced tests are designed to compare learners and rank them from highest to lowest. The purpose of this kind of test is not to measure whether students achieved the test objectives but to determine which student among a large group of students is "the best." Scores are percentile rankings that demonstrate how a student ranks in relation to others. It doesn't matter if the top score is 50 or 100 percent in the test; the student with the top score is the top performer in the group, and he or she receives the top ranking. Examples of norm-referenced standardized tests include the Law School Admissions Test (LSAT), Graduate Management Admissions Test (GMAT) and Medical College Admissions Test (MCAT). The purpose of a criterion-referenced test is thus fundamentally different from that of a norm-referenced test.

While most standardized and classroom tests are criterion-referenced, they are developed through very different processes. Brown and Abeywickrama (2010) have determined six steps in the development of a standardized language test. These steps are stating the purpose of the test, writing test specifications, writing test items, evaluating test items, determining the scoring procedures and validating the test. The stages are appropriate for communicating large amounts of information about the test to the multitude of people involved in developing them. However, while classroom test development may also involve multiple stages, it is often abbreviated for practical reasons. For example, most classroom tests are developed by a single teacher. As a result, the teacher does not need to write test specifications to be shared among many developers. Teachers may not have time to test items with native speakers as recommended by Hughes (2003). And they may not spend time validating the test through a variety of measures to prove that it is useful. Therefore, the test development processes for these two types of tests contrast significantly.

Finally, classroom and standardized tests are distinct in their impact. In the language testing field, "impact" is often replaced with the term *washback*, which is defined as the influence of testing on teaching and learning (Alderson and Wall, 1993). Washback encompasses effects that are both personal and wide-ranging. Consequently, these two types of tests can be contrasted based on what's at stake, the extent of feedback and the level of test preparation required; each of these considerations falls under the umbrella of washback.

While it may be important for a student to do well on classroom tests, the results are generally low-stakes. Students are often assessed multiple times during a course, so each test score is less likely to have a significant impact on the students' final grades. If students perform poorly on one test, they might be motivated to study harder for the next test, and they are still likely to pass the course. Consequently, students may be less anxious about taking a classroom test. In contrast, the score from a standardized test may determine whether students are admitted to a desirable university or obtain higher-paid employment. As a result, these tests are considered high-stakes. Students are often stressed by the one-time-only nature of standardized tests, whose scores influence their futures. Clearly, classroom tests are low-stakes compared to high-stakes standardized tests.

Classroom and standardized tests are distinguishable by the extent of the feedback provided with the scores. Classroom instructors, who are often dedicated to their students' success, may spend hours grading and responding to errors in the hope that students benefit from their efforts. Class time may be spent reviewing test content when the tests are returned to the students. Instructors provide extensive feedback and content review to improve student knowledge and skill; feedback therefore serves a formative purpose. However, this is not the concern of the raters who score standardized tests. They are required to produce consistent scores but not comment on student proficiency. Students may receive a single score with little or no indication of their strengths or weaknesses. The purpose of these scores is simply to quantify students' proficiency and not to provide information about how to do better next time. In this way, classroom tests often provide formative assessment while standardized tests do not.

Test preparation for these two types of testing will also vary. For classroom tests, students are likely to study on their own, or perhaps with another student or a group of students. They use their textbooks and class notes to review content that will be tested. In contrast, students studying for a standardized test usually have several options. They can take a test preparation course, either online or in a classroom. They can purchase a test preparation book or practise sample tests online. They might even go online to read blogs by students who have already completed the same test. Of course, they may decide to study on their own; however, in most cases, a wide range of study options is available. Therefore, classroom and standardized tests also differ in the study options open to students who take them.

In summary, classroom and standardized tests may be compared and contrasted to gain a greater understanding of their purposes, feedback and impact (or washback). While most classroom tests and many standardized tests are criterion-referenced, teachers often provide formative assessment on classroom tests, which are low-stakes compared to standardized tests. High-stakes standardized tests rarely result in substantive feedback. While these two types of tests are distinct, they both serve a useful purpose within the educational community.

Bibliography

Alderson, J., & Wall, D. (1993). Does washback exist? *Applied Linguistics, 14*, 115–129.

Brown, D., & Abeywickrama, P. (2010). *Language assessment: Principles and classroom practices* (2nd ed.). White Plains, NY: Pearson Longman.

Cheng, L., & Curtis, A. (2004). Washback or backwash: A review of the impact of testing on teaching and learning. In L. Cheng, Y. Watanabe, & A. Curtis (Eds.), *Washback in language testing* (pp. 3–18). Mahwah, NJ: Lawrence Erlbaum Associates.

Hughes, A. (2003). *Testing for language teachers* (2nd ed.). Cambridge, UK: Cambridge University Press.

Zwaagstra, M. (2011, October). Standardized testing is a good thing. *Frontier Centre for Public Policy: Policy Series* 119. Retrieved from http://www.fcpp.org/files/1/PS119StandardizedTesting.pdf

MODEL 5 How to Write a Report

A report explains an existing complex situation and makes recommendations about how to improve it. The following guidelines will help you write an effective report.

- Divide the report into sections. Each section begins with a section title or heading. Many reports are divided into introduction, methods, challenges and recommendations sections. However, your section titles will depend on the information that you need to explain. In the example report, the sections are *introduction, driving forces, description of an existing test* and *recommendations*.
- Select logical section titles.
- In the introduction, define important terms and explain why the situation is complex.
- In methods, explain how you gathered information about the situation.
- In the challenges section, explain the problems or challenges that result from the complexity of the situation.
- In the recommendations section, make recommendations about how to improve the situation. Predict the benefits that will result from the adoption of the recommendations.
- You may include direct or indirect quotations in any of these sections.

Example Report

Would an English-language proficiency test help solve communication problems at the Global Information Systems Technology company?

WRITER'S PLAN	
INTRODUCTION	• Global Information Systems Technology (GIST): sells information technology systems worldwide • working language English • wants to implement an English training program and an oral proficiency test • test a requirement before assignment to key English accounts • quotation from director of Human Resources • definition of a standardized test
DRIVING FORCES	• not all employees communicating well in English • problems with daily communication (example) • problems with large account management (example) • problems with marketing and sales (example) • quotation from director of marketing and sales
DESCRIPTION OF AN EXISTING TEST THAT COULD ADDRESS THE DRIVING FORCES	• Public Service Commission of Canada (PSCC) • describe Second Language Evaluation Test of Oral Proficiency • quotation from director of Second Language Assessment Program at the PSCC • quotation from test-taker
RECOMMENDATIONS	• GIST implement a program of English training and an oral proficiency test similar to the PSCC

The Need for an English Oral Proficiency Test for the Global Information Systems Technology (GIST) Company

Report submitted by Second Language Assessment Inc.

Introduction

Global Information Systems Technology (GIST) is a company that sells information technology systems to governments around the world. The company specializes in communication facilitation among government employees as well as government-to-public information flow. It employs 12,000 people in twenty different countries and operates in high-stress and confidential environments.

Many GIST employees are multilingual; however, the working language in the company is English, and the majority of business transactions are conducted in that language. GIST offers a training program for employees wishing to improve their English skills. It now wants to adopt an English oral proficiency test to measure the fluency of its employees after program completion and before salespeople are assigned to important English accounts. Janet Turner, director of Human Resources for GIST, indicates how important it is to adopt a reliable oral proficiency test. "Our employees are highly trained in information systems technology, and they are hired for their expertise, but increasingly we need them to be skilled in English as well—to communicate accurately in English to support our clients. A standardized oral English proficiency test will help us achieve improved English fluency in our employees."

A standardized test, produced by test development experts and scored by trained raters, will support GIST in its goal to reliably measure the English oral proficiency of its employees.

Driving forces

Not all GIST employees are communicating well in English. Three recent critical incidents are driving the move to adopt an oral English proficiency test.

1. A month ago, lack of communication between two teams working on similar projects in different countries resulted in a duplication of effort that cost GIST one million dollars. Failure to speak fluent English resulted in weak communication between teams.
2. Last quarter, GIST lawyers wrote a contract that contained an error due to inaccurate communication between the lawyers and the account negotiation team. GIST was forced to pay $1.5 million to cover the cost of the error.
3. Recently, GIST's marketing team was unable to close a deal in an English-speaking country because the government purchasing team did not believe GIST's technical support people could communicate accurately in English. Had the deal been completed, GIST would have gained a $125 million account.

The frustrated director of Marketing and Sales, Eric Stauffer, claims that poor oral English proficiency is costing the company. "If we can't speak English, we can't make money, or at least, not as much money," he said. "It's hurting us financially."

Description of an existing test: PSCC test of oral proficiency

The Public Service Commission of Canada (PSCC) designed a test of second-language oral proficiency in 2008 in response to the latest research in language assessment.

A team of applied linguists, second-language test developers and psychometric professionals developed the test according to a needs analysis based on the language demands of the tasks employees must perform. "The development of this test was a thorough process," reports Marie Brisson, head of PSCC Second Language Assessment Branch. "We piloted the test extensively before implementation, and it can measure oral skill level proficiency with great accuracy." She indicated the test is used to test oral proficiency in both English and French.

The four-stage test is conducted one-on-one; an individual candidate interacts with a language assessor. The first stage requires candidates to answer questions about familiar situations at work or volunteer activities. The second stage involves listening to pre-recorded voice-mail messages and work conversations. Candidates must answer questions about what they have heard. The third stage requires employees to talk for several minutes on a topic determined by the assessor and answer several questions about the presentation. In the final stage, the candidate listens to a pre-recorded conversation about work, summarizes the content and answers questions. The level of difficulty increases from stage to stage, and the assessor may stop the test at any stage if he believes the candidate's proficiency has been fully demonstrated.

"This test allowed me to show what I was capable of," Carolyn Stitt said. She was one of the first employees to pilot the test to measure her proficiency in French. "The test content reflects the kinds of things I have to do in my job, so the test really makes sense. Preparing for it helps you speak better in your second language."

Recommendations

1. It is recommended that GIST develop an English-language oral proficiency test to improve the English-speaking skills of its employees.
2. Before the test is developed, GIST should complete a language analysis of the tasks required of its employees. Test tasks should then reflect the requirements of the workplace.
3. The overall test structure should follow the model of the PSCC Test of Oral Proficiency.
4. The test should be piloted and revised as required before full implementation.
5. GIST should hire English assessor experts to ensure test scores are accurate and reliable.

MODEL 6 How to Write a Persuasive Essay

Persuasive essays are written to persuade, or convince, people that a particular opinion about a topic is correct. The following guidelines will help you write an effective persuasive essay.

- Like all essays, a persuasive essay must have three general sections: an introduction, a body and a conclusion. You may not use these section titles as headings in the essay.
- The introduction announces the topic of the essay. Although there are many good ways to start an essay, the introduction usually begins with a general

statement about why the topic is important. The introduction might also begin with a definition.

- The introduction finishes with a *thesis statement*. A thesis statement is a sentence that includes the topic of the essay and the opinion that the essay will present. It may or may not include the main reasons why the opinion of the essay is correct.
- The body of the essay will contain a number of paragraphs. For a short persuasive essay, usually each paragraph explains one reason why the essay opinion is correct.
- In the body of the essay, you may include paraphrases and summaries of other writers' ideas to support your points.
- Each body paragraph should start with a topic sentence that clearly indicates the topic of the paragraph. You can do this by repeating key words (or synonyms of the key words) from the thesis.
- Each body paragraph should finish with a sentence that makes the point of the paragraph clear.
- The conclusion summarizes the main reasons why the essay opinion is correct. It often finishes with a sentence that restates (but does not repeat) the thesis.

Example Persuasive Essay

Standardized language tests are harmful. Agree or disagree and explain why.

WRITER'S PLAN		
INTRODUCTION	• definition of standardized test (Zwaagstra, 2011) • controversial • do more harm than good	
BODY	STANDARDIZED TESTS ARE HARMFUL	STANDARDIZED TESTS ARE USEFUL
– TIME	• teachers must teach to the test • take up time that could be better spent on learning (BCTF, 2009)	• if tests and teaching and real-world tasks are aligned, then the tests are useful (Zwaagstra, 2011)
– COST	• too expensive • PISA cost to test 1,500 students: US $700,000 (Schneider, 2009) • total cost (470,000 students participating in 2009): $219 million	• similar to the drug enforcement argument: too expensive, so we shouldn't do it • consequences of not using them
– POWER AND CONTROL	• create power imbalances between testers and test-takers • tests undemocratic (Shohamy, 2001)	• test administrators now follow Shohamy's recommendations • standardized testing now more democratic
– MORALITY	• morality of testing • tests establish criteria that measure worth of students • destroy teacher-student relationship (Johnston, 2003)	• objective measure of language competency still needed
CONCLUSION	• administration must make standardized tests effective so that – time spent on test preparation is useful and not wasted – administrative costs do not exceed the usefulness of test scores – tests are not simply tools used to control power and a social agenda • tests are viewed as one way to measure proficiency but do not reflect the total worth of an individual	

Are Standardized Tests Harmful?

Zwaagstra (2011) states that standardized tests are distinct from classroom tests because they are developed by expert test developers, written by students at a set time in their learning and scored by trained raters in a single location. There is a great deal of controversy about standardized tests and whether they are harmful or useful. However, while the administration of standardized tests may be flawed, their use is essential.

One of the greatest objections to standardized tests is the time required to prepare students for them. The British Columbia Teachers' Federation expresses this view in its objections to provincial standardized tests (BCTF, 2009). It argues that time spent preparing students to write the tests is time that could be better spent on teaching and providing students with feedback that will help them learn. Their webpage states that the standardized tests assess only a small part of their provincial curriculum, and that preparing students to take the tests emphasizes those elements of the curriculum that are tested, at the expense of others.

This argument commands respect as it demonstrates the teachers' desires to do the best for their students, yet the solution is not to reduce the use of standardized tests. Instead, the tests should be redesigned, with the assistance of federation members, to assess curricular elements that teachers feel are important to their students' progress. As Zwaagstra (2011) points out, once the standardized tests align with the provincial curriculum, the time required to prepare students for the test will no longer detract from regular teaching. Teaching to the test and teaching the curriculum will be one and the same. As a result, this argument should not be used to reduce the use of standardized tests.

It is common to hear the argument that the costs of standardized testing outweigh their benefits. In an article published in *Educationnext*, Schneider (2009) estimates that the cost of administering the Programme for International Student Assessment (PISA) tests to 1,500 students (the minimum number required for inclusion in the program) is US $700,000. While PISA does not release the total costs of its standardized testing program, if Schneider's cost estimate is correct, it would have cost US $219 million to test the 470,000 students in the seventy-four countries that participated in PISA 2009 (Statistics Canada, 2010). It could reasonably be argued that this money might be better spent in some other way.

However, this line of reasoning is similar to the argument that countries should allow the use of drugs for non-medicinal purposes, because it costs too much to enforce laws against such use. Yet, countries continue to pay the costs of enforcing these laws because the alternative is undesirable. Similarly undesirable, the consequences of eliminating standardized tests would mean that applicants could be hired or admitted to positions for which they are unqualified; schools would stop trying to improve the quality of their education. Consequently, the cost of administering standardized tests can not be used to justify their elimination.

In her article "Democratic Assessment as an Alternative," Shohamy (2001) reasons that standardized tests support power imbalances that exist between test administrators and students. She suggests that those who create and administer standardized tests hold power over students, who have less power. She views these tests as undemocratic, stating that they value a narrow range of knowledge and ignore knowledge that falls outside that range. This effect devalues the knowledge of students and makes them subservient to powerful test administrators.

Shohamy's belief that standardized tests are undemocratic is often cited by other researchers, suggesting that her points have meaning for many people. And in fact, her arguments have encouraged test administrators to adopt a critical language-testing approach that involves students in test creation, ensures designers develop fair tests and requires test administrators to work continuously to improve test quality. Shohamy's writing has been influential at improving the quality of standardized tests to the point where they are now more democratic than before.

Johnston (2003) expresses a concern when he writes about the morality of standardized testing. He believes that standardized tests are used to compare students, and successful students are assumed to have desirable characteristics while less successful students are devalued. He points to teacher-student relationships, which he says are often supportive in the classroom yet become mistrustful and suspicious in a testing situation. He suggests that the decision to use standardized tests is a moral one. Although the morality of testing is important to consider, Johnston's concerns do not eliminate the need for objective measures of language competency. When principals hire teachers, employers hire translators or schools admit students, they must know whether those applicants can meet the proficiency requirements of the position. It would not be reasonable (or moral) to hire a French teacher without knowing that person's proficiency in French.

Arguments against standardized testing have merit, but this does not mean that these tests are harmful. Standardized test administrators must work to minimize the potentially harmful effects of the tests and maximize their usefulness. In this way, time spent on test preparation is not wasted, administrative costs do not exceed the usefulness of test scores and tests become more than tools used by powerful majority groups to enforce a social agenda. In addition, standardized test results should be recognized for what they are: measures of proficiency rather than a measure of an individual's worth. Current test administrators confront these challenges to standardized testing and produce useful results that allow educational institutions and employers to make good decisions about whom to admit and hire.

References

BC Teachers' Federation. (2009, December 9). BCTF concerns about the foundation skills assessment. Retrieved from http://www.bctf.ca/IssuesInEducation.aspx?id=5728

Johnston, B. (2003). The morality of testing and assessment. In *Values in English language teaching*. Mahwah, NJ: Lawrence Erlbaum Associates.

Schneider, M. (2009, Fall). The international PISA test: A risky investment for states. *Educationnext 9*(4). Retrieved from http://educationnext.org/the-international-pisa-test/

Shohamy, E. (2001). Democratic assessment as an alternative. *Language Testing, 18*(4), 373–391.

Statistics Canada. (2010). Measuring up: Canadian results of the OECD PISA study. The performance of Canada's youth in reading, mathematics and science. 2009, First results for Canadians aged 15. (81-590-XPE no.4). Ottawa, ON: Statistics Canada.

Zwaagstra, M. (2011, October). Standardized testing is a good thing. *Frontier Centre for Public Policy: Policy Series* 119. Retrieved from http://www.fcpp.org/files/1/PS119StandardizedTesting.pdf

MODEL 7 How to Write an Explanatory Synthesis Essay

An explanatory synthesis essay shows how information from one source applies to another source. One source may be theoretical while the other source may describe an individual's experience. The goal of this type of essay is to apply theory to experience.

- Like all essays, an explanatory synthesis essay must have three general sections: an introduction, a body and a conclusion. You may not use section titles as headings in the essay.
- The introduction announces the topic of the essay. Although there are many good ways to start an essay, the introduction usually begins with a general statement about why the topic is important.
- The introduction finishes with a *thesis statement*. A thesis statement is a sentence that includes the topic of the essay and the opinion that the essay will present. The opinion expresses whether theory (from the first source) applies, or does not apply, to experience (from the second source). It may or may not include the main reasons why the opinion of the essay is correct.
- The body of the essay contains a number of paragraphs. As in other types of essays, each paragraph usually explains one reason why the essay opinion is correct.
- Each body paragraph should start with a topic sentence that clearly indicates the topic of the paragraph. You can do this by repeating key words (or synonyms of the key words) from the thesis.
- Within each paragraph, refer to both your sources. Start by referring to your first source, use a transition phrase or sentence, and then refer to your second source.
- Each body paragraph should finish with a sentence that makes the point of the paragraph clear.
- The conclusion summarizes the main reasons why the essay opinion is correct. It often finishes with a sentence that restates (but does not repeat) the thesis.

Example Explanatory Synthesis Essay

Summarize Johnston's (2003) article on the morality of testing and assessment and apply it to your partner's English-language testing experiences.

SUMMARY OF INFORMATION TO BE SYNTHESIZED	
REFERENCE	Johnston, B. (2003). The morality of testing and assessment. In *Values in English language teaching*. Mahwah, NJ: Lawrence Erlbaum Associates.
ARTICLE	• assessment a moral activity • testing assigns value or worth with serious consequences for students • damages teacher-student relationship • measures only knowledge teacher values • test preparation courses unethical
STUDENT EXPERIENCE	• Ayse Mehdi, age 22, from Saudi Arabia • Government-funded scholarship for a year of English-language training and two years of Master of Engineering degree • must pass English-language program with 75 percent and iBT TOEFL with a score of 90 • English test scores must be submitted within one year

WRITER'S PLAN		
INTRODUCTION	• describe student learner, goals, motivation, funding and standardized tests required • apply theory to student experience	
BODY	**ARTICLE**	**STUDENT EXPERIENCE**
– CONSEQUENCES	• standardized tests have serious consequences • student worth dependent on scores	• under pressure to improve • will feel she has failed herself and her family • would lose government funding • future plans would change
– TEACHER-STUDENT RELATIONSHIP	• teacher-student relationship important • supportive in class • testing destroys relationship	• enjoys teachers and classes • does not view the test precautions as indications of lack of trust • if she doesn't pass will be angry with instructors
– KNOWLEDGE TO BE TESTED	• tests only measure what teachers value	• knowledge gained outside classroom not tested: "I feel like a coffee" example
– TEST PREPARATION	• test preparation unethical; attempts to improve scores without improving proficiency	• doesn't care that the test preparation is "unethical"; believes her teachers are helping improve her proficiency
CONCLUSION	• some moral implications of testing reflected in student experience, some not	

The Impact of Testing on an English-Language Learner

Ayse Mehdi is a twenty-two-year-old from Saudi Arabia. She is in Canada to learn English in the hope of being admitted to a university to study for a master's degree in Engineering. Her studies are funded by a three-year scholarship from the Saudi Arabian government, allowing her one year of English-language study and two years to complete a master's degree. In order to gain admission to a Canadian university, she must achieve above 75 percent in the advanced level of her English-language program and score a 90 on the iBT TOEFL exam. She has one year to complete these English-language requirements. If she does not succeed, she will lose her scholarship and be forced to return home without starting a master's degree. It appears that the stakes are high for Ayse. Johnston (2003) has written about the moral element of language testing and the impact tests can have on English-language learners. The purpose of this paper is to determine if Johnston's concerns about language testing are relevant to Ayse's experience.

Johnston claims that standardized tests of the kind Ayse must complete have serious consequences for a student. He maintains that students who succeed on standardized tests are valued by society; failure on these tests means that they are less valued. He points out that learners who don't succeed on standardized tests might do well in other contexts. For example, a learner might fail a test but nevertheless find a good job. Johnston's belief is that tests are only one measure of a student's value even though the results may have a significant influence on his or her future. As for Ayse, she is under pressure—from herself, her family and her government—to improve her English this year. If she does not succeed, she says she will consider herself a failure, and her family will also be unhappy. She will lose her government funding and will probably not have another opportunity to earn a master's degree. Certainly her sense of self-worth will be diminished if she does not meet the test requirements. While she may realize that test failure doesn't represent her true worth, low test scores will mean a significant change in her future plans. With regards to Ayse's experience, Johnston's point appears relevant.

One of Johnston's main points is that the student-teacher relationship is transformed by testing. During regular class time, teachers are supportive of student effort and learning. Testing damages this relationship. For example, in test situations, teachers request all student material be put away, they may search a student's dictionary to make sure no notes have been added, and they may not allow students to leave the room alone during the exam. These precautions against cheating imply that teachers don't trust students. According to Ayse, she enjoys her English classes and likes her instructors. She said that her instructors give her extensive feedback on her writing and speaking, and she feels that they are working hard to improve her English. She does not view the test precautions described by Johnston as indications that her teachers don't trust her. She believes these actions are necessary to create fair test conditions. However, when asked what would happen if she didn't get 75 percent on her final exam, Ayse said she would be angry with her instructors. She suggested that if she got below 75 percent, her instructors would have failed her. Consequently, although Ayse does not feel that the testing situation indicates instructors don't trust students, a low final test score would negatively influence her relationship with them.

In any context, a test can measure only small samples of student proficiency due to time constraints. As a result, tests measure only the knowledge that test developers believe is important (Johnston, 2003). Knowledge that lies outside the test domain may be just as significant for students, but this is not recognized in a standardized test. Ayse realizes that this is the case for her as well. The previous day, she had learned the meaning of the expression, "I feel like a coffee," from her homestay family, and she was excited to finally understand the phrase. She had not understood that it meant the speaker wanted a coffee; she had thought it meant the speaker felt warm. This expression was particularly useful to her, and she used it during our meeting. However, it is unlikely this knowledge, despite its usefulness, will be tested. Johnston's argument that tests value a narrow range of knowledge is accurate in Ayse's experience.

Finally, Johnston writes that test preparation courses for standardized tests are unethical because they attempt to improve scores without improving student proficiency. In most cases, test preparation courses are intensive courses. It is unlikely that language proficiency will improve over a weekend, for example. Ayse has registered for a TOEFL test preparation class that she will take over the next two weekends. In response to a question about whether she felt the course was unethical, Ayse said she doesn't think about it. While the course is expensive, she simply wants a high score on the test. She believes her work in the advanced-level English program is improving her proficiency; she expects the English program and the TOEFL test preparation course together will ensure a high score. So, Johnston's concern about the ethics of test preparation courses is not a concern for Ayse.

In conclusion, Johnston writes about the moral implications of standardized testing. His work exposes issues such as the consequences of testing, the transformative influence of testing on student-teacher relationships, the emphasis on narrow bands of valued knowledge and the ethics of test preparation courses. These are significant concerns, and Ayse herself recognizes most of them. She is aware of the serious consequences of her test scores and agrees that her relationship with her instructors may change if she does not succeed. She does understand that the knowledge that will be tested is only a fraction of her overall knowledge and may not be the knowledge she finds useful on a day-to-day basis. She is not worried about the ethics of test preparation; she is reasonably focused on obtaining a high score on her tests. Ayse's experience therefore demonstrates many, but not all, of Johnston's concerns.

Reference

Johnston, B. (2003). The morality of testing and assessment. In *Values in English language teaching*. Mahwah, NJ: Lawrence Erlbaum Associates.

MODEL 8 How to Write a Problem-Solution Essay

A problem-solution essay describes a problem and provides a possible solution.

- Problem-solution essays have six sections: introduction, description of a situation, statement of the problem, description of a solution, evaluation of the solution and conclusion. You may not use section titles as headings in the essay.
- The introduction announces the topic of the essay. Although there are many good ways to start an essay, the introduction usually begins with a general statement about why the topic is important.
- The introduction finishes with a *thesis statement*. A thesis statement is a sentence that includes the topic of the essay and the opinion that the essay will present. The expressed opinion indicates whether a solution is possible or whether one solution is better than another.
- The body of the essay contains the components of a problem-solution text: description of a situation, statement of the problem, description of a solution, evaluation of the solution.
  - The description of the situation may have the characteristics of a short descriptive essay.
  - The statement of the problem may have the characteristics of a challenges section of a report.
  - The description of a solution may have the characteristics of a process essay (if the solutions require multiples steps). If you write about two (or more) solutions, the section may have characteristics of a compare and contrast essay.
  - The evaluation of the solution(s) may include expressions of critical thinking, especially if the solution does not solve all elements of the problem or if one solution is inferior to another.
- The conclusion may have the characteristics of a persuasive essay as you try to convince the reader that one solution is better than another. The conclusion often finishes with a sentence that restates (but does not repeat) the thesis.

Example Problem-Solution Essay

Given that the overreliance on summative assessment is becoming a problem for English-language learners, propose and evaluate a solution to this problem.

WRITER'S PLAN	
INTRODUCTION	• definitions of summative and formative assessment (Brown and Abeywickrama, 2010)
SITUATION	• educational system driven by summative assessment • students constantly taking tests and exams to provide data on qualifications
PROBLEM	• overuse of summative assessment • students study for exams and forget • students don't receive feedback • students who don't do well on exams disadvantaged
SOLUTION	• move to more formative assessment • evidence of the assessment bridge (Colby-Kelly and Turner, 2007)
EVALUATION	• teachers worry feedback embarrasses students • students believe teachers not critical enough in evaluations
SOLUTION	• dynamic assessment description (Lantolf and Poehner, 2008)
EVALUATION	• hard to separate student ability from teacher assistance
CONCLUSION	• trend in assessment moving away from summative assessment • better for teaching, learning and students

Formative Assessment as a Response to Summative Assessment

In the field of testing, assessments can be divided into two categories: summative and formative. According to Brown and Abeywickrama (2010), summative assessment is designed to summarize a student's achievement. It is typically an end-of-term test, has a high point value and is high-stakes. The score of a summative assessment is recorded on a student's transcript, without any effort to provide feedback on his or her strengths or weaknesses. The purpose of a summative assessment is to produce a score for administrative purposes. In contrast, formative assessments are intended to facilitate student learning. They are typically end-of-unit tests, or assignments, they have lower point values and are comparatively low-stakes. The score of a formative assessment becomes part of a student's final grade, but the test's main purpose is to inform a student of his or her strengths or weaknesses.

In many countries, educational systems are driven by summative assessment. Students of all ages require scores in order to determine their educational progress. Those with high scores attend better schools and the best post-secondary institutions while those with lower scores are streamed into regular or remedial classes with fewer opportunities for enrichment. Students are constantly being tested to generate scores.

Educational administrators often make admission decisions based on a single score; that score must reflect the sum total of a student's skills and abilities. That score determines a student's future.

Is it really fair to judge a student's admissibility based on a single score? Could any single score, no matter how it is calculated, possibly reflect the complexity of abilities that any human possesses? This is the defining problem that results from an overuse of summative assessment. However, other significant issues also stem from excessive summative assessment. For example, students often prepare for summative exams by "cramming"—studying long hours and memorizing facts. This is not the best way to encourage a deep understanding of content. Students who cram for exams often quickly forget key concepts. Summative assessments are not intended to provide detailed feedback to students, so students lose the opportunity to learn from their work and from their instructors' expertise. Finally, some students simply don't score well on exams but do much better on assignments. These students are severely disadvantaged by an educational system's focus on summative test scores.

In the field of second-language learning and teaching, researchers and teachers are looking for ways to reduce the reliance on summative testing and develop alternative assessments that provide more feedback to students and allow them multiple opportunities to demonstrate mastery of core concepts. Both formative and dynamic assessment offer new solutions to the problem of overreliance on summative assessment.

Formative assessment, or assessment to enhance student learning, is also referred to as *assessment for learning* (AFL). Colby-Kelly and Turner (2007) state that AFL is characterized by increasing involvement of students in their own assessment. This includes self- and peer assessments as well as teacher feedback that enhances student performance and motivates students. Teachers who practise AFL modify their lessons based on the results of assessment; if results indicate students need more work on a particular concept, teachers revisit that concept to facilitate student learning. Colby-Kelly and Turner's study of a pre-university English for Academic Preparation program that employed formative assessment suggests that AFL can create conditions for enhanced motivation and learning.

One of the challenges of implementing AFL in the second-language classroom resulted from the conflict between theory and practice. In theory, teachers supported the use of self- and peer assessments and acknowledged their potential for involving students in their own assessment. In practice, teachers most often provided feedback directly to students, without emphasizing self- and peer assessment. Also, teachers worried that providing feedback might embarrass students; some teachers waited until class was over before speaking with students one-on-one in the hallways. Two students in the study responded that they found teacher feedback overly supportive; they felt that teachers were constantly encouraging and that teachers would be unlikely to provide negative feedback. While the benefits of AFL are substantial, Colby-Kelly and Turner's investigations point to challenges with its implementation.

Another movement in the second-language assessment field is a trend toward dynamic assessment, also a reaction to summative and standardized testing. Dynamic assessment (DA) involves diagnostic tests that are administered early in the term and designed to provide feedback and inform teacher planning. In their overview of DA, Lantolf and Poehner (2008) state that DA involves teacher mediation of student response. This explanation becomes clearer if DA is compared with summative assessment. Consider a speaking test in which a student speaks one-on-one with a teacher who assesses the student's speaking ability. In a summative test, the teacher has no flexibility to modify questions or responses to students, even if a student appears confused or answers incorrectly. With DA, the teacher could modify a response, asking the student to explain why he or she is answering in this way or encouraging a more detailed response. Teachers who use DA maintain they have a better understanding of student ability because they interact with the student during assessment.

While DA offers hope for improved diagnostic tests that can support student learning and inform teacher planning, critics suggest that it is hard to determine the student's ability to perform independently (Lantolf and Poehner, 2008). Teachers who use this approach to diagnostic testing acknowledge that some students require more help than others to complete the assessment. As a result, the assessment may not produce consistent scores.

Both AFL and DA are current trends in the assessment field, which respond to the overuse of summative testing in educational systems around the world. Although these approaches have implementation challenges, they offer new hope for more student-centred assessment that encourages feedback and enhances student learning and motivation.

Bibliography

Brown, D., & Abeywickrama, P. (2010). *Language assessment: Principles and classroom practices* (2nd ed.). White Plains, NY: Pearson Longman.

Colby-Kelly, C., & Turner, C.E. (2007). AFL research in the L2 classroom and evidence of usefulness: Taking formative assessment to the next level. *Canadian Modern Language Review*, *64*(1), 9–37.

Lantolf, J.P., & Poehner, M.E. (2008). Dynamic assessment. In E. Shohamy, & N.H. Hornberger (Eds.), *Encyclopedia of language and education*, 2nd ed., Vol. 7: *Language testing and assessment*, pp. 273–284. New York, NY: Springer.

Poehner, M.E., & Lantolf, J.P. (2005). Dynamic assessment in the language classroom. *Language Teaching Research*, *9*(3), 233–265.

Vygotsky, L.S. (1998). *The collected works of L.S. Vygotsky. Volume 5, Child Psychology*. R.W. Rieber (Ed.). New York, NY: Plenum Press.

PHOTO CREDITS

ALAMY

pp. ix, 124–125, 146, 147 © Cobis Premium RF; p. 91 © VIEW Pictures.

CORBIS

Cover, p. iii © Corbis.

COURTESY OF UNIVERSITY OF BRITISH COLUMBIA

pp. 77, 78 © Don Ehardt, UBC; p. 80 © Martin Dee, UBC.

SHUTTERSTOCK

pp. viii, ix, 100–101, 123, 147 © ra2studio; pp. ix, 148–149, 169, 193 © Nils Z; pp. ix, 170–171, 192, 193 © Dariush M; p. 3 © pkchai; p. 5 © Lichtmeister; p. 6 © David P. Lewis; p. 8 © Yuri Arcurs; p. 15 © Milan Vasicek; p. 20 © Elena Elisseeva; p. 23 © Mohamed Elsayyed; p. 24 © Glynnis Jones; p. 31 © MartiniDry; p. 34 © StockLite; p. 36 © Diego Cervo; p. 38 © Yuri Arcurs; p. 54 middle © Petroos; p. 54 bottom © Frank Anusewicz; p. 58 © Anmor Photography; p. 62 © Otmar Smit; p. 64 © zentilia; p. 66 © Olena Mykhaylova; p. 69 © T.W. van Urk; p. 70 © Ak W; p. 75 © auremar; p. 82 © think4photop; p. 83 © sunxuejun; p. 85 © tristan tan; p. 89 © Vitaliy Krasovskiy; p. 96 © Goran Bogicevic; p. 103 © DanielW; p. 109 © ARENA Creative; p. 112 © Oleg Zabielin; p. 121 bottom © EuToch; p. 122 © Buida Nikita Yourievich; p. 128 © Mikhail Zahranichny; p. 136 © AlenD; p. 141 © Christian Bertrand; p. 149 © Marc Pagani Photography; p. 165 © Herbert Kratky.

THINKSTOCK

pp. viii, 2–3, 25, 51; pp. viii, 26–27, 50, 51; pp. viii, 52–53, 73, 99; pp. viii, 74–75, 98, 99; p. 7; p. 11; p. 16; p. 17; p. 18; p. 21; p. 28; p. 30; p. 33; p. 41; p. 45; p. 47; p. 49; p. 54; p. 56; p. 57; p. 61; p. 63; p. 68; p. 87; p. 88; p. 92; p. 93; p. 94; p. 95; p. 104; p. 105; p. 106; p. 108; p. 110; p. 111; p. 114; p. 117; p. 121 top; p. 125; p. 127; p. 129; p. 130; p. 132; p. 135; p. 137; p. 139; p. 140; p. 143; p. 145; p. 151; p. 153; p. 154; p. 155; p. 156; p. 158; p. 159; p. 160; p. 163; p. 166; p. 174; p. 175; p. 176; p. 177; p. 178; p. 180; p. 181; p. 184; p. 185; p. 187; p. 188; p. 189; p. 190; p. 191.

NOTES